MW00877463

THE GRAND JURY ROOM

THE CASE FOR CHRISTIANITY

A CROSS EXAMINATION

DON STEWART

The Case For Christianity:
A Cross Examination
By Don Stewart

© 2016 Don Stewart

Published By Educating Our World
www.educatingourworld.com

English Versions Cited

The various English versions which we cite in this book, apart from the King James Version, all have copyrights. They are listed as follows.

Verses marked NRSV are from the New Revised Standard Version, copyright 1989 by Division of Christian Education of the National Council of the Churches of Christ in the USA. Used by permission. All rights reserved

Verses marked NIV are taken from the HOLY BIBLE, New International Version 2011, Copyright 1973 1978, 1984, 2011 by International Bible Society. Used by permission of Zondervan Publishing House. All rights reserved

Verses marked ESV are from The Holy Bible English Standard Version™ Copyright © 2001 by Crossway Bibles, a division of Good News Publishers All rights reserved.

Scripture quotations marked (NLT) are taken from the Holy Bible, New Living Translation, copyright 1996. Used by permission of Tyndale House Publishers, Inc., Wheaton, Illinois 60189. All rights reserved.

Scripture quotations marked "NKJV" are taken from the New King James Version. Copyright © 1982 by Thomas Nelson, Inc. All rights reserved. Used by permission.

Scripture quotations marked CEV are taken from the Contemporary English Version (CEV) copyright American Bible Society 1991, 1995
Scripture taken from THE MESSAGE: Copyright © 1993, 1994, 1995, 1996, 2000, 2001, 2002. Used by permission of NavPress Publishing Group.

Scripture quoted by permission. Quotations designated NET are from the NET Bible Copyright © 2003 By Biblical Studies Press, L.L.C. www.netbible.com All rights reserved.

Verses marked RSV are The Holy Bible: Revised Standard Version containing the Old and New Testaments, translated from the original tongues: being the version set forth A.D. 1611, revised A.D. 1881-1885 and A.D. 1901: compared with the most ancient authorities and revised A.D. 1946-52. — 2nd ed. of New Testament A.D. 1971.

Verses marked HCSB are taken from the Holman Christian Standard Bible® Copyright © 1999, 2000, 2002, 2003 by Holman Bible Publishers. Used by permission.

GOD'S WORD is a copyrighted work of God's Word to the Nations. Quotations are used by permission. Copyright 1995 by God's Word to the Nations. All rights reserved.

TABLE OF CONTENTS

CHAPTER 1: APOLOGETICS:
THE DEFENSE OF THE CHRISTIAN FAITH 5

CHAPTER 2: SETTING THE RECORD STRAIGHT:
WHAT CHRISTIANITY IS AND WHAT IT IS NOT 27

CHAPTER 3: INTRODUCING THE CASE FOR CHRISTIANITY:
THE CHRISTIAN FAITH IS SENSIBLE 39

CHAPTER 4: THE RELIABILITY OF THE NEW TESTAMENT TEXT:
HAS NOT BEEN CHANGED THROUGHOUT TIME 47

PART 1: ESTABLISHING THE TEXT OF THE NEW TESTAMENT: HOW WE KNOW THE TEXT IS ACCURATE

PART 2: THE VARIANT READINGS IN THE TEXT: WHY DO THE MANUSCRIPTS READ DIFFERENTLY?

CHAPTER 5: THE HISTORICAL ACCURACY OF THE NEW TESTAMENT:
MATCHES UP WITH KNOWN FACTS 77

CHAPTER 6: THE MAIN CHARACTER OF THE NEW TESTAMENT:
JESUS CHRIST: THE CLAIMS MADE ABOUT HIM 109

CHAPTER 7: THE CLAIMS OF CHRIST CONSIDERED:
LOOK AT THE OPTIONS 119

CHAPTER 8: THE MIRACLES OF JESUS:
HE DEMONSTRATED AUTHORITY IN EVERY REALM 135

PART 1: WHAT ARE MIRACLES? UNDERSTANDING BIBLICAL MIRACLES

PART 2: THE EVIDENCE FOR JESUS' MIRACLES: THE NEW TESTAMENT TESTIMONY TO THE MIRACLES OF CHRIST

PART 3: OBJECTIONS TO THE MIRACLES OF JESUS: ANSWERING COMMON OBJECTIONS TO HIS MIRACLES

CHAPTER 9: PREDICTIVE PROPHECY: JESUS FULFILLED PROPHECY AND MADE PREDICTIONS THAT HAVE COME TRUE 165

PART 1: INTRODUCTION TO BIBLE PROPHECY: ONLY GOD KNOWS THE FUTURE

PART 2: PROPHECIES FULFILLED BY JESUS: SOME PREDICTIONS FULFILLED AT HIS FIRST COMING

PART 3: PROPHECIES JESUS MADE THAT HAVE BEEN FULFILLED: A LOOK AT JESUS THE PROPHET

CHAPTER 10: THE RESURRECTION OF JESUS CHRIST: HE IS THE ONLY ONE WHO HAS CONQUERED DEATH 189

PART 1: THE IMPORTANCE OF THE RESURRECTION: WHAT IS MEANS TO THE CHRISTIAN FAITH

PART 2: THE CASE FOR THE RESURRECTION: WEIGHING THE EVIDENCE

PART 3: THE INDIRECT EVIDENCE FOR THE RESURRECTION: CIRCUMSTANTIAL EVIDENCE THAT JESUS HAS RISEN

PART 4: OBJECTIONS TO THE RESURRECTION: SOME COMMON OBJECTIONS ANSWERED

PART 5: THE MEANING OF THE RESURRECTION: SO WHAT IF HE DID RISE?

CHAPTER 11: JESUS' VIEW OF THE OLD TESTAMENT: HE TOTALLY TRUSTED IT 255

CHAPTER 12: JESUS' VIEW OF HIS OWN TEACHINGS: THEY WERE ABSOLUTELY AUTHORITATIVE 265

CHAPTER 13: JESUS' VIEW OF THE NEW TESTAMENT: HE CONFIRMED IT AHEAD OF TIME 271

CHAPTER 14: SUMMARY AND CONCLUSION: THE CHRISTIAN FAITH IS TRUE 275

ABOUT THE AUTHOR 281

CHAPTER 1

Apologetics: The Defense Of The Christian Faith

Our first section introduces us to subject of the defense of the Christian faith. In this chapter, we demonstrate the need for making such a defense. We begin by pointing out the various belief options which are available to humans. Some people believe in God, others do not. Some people believe in many gods, others worship only one God. To many, the one God who exists is an impersonal being. However, others view Him as personal.

With so many options, the Christian must have an explanation, as well as a defense, as to why one should believe in the God of the Bible.

In our next section, we move to the subject of defending the Christian faith. We examine all the passages in the New Testament where the word "defense" is used. Our study will discover that it is a biblical practice to defend the belief in Jesus as the Christ. This includes presenting evidence as well as answering objections.

Our final section looks at the ways in which Bible-believing Christians go about defending the faith. Believers fall into two basic categories—those who do not think we should provide any reasons for our belief in God and in the trustworthiness of Scripture and those who do believe that we should give reasons for faith as well as answer objections. We examine each perspective and conclude that the biblical practice is to proclaim the message of Jesus, give reasons for belief, and answer any objections which may arise.

PART 1: THE CENTRAL ISSUE: HUMANS HAVE MANY BELIEF OPTIONS

As we begin our examination of the claims of the Christian faith we must first look at the need to make such an inquiry. Why should anyone investigate the evidence to see whether or not Christianity is true?

The answer to this question can be simply stated: There are varieties of choices that we, as human beings, have with respect to the existence or non-existence of God or gods. Christianity is only one of these many options.

In addition, the Christian faith makes some unique claims about itself. Indeed, it claims that only one God exists and that it is the only way to reach the one God. For these reasons, it must be carefully examined along with the other belief options of humanity.

THE CHOICES THAT ALL HUMANS HAVE

Humanity has the following choices when it comes to believing in the existence or non-existence of God or gods.

AGNOSTICISM–I DO NOT KNOW IF GOD OR GODS EXISTS

Agnosticism says, "I do not know if God or gods exist." Some agnostics believe that it is not possible to know if a divine "being" or "beings" exist. Their view is that one cannot know anything about these matters. On the other hand, there are those agnostics who think that knowledge about God is possible, yet they are not convinced that there is enough evidence to prove the case. Whatever the exact position may be, an agnostic claims no knowledge, one way or the other, about the existence of God.

ATHEISM OR THEISM–I KNOW WHETHER GOD OR GODS EXIST

Contrary to agnosticism, which says it does not know, are theism and atheism. Both of these groups claim to have knowledge about the existence of a supernatural being or beings. The atheist knows that God or gods do not exist. The theist knows that God or gods do exist.

Of course, the atheist cannot really know for certain that God does not exist. Only someone who has all knowledge or is everywhere present in the universe could know this. The only being who has these credentials is God Himself!

POLYTHEISM OR MONOTHEISM–DOES ONE GOD OR MANY GODS EXIST?

Those who believe in the existence of God must decide whether they believe in polytheism or in monotheism. Polytheism believes in the existence of many gods, though a polytheist may choose to worship only one of these gods (this is known as henotheism). On the other hand, a monotheist believes only one God exists—no other so-called gods have any real substance

PANTHEISM OR A PERSONAL BEING–IS THE ONE GOD PERSONAL OR IMPERSONAL?

If only one God exists, then it must be determined whether that one God is a personal or impersonal being. Pantheism (God is equal to everything) believes that the one God who exists is impersonal—he has no personal existence apart from creation. Creation and God are basically one-in-the same. Those who believe in a personal God make a distinction between God and His creation—God exists separately from that which He created.

DEISM OR A PERSONALLY INVOLVED GOD–IS THE ONE GOD INVOLVED WITH HUMANITY?

If only one God exists, and this one God is a personal God, then our next question considers His involvement in our world. Is the one God intimately involved in the affairs of humanity? Deism says that God is not involved with humanity. God started everything in the beginning and then backed off from His creation. In other words, He is no more than an onlooker. This is opposed to a God who is personally involved in the lives of the beings He created (such as the God revealed in the Bible).

UNITARIANISM VERSUS TRINITARIANISM–IS THE ONE GOD ONLY A UNITY OR A TRINITY?

We now come to our final option. If there is one personal God who exists, and He is intimately involved in the affairs of humanity, is this God a unity or a Trinity? Is there only one person, or is there a plurality of persons, or centers of consciousness, within the nature of the one God?

These are the various belief options that humans have. Each human being will basically fit into one of these categories with respect to his or her belief about the existence or the non-existence of God or gods.

With so many belief options that are possible, certain questions naturally arise for the Christian: Why believe in Jesus Christ? What makes Christianity different than these other possibilities?

It is, therefore, the responsibility of the Christian to respond to these types of questions.

APOLOGETICS—THE CHRISTIAN RESPONSE TO OBJECTIONS

The job of defending the Christian faith, and answering questions such as these, is known as apologetics. One person has defined apologetics as "proving what you never doubted by arguments you don't understand." This, however, is certainly not the case!

Our English word "apologetics" comes from two Greek words—the noun apologia and the verb *apologeomai*. In the New Testament era, these words meant, "to give a defense or a reply." They are found some eighteen times in the New Testament.

THE NOUN "DEFEND" AS USED IN THE NEW TESTAMENT

The noun apologia is used eight times in the New Testament. These references are as follows.

First, we find Paul offering a defense concerning accusations against him. The Bible says.

> "Brothers and esteemed fathers," Paul said, "listen to me as I offer my defense" (Acts 22:1 NLT).

The Apostle Paul is offering a defense to certain things he was wrongly accused of.

In another instance, Paul is defending himself against false charges. He said.

> I told them that it was not the custom of the Romans to hand over anyone before the accused had met the accusers face to face and had been given an opportunity to make a defense against the charge (Acts 25:16 NRSV).

Here the word is used in the technical sense of making a defense against accusers.

In his letter to the Corinthians, Paul makes another use of this word. He wrote.

> My defense to those who examine me is this (1 Corinthians 9:3 HCSB).

Paul again is using the term in the legal sense.

In his second letter to the Corinthians, Paul uses the word in the sense of clearing oneself of charges. He wrote.

> For see what earnestness this godly grief has produced in you, but also what eagerness to clear yourselves, what indignation, what fear, what longing, what zeal, what punishment! At every point you have proved yourselves innocent in the matter (2 Corinthians 7:11 ESV).

Here Paul is using the term with reference to the Corinthians defending or clearing themselves from charges made against them.

PAUL DEFENDED THE GOSPEL

When he wrote to the Philippians, he emphasized his role as defending the gospel. Paul said.

> Just as it is right for me to think this of you all, because I have you in my heart, inasmuch as both in my chains and in the defense and confirmation of the gospel, you all are partakers with me of grace (Philippians 1:7 NKJV).

The scope of Paul's ministry concerns both the defense and confirmation of the good news. This implies that his response, or apology, was closely linked with the gospel. He also wrote to the Philippians.

> The latter do so out of love, knowing that I am put here for the defense of the gospel (Philippians 1:16 NIV).

This clearly points out his purpose—he is set for the defense of the gospel.

When he wrote his final letter, he spoke of his defense before his accusers.

> At my first defense no one stood with me, but all forsook me. May it not be charged against them (2 Timothy 4:16 NKJV).

This could mean defend or support oneself in front of hostile witnesses. In this context, it is used of an actual trial.

PETER SPOKE OF DEFENDING THE FAITH

We also find Peter using the word "defense." He wrote.

> But in your hearts sanctify Christ as Lord. Always be ready to make your defense to anyone who demands from you an accounting for the hope that is in you (1 Peter 3:15 NRSV).

This is a key verse with respect to the defense of the Christian faith. Here it is in the context of persecution. When asked, as believers we are commanded to have an answer as to what we believe, as well as why we believe.

THE VERB "TO DEFEND" AS USED IN THE NEW TESTAMENT

Now we will look at the verb translated, "to defend." The verb *apologeomai* is used ten times in the New Testament. The references are as follows.

THE USE OF THE WORD DEFENSE BY JESUS

Jesus gave instructions to His disciples in speaking in their own defense in front of the authorities. He said.

> When you are brought before synagogues, rulers and authorities, do not worry about how you will defend yourselves or what you will say (Luke 12:11 NIV).

Jesus uses "defense" here with the idea of defending the faith before institutions and authorities. Later, He said.

> Make up your minds not to prepare your defense ahead of time (Luke 21:14 HCSB).

This could be a formal defense before those who were making a legal charge against them.

ALEXANDER WANTED TO MAKE HIS DEFENSE

In the Book of Acts, we are told of a man named Alexander who wanted to make a defense in front of the people. The text says.

> And they drew Alexander out of the multitude, the Jews putting him forward. And Alexander motioned with his hand, and wanted to make his defense to the people (Acts 19:33 NKJV).

Alexander was attempting to respond to the charges made against him.

PAUL DEFENDED HIMSELF BEFORE THE GOVERNOR

When the Apostle Paul appeared before the governor, he made his defense. The Bible says.

> When the governor motioned for him to speak, Paul replied: "I know that for a number of years you have been a judge over this nation; so I gladly make my defense" (Acts 24:10 NIV).

Again, we have Paul's defense to charges that were brought against him. In this case, it was before the governor.

In another instance, the Apostle Paul defended himself. The Book of Acts records it as follows.

> Paul said in his defense, "I have in no way committed an offense against the law of the Jews, or against the temple, or against the emperor" (Acts 25:8 NRSV).

Paul is responding to the specific charges that he has committed offenses either against the Jews, their religion, or Rome.

When Paul came before Agrippa the King, he was allowed to defend himself. Scripture says.

> Then Agrippa said to Paul, "You may speak in your defense." So Paul, with a gesture of his hand, started his defense (Acts 26:1 NLT).

He then began his legal defense before King Agrippa. He said.

> King Agrippa, I consider myself fortunate to stand before you today as I make my defense against all the accusations of the Jews (Acts 26:2 NIV).

Again, we have another use of the term in the sense of a legal defense. Paul makes his defense before Agrippa. Verse twenty-two is the key to understand of what his defense consisted. It says.

> God has been helping me to this day so that I can stand and testify to important and unimportant people. I tell them only what the prophets and Moses said would happen (Acts 26:22 God's Word).

Paul argues that he is teaching nothing different than what is found in Moses (the Law) and the Old Testament prophets. His defense received the following response.

> Now as he thus made his defense, Festus said with a loud voice, "Paul, you are beside yourself! Much learning is driving you mad!" (Acts 26:24 NKJV).

Here Paul is interrupted by Festus as he is making his defense.

In Paul's letter to the Romans, he speaks of the law of God which has been written on the human heart. He said.

> They show that what the law requires is written on their hearts, to which their own conscience also bears witness; and their conflicting thoughts will accuse or perhaps excuse them (Romans 2:15 NRSV).

The thoughts of humans can either bring an accusation or a defense.

Finally, Paul wrote to the Corinthians about the apostles defending themselves.

> Have you been thinking all along that we have been defending ourselves before you? We are speaking in Christ before God. Everything we do, beloved, is for the sake of building you up (2 Corinthians 12:19 NRSV).

This refers to specific attacks against Paul from certain people in Corinth.

SUMMARY TO THE USE OF THE WORD DEFENSE IN THE NEW TESTAMENT

From these verses we learn that an apologist is one who gives a defense, a reply, to questions about the Christian faith. This is true whether it is answering a simple question or responding to some type of accusation. Twice, this defense was carried out in a court of law. Thus, defending the Christian faith is a New Testament practice.

THERE ARE OTHER VERSES THAT SPEAK OF DEFENDING THE FAITH

There are other verses in Scripture that speak of defending the faith. They include the following references.

1. THE FAITH HAS BEEN ONCE-AND-FOR-ALL DELIVERED

Jude wrote about the need for defending the faith. He said.

> Dear friends, although I have been eager to write to you about our common salvation, I now feel compelled instead to write to encourage you to contend earnestly for the faith that was once for all entrusted to the saints (Jude 3 NET).

The same idea is here. The faith that has been once-and-for-all delivered needs defending. Jude emphasizes that we should earnestly contend for the faith. Elsewhere he wrote.

> Show mercy to those whose faith is wavering (Jude 22 NLT).

We are to be merciful, not judgmental, to those who have honest doubts about the faith.

2. CHURCH LEADERS ARE TO TEACH THE TRUTH AND REFUTE FALSE DOCTRINE

In Paul's letter to Titus, he lists the traits of a church leader. He said.

> He must hold firmly to the trustworthy message as it has been taught, so that he can encourage others by sound

> doctrine and refute those who oppose it. For there are many rebellious people, full of meaningless talk and deception, especially those of the circumcision group. They must be silenced, because they are disrupting whole households by teaching things they ought not to teach-and that for the sake of dishonest gain (Titus 1:9-11 NIV).

The qualifications of those who lead the church include teaching sound doctrine and refuting those who disagree by defending the faith.

3. THE DEFENSE OF THE FAITH IS TO BE DONE IN LOVE

Paul stresses the personal qualities that Christians are to have as they defend the faith. He wrote the following to Timothy.

> The Lord's servants must not quarrel but must be kind to everyone. They must be able to teach effectively and be patient with difficult people. They should gently teach those who oppose the truth. Perhaps God will change those people's hearts, and they will believe the truth (2 Timothy 2:24-25 NLT).

This is so important to realize. Any defense of the faith must be done in love.

THE JOB OF THE APOLOGIST IS TO REMOVE OBJECTIONS TO CHRISTIANITY

The apologist's job is to remove roadblocks that keep people from believing in Jesus Christ. Unfortunately, people grow up with certain misconceptions about Christianity and Christ. These may include: Jesus never existed, the Bible is unreliable, the records about Jesus have been changed throughout history, miracles have been disproved, etc.

These accusations must first be answered before these people can hear the gospel. Apologetics, therefore, is not the gospel, but rather consists of answering questions and objections so that people are then able to hear the good news of Christ.

Of course, if someone does not have these objections and wishes to hear the gospel, then, by all means, the gospel should be preached to them. In these cases, it is not necessary to provide reasons for belief if the person is ready to believe the message of Jesus.

1. THE GOAL—BRINGING PEOPLE TO JESUS CHRIST

The ultimate goal in answering doubter's questions is to bring that person to faith in Christ. We want unbelievers to see themselves as lost sinners needing a Savior. This is what the apologist is trying to accomplish. It is not attempting to win arguments or to prove how smart we are.

2. THE APOLOGIST DEFENDS THE CENTRAL BELIEFS OF CHRISTIANITY

The defense of the faith also consists of the clarification of the gospel message and the belief system of Christians. There is a core belief system that needs to be defended. These beliefs include: salvation by grace through faith, Jesus Christ is the only way to know God and the Bible is the final authority on all matters of faith and practice. The apologist proclaims these beliefs and defends them against attack.

3. THE ATTACKS AGAINST CHRISTIANITY ARE EVER-CHANGING AND GROWING

In addition, each generation of believers must respond to the attacks of their own particular generation. For example, the first Christians were accused of atheism because they did not worship the gods of Rome as well as being cannibals because they "ate the body of Jesus" at the Lords Supper! They had to respond to those accusations.

Today, believers do not have to defend themselves against these specific attacks but rather we have to respond to new and ongoing attacks.

The attacks change from generation to generation, yet the doubts continue to surface in the form of the same question, "Has God really said?" This question, originally asked by the serpent in the Garden of

Eden, is still being asked today in one form or another. Has God really spoken to the human race and are His words recorded in the Bible? This is the question that Christians must answer!

THE TWO APPROACHES TO DEFENDING THE FAITH

Among believers, there are two different approaches to the way the Christian faith is defended—the presuppositionalist and the evidentialist. They can be summarized as follows.

THE PRESUPPOSITIONALIST APPROACH: NO DEFENSE IS NEEDED

The presuppositionalist defends the Christian faith by first making several assumptions that are not up for discussion or debate. They assume that the God of the Bible is the only God who exists and that the Bible is His sole revelation to the human race. These truths are assumed to be true— they cannot be tested or challenged. Rather, they are to be believed as a starting point for all discussion.

Therefore, the presuppositionalist will not attempt to answer any objections to these truths, nor will they give any reason as to why they should be believed. The reason why this position is taken is due to the way the presuppositionalist understands human beings and our sinful nature.

The presuppositionalist holds to the view that the fall of humanity, as is recorded in Genesis chapter three, made human beings incapable of responding to God. Therefore, God must regenerate, or save them, before they can understand anything about Him. Unbelievers, by definition, are not capable of responding to the evidence for the Christian faith because of their fallen nature. Evidence for the Christian faith can only be understood after someone has trusted Jesus Christ, not before.

Furthermore, giving evidence for faith places human reason as the final determiner of what is true. We should place God's Word as the final standard and not allow humans to determine whether or not the Bible is true.

Therefore, the presuppositionalist preaches the gospel to unbelievers. Those who are the elect will respond in faith. Those who are not the elect will not. Consequently, the presuppositionalist does not bother giving any evidence or answering any objections.

THE EVIDENTIALIST APPROACH: ANSWERS SHOULD BE GIVEN

The evidentialist sees things differently. They believe that the non-Christian can respond to evidences brought forward to show the reasonableness of the Christian faith. Non-believers should have their objections answered. They deserve to hear the clear and convincing evidence that is available to substantiate the Christian faith.

The evidentialist like the presuppositionalist assumes that God exists and that the Bible is His sole revelation to humanity. But unlike the presuppositionalist, the evidentialist will provide reasons as to why these truths are to be believed and will answer objections brought forward by skeptics.

The evidentialist believes that the Holy Spirit takes the arguments used to support the gospel and convicts the unbeliever of sin while the presuppositionalist uses the Bible alone. The evidentialist believes that giving reasons for faith is not fighting against the work of the Holy Spirit.

Simply stated, the evidentialist will answer the questions of unbelievers. Indeed, they will start with where the unbeliever is at and attempt to answer their objections with the goal of leading them to Christ. On the other hand, the presuppositionalist will make the unbeliever accept the existence of the God of the Bible and the truth of the Word of God before any discussion can begin.

Obviously, the way in which we preach the gospel and tell others about Jesus will depend upon which of these two positions we hold. The evidentialist will preach the good news and answer questions while the presuppositionalist will merely preach the good news without answering any of the objections of the unbelievers.

THE EVIDENTIALIST APPROACH IS THE BEST

Therefore, we must make a choice between the evidentialist and the presuppositionalist position. Why not, like the presuppositionalist, just proclaim the gospel? Why bother with arguing with people and presenting evidence? The presuppositionalist would say that giving reasons for the faith is a waste of time. The best option is to just preach the gospel and pray for that person to respond to the simple message.

However, this is not the biblical approach for the following reasons.

1. GOD GAVE US OUR MINDS TO THINK AND REASON

The Bible says that God created humans with the ability to think and reason. If we devalue the use of the mind, then we are despising one of the gifts that God has given humanity. Jesus emphasized that we are to love the Lord with our entire mind. Matthew records him saying the following.

> He said to him, "You shall love the Lord your God with all your heart, and with all your soul, and with all your mind" (Matthew 22:37 NRSV).

We are to use our mind in our love for the Lord. This includes weighing and evaluating the evidence for the Christian faith.

2. THE GOSPEL MESSAGE ITSELF CAUSES US TO THINK

The message of Christ is addressed to the minds of its listeners. We must use our minds to weigh and evaluate the evidence concerning Christ. God does not bring anyone into His kingdom by bypassing the mind.

3. THE NEW TESTAMENT IS CAREFULLY AND LOGICALLY WRITTEN

We also find that each New Testament book has been carefully written and thought out. The arguments for Jesus being the Christ are not emotional but rather are reasonable and logical. The expectation is that the reader will be able to follow the line of argumentation and then respond in belief.

4. EXPERIENCE MUST BE BASED UPON TRUTH

While emotions do play an important part in Christian experience they are always linked to a sound mind and to sound preaching. Nowhere do we find the writers appealing to experience alone as the test of truth.

5. WE ARE COMMANDED TO HONESTLY INVESTIGATE THE EVIDENCE

In fact, the Bible encourages honest investigation of the message of Christ. When people have legitimate questions concerning the Christian faith, they deserve to be given honest answers. We should not tell them, "Just believe," or "You have to take it by blind faith." The Bible never encourages this type of response. Paul wrote.

> But test everything that is said. Hold on to what is good (1 Thessalonians 5:21 NLT).

Another New Testament writer, John, put it this way.

> Beloved, do not believe every spirit, but test the spirits, whether they are of God; because many false prophets have gone out into the world (1 John 4:1 NKJV).

The Apostle Paul encouraged the church at Corinth to judge, as sensible people, the things that he said. He wrote.

> You are reasonable people. Decide for yourselves if what I am about to say is true (1 Corinthians 10:15 NLT).

Notice that Paul said they were reasonable people who could make their own decisions.

An important verse with respect to defending the faith is 1 Peter 3:15.

It reads as follows.

> Instead, you must worship Christ as Lord of your life. And if you are asked about your Christian hope, always be ready to explain it (1 Peter 3:15 NLT).

This verse commands Christians to know what they believe about God, why they believe it, and then be able to give an answer to those who ask questions about what and why they believe.

6. THE PATTERN OF THE NEW TESTAMENT IS TO GIVE INTELLIGENT ANSWERS

Furthermore, we find those in the New Testament giving intelligent answers to the questions asked about Jesus Christ and the Christian faith. In the Book of Acts, we read.

> As usual, Paul went into the synagogue. On three consecutive days of worship, he had discussions about Scripture with the synagogue members. He explained and showed to them that the Messiah had to suffer, die, and come back to life, and that Jesus the person he talked about, was this Messiah (Acts 17:2,3 God's Word).

This passage tells us that Paul held discussions with the unbelievers from the Scriptures. He took the time to listen to their questions and then give them answers.

When the Apostle Paul was in Athens, he went to Mars Hill. At that place he gave answers to the honest questions of the skeptics (Acts 17:16-34). Nowhere do we find him encouraging people to embrace the Christian message with blind faith or merely upon some religious experience.

In another example, we find that the apostle Paul spent a year and a half teaching the people at the church in Corinth. In the Book of Acts, we read the following.

> Paul lived in Corinth for a year and a half and taught the word of God to them (Acts 18:11 HCSB).

When Paul brought the good news to Ephesus, he hired a lecture hall. Then for two years he taught the people daily, proclaiming the message of Christ and answering the people's objections and questions. We also read in the Book of Acts.

> When some stubbornly refused to believe and spoke evil of the Way before the congregation, he left them, taking the disciples with him, and argued daily in the lecture hall of Tyrannus. This continued for two years, so that all the residents of Asia, both Jews and Greeks, heard the word of the Lord (Acts 19:9,10 NRSV).

In the Book of Acts, we read the following about the Berean Jews. It says.

> Now the Berean Jews were of more noble character than those in Thessalonica, for they received the message with great eagerness and examined the Scriptures every day to see if what Paul said was true (Acts 17:11 NIV).

The biblical writers applaud this type of behavior—the searching of the Scriptures to find out the truth. Furthermore, this type of response to unbelievers is the job of every believer—not just the specialist.

7. THE EXAMPLE OF JESUS WITH DOUBTING THOMAS

We also want to look at the way in which Jesus dealt with those who had doubts. The Bible says that when Jesus first appeared to His disciples after His resurrection, Thomas was absent. When the other disciples told Thomas they had seen the risen Lord, he wanted more than their word. Indeed, he wanted to see the evidence. The Bible says.

> So the other disciples told him, "We have seen the Lord." But he said to them, "Unless I see in his hands the mark

> of the nails, and place my finger into the mark of the nails, and place my hand into his side, I will never believe" (John 20:25 ESV).

When Jesus appeared eight days later, this time with Thomas present, He offered to show Thomas His scars. The Bible says.

> Then he said to Thomas, "Put your finger here, and see my hands; and put out your hand, and place it in my side. Do not disbelieve, but believe" (John 20:27 ESV).

We note that Jesus did not rebuke Thomas for wanting to see the risen Lord with his own eyes. Rather, Jesus offered to Thomas the opportunity to touch the imprints of the wounds. Jesus gave Thomas the evidence which he wanted. In the same manner, we should offer for those who doubt, the evidence which God has provided for us. It is not lack of faith to ask for sufficient evidence to trust Christ.

However, when the evidence is given, the person is then responsible to act upon it. It is proper for doubters to ask for evidence that meets a reasonable standard of proof. Unfortunately, many times, unbelievers ask for an impossible standard of proof before they claim they will believe. For example, they may say, "I will not believe in God unless He personally appears to me." This will not happen—neither will it remove the responsibility of the doubter to believe in Christ. God has already provided sufficient evidence for humans to believe. It is now the responsibility of each person to act upon that evidence.

8. WE SHOW THE WORLD THAT CHRISTIANITY HAS THE ANSWERS

Finally, giving reasonable answers to the objections of unbelievers is important because the world needs to know that Christians do indeed have the answers. The agnostic, atheist, those of other religions, and the cultists all need to know that the answers to their deepest questions about God and themselves are found in the Bible and in it alone. To do this, we must take the time to demonstrate that the Christian faith is a rational, intelligent system.

CONCLUSION: GOD DOES NOT NEED OUR DEFENSE HOWEVER, HE COMMANDS US TO DO IT

God certainly does not need our defense of Him. In fact, God does not need anything. The Apostle Paul wrote.

> He himself is before all things and all things are held together in him (Colossians 1:17 NET).

The God of the Bible holds the entire universe together. He needs nothing. However, according to Scripture, we are commanded to give answers to the questions that people ask about His existence and His dealings with humanity.

To sum up, both the evidentialists and the presuppositionalists believe the same things about the nature of the Bible and the Person of Jesus Christ. Also, there is no difference in their ultimate goals—to preach the gospel, see people come to Christ, and ultimately give glory to God. The only real difference between these believers is the way in which these goals are accomplished. The presuppositionalist starts by assuming the existence of God and the truthfulness of the Scripture. All discussion with unbelievers must begin with these assumptions.

On the other hand, while the evidentialist believes the exact same thing as the presuppositionalist, the evidentialist will discuss evidence for God's existence and the reliability of the Bible with the non-believer. Questions from the non-believer about these issues will be answered, not ignored.

Therefore, an apologist clarifies and defends biblical Christianity. On the positive side, it is the setting forth of evidences for the Christian faith. On the defensive side, apologetics defends the gospel against the attacks of unbelievers. While some Christians do not believe in answering the objections of unbelievers this is not the biblical approach.

We are to tell people not only what we believe but also we are to tell them why they should believe. Unbelievers who ask honest questions deserve to receive honest answers.

SUMMARY TO CHAPTER 1
APOLOGETICS: THE DEFENSE OF THE CHRISTIAN FAITH

In our first chapter, we have looked at some introductory issues with respect to the defense of the Christian faith. From what we have discovered, we can make the following observations.

1. First, we have discovered that humans have different belief options about God. They include the following.

Agnosticism—I do not know if God or gods exist.

Atheism—I do know—God or gods do not exist.

Theism—I do know—God or gods do exist.

Polytheism—Many gods exist.

Henotheism—The henotheist worships only one of the many gods who exist.

Monotheism—Only one God exists.

Pantheism—All things that exist are part of God. Therefore, God is impersonal.

Deism—The one God who exists is personal, yet He is not involved with humanity.

Personal Theism—The one personal God is intimately involved with humanity.

Unitarianism—God is only one person.

Trinitarianism—The one God who exists, is, by nature, a Trinity—three distinct Persons within the nature of the one God.

2. The Christian response in defending the faith is known as "apologetics." It has an offensive and defensive aspect to it. There are a number of references in the New Testament to defending the faith.

3. Apologetics has the idea of defending the faith that has been once-and-for-all delivered to the saints. There is a body of truth that needs to be proclaimed and defended.

4. Apologetics is not the gospel, but defends and clarifies the biblical gospel.

5. There are two basic approaches among Christians—the evidentialist and the presuppositionalist. The presuppositionalist does not believe in offering evidences for the truth of the Christian faith while the evidentialist does.

According to the evidentialist approach, Christians must not merely preach the gospel without offering a reasonable defense when the faith is attacked or questioned. This is the approach which is consistent with the Scripture.

6. Honest questions deserve honest answers. We should not tell people "just believe."

CHAPTER 2

Setting The Record Straight: What Christianity Is And Is Not

This chapter picks up where the last one left off. It clears up a number of common misconceptions about the Christian faith.

First, we again emphasize that all religions are not ultimately saying the same thing. The differences between them are so vast that they cannot all be true at the same time. While all of them can be wrong, they cannot all be true.

Furthermore, Christianity makes specific claims that rule out the claims made in these other religions. It claims to be the only religion, or faith, which has the truth about God. Therefore, according to the Christian perspective, the idea that somehow all religions are teaching the same thing, and that all paths eventually bring humanity to the same place, is not true. This is crucial for us to understand.

Indeed, Jesus made Himself the issue, not His teachings. People will spend eternity with God or apart from Him based upon their response to the claims of Jesus Christ.

Once this is established, we then go on to demonstrate that Jesus Christ did not merely make these claims about Himself, He backed up His claims with objective evidence. This is where Jesus is different from other religious leaders. He not only made the claims, He proved that He had the right to make these claims.

Before we examine the case for Christianity there are a few more introductory matters that need to be covered. This chapter covers those issues. They are as follows.

ALL RELIGIONS ARE NOT ULTIMATELY SAYING THE SAME THING

Though humans have many different belief options do these choices really matter? Is it possible that all these different belief systems (Buddhism, Hinduism, Islam, Christianity, etc.) are ultimately saying the same thing? If this is the case, then why make such a big deal out of Christianity?

Often we hear it asked in this manner, "Why make such a big issue about Jesus Christ and Christianity? All religions ultimately teach the same thing. Was not Jesus basically saying the same thing as Buddha, Confucius, Muhammad, and the other founders of great religions? They all teach that God is love, that we are to love our fellow humans, and that we should give of ourselves for others, do they not? If this is the case, then why single out Christianity for special attention?"

1. ALL RELIGIONS ULTIMATELY CONTRADICT EACH OTHER AT THEIR MAIN POINTS

The answer is simple: the Muslims, Buddhists, Christians and other religious groups cannot all be experiencing the same God because the way they define God contradicts each other. For example, Buddhism believes in an impersonal God—it does not separate God from creation, they are one-in-the same. However, Christianity believes and teaches that God is personal—He is not the same essence as His creation but has a separate existence from it. There are many such examples of major differences between the various religions.

Since the various religions teach different and contradictory things about the nature of God, and how a person can get to know Him, they cannot all be true at the same time. They can all be wrong, but they cannot all be true. It is impossible for God to be personal and impersonal at the same time. Hence, to say that all religions are ultimately the same shows a lack of understanding of these religions and what they are teaching.

Remember: The main question that needs to be addressed concerning the various religions is not, "Do they contain some truth?" The real issue is, "Can they save?"

2. CHRISTIANITY IS UNIQUE AMONG THE WORLD'S RELIGIONS IN ITS CLAIMS

Next, we must consider the unique claims of Jesus. He said.

> I am the way, and the truth, and the life. No one comes to the Father except through me (John 14:6 ESV).

Jesus claimed to be the exclusive way in which a person can know the only God who exists. Therefore, according to the Christian faith, any religion, which teaches another way to know God, is, at that point, incorrect. This claim of Jesus does not make it true in-and-of itself, however it does rule out the possibility of Christianity being compatible with any other religion.

3. JESUS IS IN A DIFFERENT CLASS THAN THE FOUNDERS OF OTHER WORLD RELIGIONS

Throughout history many religious leaders have come on the scene and attracted large followings—the Buddha, with his teachings on how to cope with life's suffering, gained millions of adherents. Confucius, with his precepts on how members of society should get along with each other, likewise numbers his followers in the millions. The same can be said for Muhammad and the religion of Islam. Yet, Jesus has demonstrated that He is in a different class from these, as well as all the other founders of the major religions of the world.

4. THE PERSON OF JESUS CHRIST IS THE ISSUE: NOT HIS TEACHINGS

Several things make Jesus different. First, He made Himself the issue while other leaders made their teachings the prime concern. Central to religions such as Buddhism, Islam, Sikhism, Confucianism, etc. are the teachings. What is stressed, in these religions, are the things these founders taught—not so much who they were. The teachers, therefore, are secondary to the teachings.

However, in Christianity, the opposite is true. The all-important issue is not so much what Jesus taught, as whom He claimed to be. The religious leaders of His day became infuriated when He claimed authority over everything. When Jesus healed on the Sabbath, contrary to their tradition, they became incensed. The Bible says.

> Some of the Pharisees said, "This man is not from God, for he does not observe the sabbath." But others said, "How can a man who is a sinner perform such signs?" And they were divided (John 9:16 NRSV).

Jesus answered this charge by declaring the following.

> For the Son of Man is Lord of the Sabbath (Matthew 12:8 HCSB).

Jesus Christ is Lord of all.

5. JESUS MAKES A DIFFERENCE

This is one of the major differences between Jesus and the founders of other religions—He made Himself the issue. We find Jesus asking His disciples the following question.

> Who do you say I am? (Matthew 16:15 NLT).

He asked this question to secure a commitment, either for Him or against Him. We do not find the founders of the other world religions doing such a thing.

When the Jewish religious leaders brought Jesus to Pontius Pilate, their accusation against Him was as follows.

> By our laws he ought to die because he called himself the Son of God" (John 19:7 NLT).

Therefore, contrary to the founders of all the other major religions, it is the identity of Jesus Christ, not His teachings, that is the major issue.

6. JESUS DEMONSTRATED HIS AUTHORITY

Another aspect that separates Jesus from other religious leaders is that He demonstrated He had authority to make such monumental claims. While other religious leaders have made great claims, they have given no legitimate evidence to substantiate them. Jesus, on the other hand, backed up His claims with objective proof.

THE DIFFERENCE THAT JESUS MAKES IS ILLUSTRATED

The account of Jesus healing a paralyzed man illustrates this point. When this man was brought before Him, Jesus said.

> Friend, your sins are forgiven (Mark 2:5 God's Word).

This claim to forgive sins upset the religious rulers. Mark records the following response.

> Some scribes were sitting there. They thought, "Why does he talk this way? He's dishonoring God. Who besides God can forgive sins?' (Mark 2:6,7 God's Word).

They said it is only God who can forgive sins.

ONLY GOD CAN FORGIVE SINS

They were absolutely right in their assertion that only God could forgive sins. The prophet Isaiah records God as saying:

> I, I am He who blots out your transgressions for my own sake, and I will not remember your sins (Isaiah 43:25 NRSV).

But making the claim to forgive sins is something that cannot be publicly verified. How could anyone have known that Jesus had this authority? Realizing this to be the case, Jesus responded.

> Jesus knew what they were discussing among themselves, so he said to them, "Why do you think this is blasphemy? Is it easier to say to the paralyzed man, 'Your sins are forgiven' or 'Get up, pick up your mat, and walk'? I will prove that I, the Son of Man, have the authority on earth to forgive sins." Then Jesus turned to the paralyzed man and said, "Stand up, take your mat, and go on home, because you are healed!" The man jumped up, took the mat, and pushed his way through the stunned onlookers. Then they all praised God. "We've never seen anything like this before!" they exclaimed (Mark 2:8-12 NLT).

We note how Jesus dealt with the situation. He asked, "Which is easier to say, 'Your sins are forgiven or rise up and walk?'" It is much easier to say, "Your sins are forgiven" because no one can tell, at that moment, whether or not they have been forgiven. There is no observable sign that accompanies the forgiveness of sin.

EVERYONE WILL KNOW THAT JESUS CHRIST HAS THE AUTHORITY

But, if someone says to a paralyzed man, "Rise up and walk," it will immediately become apparent to everyone whether or not the person has the ability to supernaturally heal. When Jesus instantly healed the paralytic, He showed the religious rulers He had God's authority—since this miracle occurred where everyone could see it with their own eyes.

Jesus, therefore, demonstrated His authority in the observable realm. It also illustrated the fact that He also had supernatural authority to forgive sins in the realm we cannot see—the invisible realm.

Therefore, Jesus did not merely make claims about Himself. Indeed, He backed up those claims with observable miracles, which testified, to His power and authority.

7. FULFILLED PROPHECY SEPARATES JESUS FROM OTHER RELIGIOUS LEADERS

Another thing that separates Jesus, from other founders of the great religions of the world, is that He fulfilled predictions about Himself that were written hundreds of years before He came. No one else can claim anything like this. Since the evidence is so vast, we will devote an entire chapter in our book to show the remarkable fulfillment of prophecy in the life of Jesus.

8. JESUS CHRIST CAME BACK FROM THE DEAD

A final fact, which separates Jesus from all others, is that He conquered the ultimate enemy that everyone faces—death. By coming back from the dead, He provided a solid answer to the question, "What will happen to us when we die?" No other religious figure has returned from the dead to verify his claims except Jesus of Nazareth. As we shall later see, the evidence that Jesus came back from the dead is sufficient to convince even the most skeptical.

9. THE CLAIMS OF JESUS CAN BE TESTED

In addition, the bodily resurrection of Jesus can be tested by the most rigorous historical methods. While many other religious traditions have an idea of spirit resurrections (an untestable hypothesis), only the New Testament proclaims a bodily resurrection that passes all tests of historical reliability. This provides the believer with a genuine hope of life beyond the grave.

Thus, the resurrection of Jesus Christ separates Him from all other religious figures, past or present, for He conquered the greatest enemy we all face—death.

Therefore, Jesus is different from the founders of other religions in at least four ways. They include the following.

He made Himself the issue instead of His teachings.

He backed up His claims with observable miracles.

He fulfilled predictions made about His life and His ministry. These predictions were made hundreds of years before He was born.

He conquered death to verify that He was the unique Son of God.

These four things separate Jesus from any other religious leader past or present.

ACCORDING TO SCRIPTURE, TRUTH IS ABSOLUTE

We now move on to the next obvious question, "So what if Jesus is unique? Does it really make a difference?" A popular response to this question is, "I'm glad Jesus has helped you, you need help! But don't tell me I have to believe in Him. What is true for you may not be true for me. It's enough that a person believes in something but ultimately it does not matter what you believe."

1. IT IS THE OBJECT OF FAITH THAT IS IMPORTANT

The Bible refutes this kind of thinking. It is important what we believe. In the New Testament, it is always the object of faith—Jesus Christ—and not faith itself, which is stressed. As far as the Bible is concerned, correct belief is crucial. The New Testament teaches that right belief consists of several things.

FAITH MUST BE IN THE GOD OF SCRIPTURE

First, faith must be in God, but not just any god. Faith must be placed only in the God of the Bible—He is the only God who exists. There are no others.

FAITH MUST BE IN HIS SON: JESUS CHRIST

Second, faith must be placed in God's Son, Jesus Christ. It is impossible to have a relationship with the true God apart from the Person of Jesus Christ. The Bible says.

> But to all who received him, who believed in his name, he gave power to become children of God (John 1:12 NRSV).

In another place, it states the following.

> No one who denies the Son has the Father; everyone who confesses the Son has the Father also (1 John 2:23 NRSV).

According to the Bible, anyone who claims to know God, and yet does not believe in Jesus, does not know God. You have to have both the Father and the Son.

FAITH IS MORE THAN MERE MENTAL ASSENT

Furthermore, faith in Jesus is more than merely acknowledging intellectually that He existed or that He is the Lord. James wrote about this type of ineffective faith. He compared it to the belief that demons have. He wrote.

> You believe that there is one God. You do well. Even the demons believe—and tremble (James 2:19 NKJV).

The demons know who Jesus is—God the Son, the Savior of the world. But merely knowing these things and other facts about Jesus does not do them any good—they have no relationship with Him. Biblical faith consists of trusting Jesus as Savior—not simply acknowledging Him with the intellect.

Therefore, it does matter what a person believes. Faith must be placed in God's Son—Jesus Christ—or else there is no forgiveness.

2. THE BIBLE ENCOURAGES PEOPLE TO USE THEIR MINDS WHEN CONSIDERING THESE ISSUES

Though the Bible encourages people to put their faith in Jesus, it is neither blind nor irrational faith. No one is asked to sacrifice his or her intellect when they put their faith in the God of the Bible. Christian faith is intelligent faith.

3. THE BIBLE REVEALS WHAT GOD HAS DONE IN HISTORY

Christian faith is a "reasonable" or an "intelligent" faith because it is based upon the firm foundation of what God has done in the past. The Lord has revealed Himself to humanity and that revelation is recorded in the Holy Scriptures. The Bible tells us what God requires of us and that we are to respond to Him by faith. In doing so, we are never expected to stop thinking or to act irrationally. Isaiah the prophet records the Lord as saying.

> Come now, and let us reason together (Isaiah 1:18 KJV).

Jesus emphasized that coming to God involves the mind as well as the heart and soul. Matthew writes.

> Jesus said to him, 'You shall love the LORD your God with all your heart, with all your soul, and with all your mind' (Matthew 22:37 NKJV).

When Jesus had a conversation with one of the teachers of the law, He equated intelligence with knowing God. Mark writes.

> When Jesus saw that he had answered thoughtfully, he said to him, "You are not far from the kingdom of God." Then no one dared any longer to question him (Mark 12:34 NET).

The New International Versions puts it this way

> When Jesus saw that he had answered wisely, he said to him, "You are not far from the kingdom of God." And

> from then on no one dared ask him any more questions (Mark 12:34 NIV).

An intelligent response from this person caused Jesus to remark that this man was close to the kingdom of God. This is another indication that the Bible encourages people to use their minds when examining the evidence for the Christian faith.

4. THE APOSTLES KNEW THE EVENTS THEY PREACHED AND WROTE ABOUT WERE TRUE

The writers of the New Testament knew the events they preached, and wrote about, actually occurred—because they were eyewitnesses to these events. Simon Peter showed that the New Testament authors were aware of the difference between mythology and fact. He wrote.

> For we were not making up clever stories when we told you about the power of our Lord Jesus Christ and his coming again. We have seen his majestic splendor with our own eyes. And he received honor and glory from God the Father when God's glorious, majestic voice called down from heaven, "This is my beloved Son; I am fully pleased with him" (2 Peter 1:16-17 NLT).

They knew what myths were, and they knew what they had experienced. They testified that the things they had experienced were not myths, but reality. Consequently, they welcomed an honest investigation of the facts. Blind faith was never encouraged.

SUMMARY OF THE CHRISTIAN POSITION

Therefore, the Christian position can be summed up as follows: If the God of the Bible is the true God, then every subject explored will only confirm, not contradict, His written revelation. The Christian is not afraid of any issue that may come up.

THE EVIDENCE IS SUFFICIENT TO BELIEVE IN CHRIST

Finally, as we examine the case for Christianity we will discover that the evidence is more than sufficient to believe. When all the evidence is in, it will be clear that the Christian faith is true—Jesus is the one whom He claimed to be. Therefore, each individual must ultimately make a decision concerning Him.

The rest of this book will present some of the evidence for "The Case for Christianity."

SUMMARY TO CHAPTER TWO
SETTING THE RECORD STRAIGHT

From our examination of further introductory issues with respect to the Christian faith, we can make the following concluding observations.

1. All religions are not ultimately saying the same thing.

2. Christianity is unique among the world's religions.

3. Jesus demonstrated Himself to be different from any other religious figure.

4. Scripture teaches that truth is absolute, it does matter what we believe.

5. The Bible encourages people to think about these matters—to use their mind.

6. When all the facts are in, the evidence is sufficient to believe in Christ. Therefore, the Christian is not afraid of answering any question the doubter may ask.

Consequently, giving evidence for belief in Jesus will strengthen the faith of the believer and will show the unbeliever that Christianity is based upon fact. It also demonstrates the need for each of us to respond to the claims of Jesus Christ.

Now that we have an understanding of the basic issues that are before us, let us move on to our case for Christianity.

CHAPTER 3

Introducing The Case For Christianity: The Christian Faith Is Sensible

In this chapter, we explain, in outline form, the case for Christianity. In brief, we go through the argument of the entire book. It will become obvious that each section is logically connected to the previous one. You will notice that we plan to begin by establishing a few necessary items.

First, we will demonstrate that the New Testament is trustworthy. It has been transmitted accurately throughout history and what it says matches up with known reality.

Once this has been established we will then observe exactly what the New Testament claims. This will introduce us to the main character, the Person of Jesus Christ and the claims made by Him and about Him. We will discover that He is the one way to reach the only God who exists.

Next, we will look at the options available to us. If in this reliable document, there are extraordinary claims made by its main character, then these claims must be addressed.

We will discover that there are only four possible responses to Jesus' claims. He never made them, legend, He made them and He knew they were false, liar, He made them and they were false, but He thought they were true, lunatic, or He made them, and they are true, Lord.

We will show that the legend hypothesis does not work. Also, the idea of Jesus being a liar or lunatic certainly does not fit the evidence. What is left is for us to believe His claims—He is Lord of all.

As we mentioned in chapter two, Jesus did not merely make claims, He backed them up with sufficient evidence. The next three chapters examine this evidence—miracles, fulfilled prophecy, and His resurrection from the dead.

Once we establish that Jesus is the One whom He claimed to be, we then look at how He viewed the Old Testament, His own teachings, and the soon-to-be-written New Testament.

Our last chapter sums up what we have learned. Again, it is important to realize that we build a case for Christianity by taking nothing for granted.

We now begin our examination of the case for the Christian faith. Our approach is simple: We are going to presume that the individual to whom we are talking to has never heard about the Bible, Jesus Christ, or Christianity.

Therefore, we will take absolutely nothing for granted. Our case for Christianity will be built without assuming any facts to be true. It is our belief that when all the evidence is in, the facts will speak loud and clear with respect to the truthfulness of the faith. The evidence will show that the Christian faith is true beyond a reasonable doubt.

Our plan is as follows.

PART 1: WE FIRST ESTABLISH THE RELIABILITY OF THE NEW TESTAMENT

Our first point is to make the determination that the New Testament is a reliable historical document—it can be trusted. The reliability will be demonstrated in two ways—its text and its history. This occurs in the following ways.

THE TEXT OF THE NEW TESTAMENT: WHAT IT SAYS HAS BEEN TRANSMITTED ACCURATELY

We will discover that the text of the New Testament has been transmitted accurately throughout history. In other words, the New Testament says the same thing today as when it was originally written—it has not been changed.

Therefore, we can trust that the message has been handed down to us correctly. While this, by itself, does not make the Bible the Word of God, or even true, it does give us confidence to move on to the next step.

NEW TESTAMENT HISTORY—THE EVENTS MATCH UP WITH KNOWN FACTS

Next, we will look at the history that the New Testament records. We will see that the historical references reported in the New Testament match up to known history. As far as we can tell, the people mentioned were real people, and the events actually occurred. Consequently, we are dealing with reality, not mythology.

Therefore, the New Testament proves trustworthy in both its text and its history. This being the case, the claims it makes deserve to be heard because everything about it tells us it is a reliable document.

PART 2: WE DISCOVER THE CLAIMS THE NEW TESTAMENT MAKES ABOUT JESUS CHRIST

Next, we move on to our second point—the claims of the New Testament. First, we determine what kind of book the Bible is, and what it has to say about itself. We need to let it tell us the story it wants to tell rather than forcing it to say something it does not say. From the New Testament, we discover two important truths about Jesus Christ. They can be summarized as follows.

JESUS IS THE ONE WAY TO REACH THE ONE GOD

We will discover that the main character of the New Testament is Jesus Christ. In fact, the entire Bible is about Him. Astounding claims are made about Jesus—He is the Savior of the world, the Son of God, the way, the truth, and the life, the only hope for salvation. According to Scripture, there is no other way to reach the only God who exists except through Jesus. This is the claim the New Testament makes about Him—it is not something that the church later invented.

JESUS IS GOD ALMIGHTY

Furthermore, the Scripture teaches that Jesus was more than a mere human—He is God the Son, the Second Person of the Trinity. He is the living God who became a human being. This is taught both directly and indirectly in the New Testament.

PART 3: THE CLAIMS MADE ABOUT CHRIST ARE EXAMINED

We then examine the claims of the New Testament about Jesus Christ. Since these claims are recorded in a document that we have already demonstrated to be reliable it its text and its historical references, these claims must be taken seriously.

Consequently, there are three possible ways to understand the claims made about Jesus that are recorded in the New Testament. They are as follows.

POSSIBILITY 1: HE NEVER MADE THE CLAIMS—LEGEND

This view holds that Jesus never made the astounding claims that are recorded in the New Testament. The claims are those of His disciples who later exaggerated His words. Therefore, the accounts about His miracles and the claims that He is the Son of God, the Savior of the world, and the only hope of humanity, are merely legendary. Basically, this point of view says that Jesus' disciples turned this simple teacher and preacher into God Himself.

However, as we shall see, this viewpoint does not fit the facts. There is not enough time for legends about Jesus to occur before the New

Testament was written. This means that the claims made about Jesus, and by Jesus, have to be dealt with. He actually made these claims.

POSSIBILITY 2: HE MADE THE CLAIMS BUT THE CLAIMS WERE NOT TRUE: LIAR OR LUNATIC

The second possibility is that He actually made the claims that are recorded in the New Testament but His claims were not true. We have two possibilities if this is the case. They are as follows.

HE COULD HAVE BEEN A LIAR

This perspective believes that Jesus was not the Son of God and that He knew He was not the Son of God, yet He lied about His true identity when He made the claims recorded in the New Testament. Therefore, He knowingly lied about who He was.

HE MAY HAVE BEEN A LUNATIC

The other possibility, if His claims were not true, holds that Jesus was not the Son of God but that He actually thought that He was. In this case, Jesus would have been deluded when He claimed to be the ultimate authority on every issue.

POSSIBILITY 3: HE MADE THE CLAIMS AND THEY WERE TRUE—LORD

The last possibility holds that Jesus actually made the claims recorded in the New Testament and these claims are true. This would make Him Lord.

After examining the three possible ways in which to assess Jesus' claims, we will find that the only one that makes sense is that He is Lord. There is no evidence whatsoever that Jesus was a liar or a lunatic.

PART 4: THE EVIDENCE FOR JESUS' CLAIMS

The fourth section will deal with the evidence concerning the claims of Christ. If Jesus is the Lord, then there should be some evidence to back up His claims.

The New Testament basically provides us with three different lines of evidence: miracles, fulfilled prophecy, and Jesus' resurrection from the dead.

MIRACLES

We will see that Jesus performed miracles as objective signs that He was indeed the promised Messiah. The number of miracles recorded, the different types of miracles, as well as the various areas of authority they covered, show that Jesus is the One whom He claimed to be—the Son of God. In addition, all attempts to explain away the miracles of Jesus miserable fail.

FULFILLED PROPHECY

Our second line of evidence will be predictive prophecy. Only God knows the future and in Scripture we have the evidence of the future having been predicted in advance.

Fulfilled prophecy shows not only that God exists, but that also He is in control of history. Consequently, we can have complete confidence in Him and His message.

THE RESURRECTION OF CHRIST

The final evidence is the most important of all—the resurrection of Jesus Christ from the dead. Without the resurrection there is no Christian faith. Happily, the evidence for the resurrection of Jesus Christ is overwhelming.

These three lines of evidence, taken together, provide a solid foundation for the believer to put their trust in Jesus as the One whom He claimed to be.

PART 5: THE BIBLE IS GOD'S WORD—JESUS SAYS SO!

We now come to our final point—the nature of the Bible. We believe it is the Word of God because Jesus says so. His understanding of Scripture will be our understanding since He has demonstrated Himself to be God's Son. To be consistent, we should hold the same view of Scripture as Jesus held.

JESUS' VIEW OF THE OLD TESTAMENT

First, we will examine Jesus' view of the Old Testament. He believed it was God's Word. His attitude toward the Old Testament was one of total trust. Since He is God the Son, He would be in a position to know whether or not the Old Testament was God's Word. He made it clear that it is.

JESUS' VIEW OF HIS OWN TEACHINGS

Next we examine how Jesus viewed His own teachings. We will find that He considered them to be authoritative. When He spoke there was no court of appeal—He was the final Word on every matter in which He dealt with! There is no doubt that He believed this about His own teachings.

JESUS' VIEW OF THE NEW TESTAMENT

Finally, we have Jesus' predictions to His disciples with respect to the New Testament. We will find that He pre-authenticated it—promising His followers that all things He taught them would be supernaturally brought back to their remembrance and the Holy Spirit would guide them into all truth.

Therefore, we can put out trust in the New Testament because Jesus authenticated it ahead of time. This is the outline for our study. We will argue the Case for Christianity in the same way in which reasonable people everywhere argue for truth in the areas such as law, history, and science.

We will examine the evidence and then draw conclusions based upon the best evidence.

We will now proceed to our first point—establishing the reliability of the New Testament.

CHAPTER 4

The Reliability Of The New Testament Text: It Has Not Been Changed Throughout Time

In this chapter, we begin our case for Christianity. Before we can examine anything that the New Testament claims about Jesus, we must first establish what the writers actually said about Him. This chapter looks at the various sources used to reconstruct the text of the New Testament.

We begin our study by looking at the necessity of recovering the original text. We then consider the three sources available to us—Greek manuscripts, versions or translations, and the writings of the early Christians, or the Church Fathers.

After listing the evidence from these sources, we compare the New Testament to other ancient works, as well as the writings of William Shakespeare. We will discover that the New Testament is in a class by itself.

We then move on to the subject of variations in the text, or variant readings. Our look at the evidence shows that the variations in the manuscripts have not changed or altered the message of Jesus. The conclusion we will make, from examining the evidence, is that the New Testament text is indeed trustworthy. Thus, we can read our English translations with confidence seeing that they are translating from the words which were originally written by the authors.

Our first order of business concerns the text of the New Testament. Is there evidence that what we read today in our modern translations is an accurate representation of what was originally written, or has the text been changed so often that we cannot trust it at all? Can we be assured that we are reading the actual words that these writers first penned, or have their writings been altered—either accidentally or on purpose? This issue is primary.

Unless we can be satisfied that the text has come down to us in an accurate manner, no reasonable case for Christianity can be established. We will discover that there is every reason to trust that the New Testament has been accurately transmitted to us.

THE STUDY OF TEXTUAL CRITICISM

In the first century, Greek was the international language. The books of the New Testament were originally written in the common Greek of the day called *koine*. Today, we do not possess the autographs (originals) of the various New Testament books but are dependent upon handwritten copies, and copies of copies to reconstruct the text. The practice of reconstructing the text of a document is known as "textual criticism."

We must note that textual criticism is not limited to the New Testament. No originals exist of any of the Greek and Latin classics, any of the writings of the early Christians, or even the works of William Shakespeare.

THE NECESSITY OF NEW TESTAMENT TEXTUAL CRITICISM

Textual criticism of the New Testament is necessary for three basic reasons. They are as follows.

1. We do not possess any of the original writings of the New Testament. We are dependent upon copies to reconstruct the text.

2. Movable type was not invented until the fifteenth century. Gutenberg's Latin Bible was printed somewhere between the years 1452 and 1456. Therefore, until about five hundred years ago, all documents were

copied by hand. The handwritten copies of the Greek New Testament are called manuscripts. The copies of the New Testament manuscripts we now possess differ in some respects from each other because of scribal mistakes that have crept into the text.

3. In the case of the New Testament there is an abundance of material to evaluate.

Therefore, the lack of the originals for any of the New Testament books, the fact that the existing manuscripts differ, and the abundance of evidence that exists, makes textual criticism, with respect to the New Testament, absolutely necessary.

Furthermore, before any type of biblical interpretation can begin, we must first determine what the text originally said. We cannot determine what the text means until we first determine what it says. This is another reason for the necessity of New Testament textual criticism.

THE PRACTICE OF TEXTUAL CRITICISM

The goal of textual criticism is to establish the original reading of the text. To accomplish this goal, the textual critic sifts through the manuscripts and carefully compares them with one another. This is to ascertain, as much as it is possible, how the variations occurred. The goal of New Testament textual criticism is to recover the original text.

THERE IS AN ABUNDANCE OF EVIDENCE TO CONSIDER

The problem with almost all ancient writings is the lack of existing manuscripts to reconstruct the text. Most ancient writings have the slimmest manuscript evidence by which scholars attempt to establish the original. In the case of the New Testament, however, there is no such problem. We are not lacking manuscripts to reconstruct the text. On the contrary, we have such an abundance of manuscripts that it makes the establishment of the text virtually certain. We can make the following observations.

THERE ARE THREE LINES OF EVIDENCE FOR THE NEW TESTAMENT TEXT

In the case of the New Testament there are three lines of evidence available to reconstruct the original. They include.

1. The Greek Manuscripts

2. The Versions (Translations)

3. The Writings Of The Church Fathers

We will consider the evidence from each of these witnesses.

The Evidence From The Greek Manuscripts

The oldest and most important evidence to reconstruct the New Testament text are the Greek manuscripts. Since the New Testament was originally written in Greek, these Greek manuscripts which have survived are the most important evidence which we have to reconstruct the true text.

We find that these manuscripts are categorized according to writing material (papyri), the style of the letters (uncial and minuscule manuscripts) and the format of the document (lectionaries).

PAPYRUS MANUSCRIPTS (THE PAPYRI)

The first group of manuscripts, the papyri, is named after the type of material they were written upon—papyrus. Papyrus was cheap writing material. The English word translated "paper" is derived from the word papyrus.

Scholars are fairly certain that papyrus is the surface upon which the originals (the autographs) of the books of the New Testament were composed. Indeed, papyrus is actually mentioned in the New Testament. John wrote.

> Though I have much to write to you, I would rather not use paper and ink. Instead I hope to come to you and talk face to face, so that our joy may be complete (2 John 12 ESV).

The word translated "paper," in this verse, is referring to papyrus. In this verse, the Greek word *chartes* is used. It referred to a sheet or role of papyrus. From this Greek term, comes the Latin word *charta* and the English words "chart," "charter", and "card."

Papyrus is extremely perishable, surviving only in warm, dry climates. Thus, we are fortunate that any papyrus fragments have survived to this day. The papyrus fragments that have survived contain some of the earliest witnesses to the New Testament text. In fact, the forty-five earliest New Testament fragments we possess were written on papyri (all dating before A.D. 300). The content in these forty-five manuscripts make up about two thirds of the New Testament text.

At the turn of the twentieth century, there were only nine known papyrus fragments that contained parts of the New Testament. There are now some one hundred and twenty-seven and counting. These papyrus manuscripts are designated by the letter "p" followed by a superscript Arabic number (e.g. p75).

UNCIALS (MAJUSCULES)

The second line of evidence to reconstruct the text of the New Testament is the uncial or inch high manuscripts. They are also called majuscules. The name uncial is derived from the inch-high size of the letters. There are approximately three hundred uncial manuscripts of the New Testament which have still survived. All of them were written upon parchment (animal skins). Many of them are ornately illustrated.

We must note that all of the papyrus manuscripts which still exist are also written in uncial script. The papyrus manuscripts are catalogued separately from the uncial manuscripts because of the two different surfaces which the text was written upon—papyrus and animal skins.

Uncial writing consists of upper-case, or capital-like, letters that are deliberately and carefully written. There was no punctuation in the sentences and no space between the words. Though there is no space between the words, it is still possible to read and understand the sentence with ease.

The uncial manuscripts were basically written between the fourth and tenth centuries—there are five fragmentary uncials that date from the third century.

As a note of interest, it has been estimated that it would have taken the hides of about three hundred and sixty sheep and goats to produce *Codex Sinaiaticus* (a fourth century uncial manuscript that contained the entire Greek Old Testament and New Testament).

THE MINUSCULES (CURSIVES)

In the ninth century A.D., uncial writing began to be replaced by a faster method known as minuscule writing. Minuscule writing was a script of smaller letters or lower case letters not as carefully executed as uncials. By using minuscule writing, books could be turned out much faster.

Minuscule writing was in use from the ninth to the sixteenth century. There are approximately two thousand eight hundred minuscule or cursive manuscripts which are known to exist.

LECTIONARIES

The fourth witness, to the New Testament text, are Scripture portions known as lectionaries. The church followed the custom of the synagogue which had a fixed portion of the Law and the Prophets read each Sabbath. In the same manner, Christians developed a practice where they would read a fixed portion of the gospels and the New Testament letters every Sunday as well as upon Holy Days. These fixed portions are the lectionaries. Fragments of lectionaries come from as early as the sixth century A.D., while complete manuscripts are found as early as the eighth century. About three hundred of the lectionary manuscripts were written with the upper case uncial script but the great majority of them were composed in the lower case minuscule script. There are about twenty-three hundred lectionary manuscripts which still exist.

Interestingly, the copies of the lectionaries which still exist reveal greater care in their copying than other biblical manuscripts. Because these sections of Scripture were to be read publicly, great care was taken to make certain they were copied correctly.

CATALOGING THE GREEK MANUSCRIPTS

Therefore, we can catalogue the manuscripts into these four groupings— papyri, uncials, minuscules, and lectionaries. The surviving Greek manuscripts can then be catalogued as follows: Uncial (about 300) Minuscule (2,813), Lectionaries (2,281), Papyri (127). That would make the total about 5,500.

It is also possible to place the Greek manuscripts into two groupings— those which have the uncial writing and those which employ minuscule writing. As we have seen, the papyri, uncial manuscripts, and about three hundred lectionary manuscripts use this more formal hand-writing style while the great majority of existing manuscripts are written in the minuscule or cursive style.

One last thing should be noted about the total number of surviving manuscripts. This is not an exact number because some of the manuscripts that are counted individually actually belong to other existing manuscripts. Because of the fragmentary nature of some of the existing manuscripts, it is not certain as to whether it is a separate manuscript or whether it is part of another manuscript which has already been catalogued.

THEY ARE NOT NECESSARILY COMPLETE MANUSCRIPTS

This brings us to an important point. When we speak of manuscripts, we are not necessarily speaking of complete manuscripts. For example, of the

5,500 Greek manuscripts that have been catalogued, most are fragmentary. Only three of the uncials are complete. There are fifty-six minuscule manuscripts that contain the entire New Testament. Two other uncial manuscripts, and another one hundred forty-seven minuscules, contain the entire New Testament except for the Book of Revelation.

Material from the gospels is found in 2,328 manuscripts, Acts and the universal letters in another 655 manuscripts, Paul's writings in 779 manuscripts, and the Book of Revelation in 287. No other ancient book has anywhere near the amount of manuscript testimony as the New Testament.

As far as the dates of these manuscripts are concerned, 125 of them are from the first five centuries (two and one half per cent of the total) while 65% of the manuscripts are from the 11th through 14th centuries. These manuscripts exist today in libraries, museums, and private collections all over the world.

THE EVIDENCE FROM THE VERSIONS (TRANSLATIONS)

Though the total number of surviving Greek manuscripts is larger than all other ancient works, they are not the only means available for reconstructing the original text. A second line of evidence by which the New Testament text can be established comes from the versions. Versions are translations of the different New Testament books into languages other than Greek. Ancient literature was rarely translated into another language—with the New Testament being an important exception.

From the very beginning, Christian missionaries, in an attempt to spread their faith, translated the New Testament into the various languages of the people they encountered. These translations, some made as early as the middle of the second century, give us an important witness to the text of that time.

We should also note that scholars usually reserve the term "manuscript" for Greek manuscripts of the New Testament, while the different copies of the versions are usually referred to as versional evidence or copies of versions. Thus, the word manuscript becomes something of a special term referring to the handwritten copies found only in Greek.

When the copies of the versions are catalogued, again we are faced with an overwhelming number (somewhere in the neighborhood of 30,000)

Because the versions are translations from the original Greek, they are not as valuable as the Greek manuscripts in reconstructing the text. However, they are an important witness to the text's reliability.

COMPARISONS OF THE NEW TESTAMENT TO OTHER ANCIENT WORKS

When the total manuscript evidence for the New Testament text (Greek manuscripts and early translations) is compared to other ancient writings the difference is striking. Consider the following evidence.

THE NEW TESTAMENT COMPARED TO OTHER ANCIENT WORKS

When the total manuscript evidence for the New Testament text (Greek manuscripts and early translations) is compared to other ancient writings the difference is striking. Note the following comparisons.

	Date Written	Earliest Copy	Time Span (Years)	Number of Copies
Euripides	450. B.C.	A.D. 1100	1500	9
Sophocles	450. B.C.	A.D. 1000	1400	193
Catullus	54 B.C.	A.D. 1550	1600	3
Homer	900 B.C.	400 B.C.	500	1800
N.T.	A.D. 40-95	A.D. 125	3	24,000

THERE ARE TWO QUESTIONS TO CONSIDER WHEN RECONSTRUCTING A TEXT

When reconstructing the text of an ancient work, two key questions need to be considered—the time span and the number of copies.

The first question deals with the time span between the date the work was completed and the earliest existing copy available to reconstruct the text. Usually, the shorter the time span the more dependable is the copy. The longer the time between the original and the copy, the more errors are apt to creep in as the text is copied and recopied.

As the above chart reveals, the time span between the composition of the New Testament and the earliest existing copy is much shorter than for these other ancient works. Using this standard of comparison, the New Testament is far superior in this regard.

HOW MANY COPIES STILL EXIST?

The second question that needs to be addressed concerns the number of copies, "How many copies are available to reconstruct the text?" The more copies available, the better off we are—since there is more evidence to help one decide what the original text said.

For example, if an ancient work were to come down to us in only one copy, there would be nothing with which to compare that copy. There is no way of knowing if the scribe was incompetent since it could not be checked against another copy.

As we have seen, the New Testament dwarfs all other ancient works with respect to the total number of manuscripts that still exist. With such a wealth of manuscript evidence, we have every right to assume that nothing has been lost from the original New Testament text. Yet, the Greek manuscripts and the various versions do not exhaust the lines of evidence for reconstructing how the text read.

THE EVIDENCE FROM THE CHURCH FATHERS

A third line of evidence, used in establishing the New Testament text, are the quotations from the writings of the early Christians known as the "church fathers." In their writings, they often quoted from the New Testament text. Every time we find a biblical quotation we have a further witness to the text.

THERE IS MUCH EARLY TESTIMONY TO THE NEW TESTAMENT

For example, seven letters have survived which were written by a man named Ignatius (A.D. 70-110). In those letters he quoted from eighteen different books of the New Testament. Every time he cites Scripture, we can observe the Greek text he was using.

Consequently, the early church fathers provide us with an excellent early witness to the text. We must be careful, however, in relying too heavily on the fathers because sometimes their quotations were paraphrases (not word for word citations) of the biblical text. In addition, the manuscripts of their writings have gone through a period of copying, during which time mistakes have slipped into the text. Nevertheless, their writings remain an important witness to the New Testament.

THERE IS OVERWHELMING TESTIMONY TO THE TEXT

The number of quotations of the church fathers is so overwhelming that, if every other source for the New Testament (Greek manuscripts, versions) were destroyed, the text could be reconstructed merely on the writings of the church fathers alone! In his book, *Our Bible—How We Got It*, Charles Leach relates the story of Sir David Dalrymple.

> Sir David Dalrymple was wondering about the preponderance of Scripture in early writings when someone asked him. 'Suppose that the New Testament had been destroyed, and every copy of it lost by the end of the third century,

> could it have been collected again from the writings of the Fathers of the second and third centuries?' After a great deal of investigation Dalrymple concluded . . . 'You remember the question about the New Testament and the Fathers? That question roused my curiosity and as I possessed all the existing works of the Fathers of the second and third centuries, I commenced to search and up to this time I have found the entire New Testament, except eleven verses'.[1]

Author Leo Vaganay remarked on the thorough research of the nineteenth century scholar John Burgon. He said.

> Of the considerable volumes of unpublished material that Dean Burgon left when he died, of special note is his index of New Testament citations by the church Fathers of antiquity. It contains sixteen thick volumes to be found in the British Museum, and contains 86,489 quotations.[2]

Today, it has been estimated that we have over one million quotations of Scripture which have survived in the writings from the early Christians!

Confidently, we can say that when the evidence from the Greek manuscripts, the versions (translations), and the church fathers is considered, any impartial person cannot help but be impressed with their abundant testimony.

THE COMPARISON OF THE NEW TESTAMENT TEXT TO THE WORKS OF SHAKESPEARE

We can go a step further and compare the New Testament to the works of William Shakespeare. He wrote thirty-seven plays in the

---

1. Charles Leach, *Our Bible—How We Got It*, Chicago: Moody Press, 1898, pp. 35, 36
2. Leo Vaganay, *An Introduction to the Textual Criticism of the New Testament*, trans. by B.V. Miller, London: Sands and Co., 1937, p. 48

seventeenth century—all after the invention of printing. The originals of Shakespeare's plays have not survived. Therefore, we are dependent upon copies to reconstruct the text. In every one of his plays there are gaps in the printed text where we do not know what was originally written. Textual scholars attempt to fill in the gaps in the printed copies by making an educated guess as to what it originally said. The New Testament, written some sixteen centuries earlier than Shakespeare, with three quarters of its history copied by hand, is in much better textual shape, needing no educated guesses to fill in the blanks.

THERE IS NO GUESSWORK NEEDED TO ESTABLISH THE NEW TESTAMENT TEXT

Since we do possess so many manuscripts, we can be assured the original text has been preserved. Consequently, we never have to revert to guessing to determine what the text originally said. The great scholar of the nineteenth century, Samuel Tregelles, wrote.

We possess so many mss, [manuscripts] and we are aided by so many versions, that we are never left to the need to conjecture as the means of removing errata [mistakes].[3]

Modern day textual scholar Michael Holmes concurs. He put it this way.

> The sheer volume of the information available to the New Testament textual critic makes it practically certain that the original text has been preserved somewhere among the surviving witnesses.[4]

The well-known textual authority, Sir Frederic Kenyon, wrote the following testimony.

---

3. Samuel Tregelles, *Greek New Testament*, Prolegomena

4. Michael Holmes, *New Testament Criticism and Interpretation*, Editors David Alan Black and David S. Dockery, Zondervan, 1991, p. 106

> The number of manuscripts of the New Testament, of early translations from it, and of quotations from it in the oldest writers of the Church, is so large that it is practically certain that the true reading of every doubtful passage is preserved in some one or other of these ancient authorities. This can be said of no other book in the world.[5]

Clearly, the text has come down to us in an accurate manner with nothing lost in its transmission.

THE TRANSMISSION OF THE NEW TESTAMENT WAS WATCHED BY DIFFERENT GROUPS

Another important point to remember is that there were different groups interested in the proper copying of the text. From the time the New Testament text was first written there were a number of different groups in the church who had differences of belief. However, to substantiate their belief, all of these different groups appealed to the same Scriptures. Consequently, they would have been vigilant in making certain that the text was not altered in any way. They would have been constantly keeping an eye on one another. This is another reason why we can be confident that nothing was added or deleted to the New Testament text.

THE VARIANT READINGS IN THE TEXT: WHY DO THE MANUSCRIPTS READ DIFFERENTLY?

Next, we deal with the often-asked question about variant readings. When two manuscripts differ on a particular word or phrase in the text, the result is known as a variant reading. The difference may be of spelling, word order, or different words used. Because of the innumerable times the New Testament has been copied in the last two thousand years,

---

5. Sir Frederic Kenyon, *Our Bible and Ancient Manuscripts*, New York: Harper and Brothers, 1941, p. 55

scribal errors have crept into the text. However, textual critics do not use the word "error" to describe these variations because the word error gives the wrong idea. This is why the term "variant reading" is used.

MOST OF THE VARIATIONS ARE UNINTENTIONAL

The scribes who did copy the text introduced changes. These scribal changes can be broken down into two basic types: unintentional and intentional. The greatest number of the variant readings which are found in the New Testament manuscripts are unintentional variants. They could creep into the text through faulty sight, hearing, writing, memory or judgment on the part of the scribe.

THERE WAS SOME INTENTIONAL VARIATIONS

Some of the variations came about intentionally as New Testament Greek scholar J. Harold Greenlee notes.

> These comprise a significant, although a much less numerous, group of errors than the unintentional changes. They derive for the most part from attempts by scribes to improve the text in various ways. Few indeed are the evidences that heretical or destructive variants have been deliberately introduced into the mss [manuscripts].[6]

Thus, the intentional variations, for the most, part, were the work of scribes attempting to make the text more readable—not change the meaning.

Bruce Metzger, the great authority on New Testament textual criticism, expands upon the intentional variations. He wrote.

> Other divergence's in wording arose from deliberate attempts to smooth out grammatical or stylistic harshness, or to

6. J. Harold Greenlee, *Introduction To New Testament Textual Criticism*, Eerdmans, 1964, p. 66

> eliminate real or imagined obscurities of meaning in the text. Sometimes a copyist would add what seemed to him to be a more appropriate word or form, perhaps derived from a parallel passage.[7]

The charge is often made that copyists radically changed the text. Again, the facts speak otherwise as Michael Holmes explains the evidence.

> Occasionally the text was altered for doctrinal reasons. Orthodox and heretics alike leveled this charge against their opponents, though the surviving evidence suggests the charge was more frequent than the reality.[8]

Therefore, the amount of intentional variation to the text was minimal. The text was carefully copied, and the Christians, who were spread out throughout the entire Roman Empire, would have made certain that changes would not be introduced.

SUMMARY TO THE VARIANT READINGS FOUND IN THE TEXT

With respect to the variations found in the New Testament manuscripts, most were unintentional. The few that were intentional consisted mostly of grammatical improvements. There is no evidence of any widespread altering of the text for doctrinal reasons.

THERE IS A SMALL PERCENTAGE OF VARIATION IN THE TEXT

Furthermore, the variant readings, whether intentional or unintentional, exist only in a very limited portion of the New Testament. The practice of textual criticism, therefore, deals with this small percentage of the biblical text. Two of the greatest textual scholars who ever lived,

---

7. Bruce Metzger, *A Textual Commentary on the Greek New Testament*, German Bible Society, Second Edition, 1994, p.3,4

8. Michael Holmes, *New Testament Criticism and Interpretation*, Editors David Alan Black and David S. Dockery, Zondervan, p. 103

Brooke Foss Westcott and Fenton John Anthony Hort, had this to say concerning the amount of variation in the New Testament manuscripts.

> If comparative trivialities, such as changes of order, the insertion or omission of an article with proper names, and the like, are set aside, the words in our opinion still subject to doubt can hardly amount to more than a thousandth part of the whole New Testament.[9]

Scholar B.B. Warfield made a similar claim. He wrote.

> [The New Testament] has been transmitted to us with no, or next to no, variation; and even in the most corrupt form in which it has ever appeared, to use the oft-quoted words of Richard Bentley, 'The real text of the sacred writers is competently exact'.[10]

Textual criticism experts, Maurice A. Robinson and William Pierpoint, note the following situation in which we find the text of the New Testament.

> For over four-fifths of the New Testament, the Greek text is considered 100% certain, regardless of which textype might be favored by any critic. This undisputed bulk of the text reflects a common pre-existing archetype (the autograph), which has universal critical acceptance.
>
> Note . . . that most of the variant readings found in manuscripts of other textypes are trivial or untranslatable. Only about 400-600 variant readings seriously affect

9. B.F. Westcott and F.J.A. Hort, *The New Testament in Greek*, New York: MacMillan, 1957, p. 565

10. Benjamin B. Warfield, *Introduction to the Textual Criticism of the New Testament*, seventh edition. London: Hodder and Stoughton, 1907, p. 14

> the translational sense of any passage in the entire New Testament.[11]

Therefore, when all the variants of the New Testament are considered we are only dealing with four hundred to six hundred places that have any affect on the translation of the text.

ONLY FIFTY VARIANTS ARE IMPORTANT

> Church historian Phillip Schaff estimated that of the four hundred variants that have affected the sense of the passages in the New Testament, only fifty of these were actually important.[12]

Facts like this led textual scholars Kurt and Barbara Aland to make the following observations concerning the text of the New Testament.

> On the whole it must be admitted that statements about the text of the New Testament whether by amateurs or by specialists, have far too rarely reflected an overall perspective. All too frequently the focus has been on variants found in particular manuscripts or editions. This is true for even the most fundamental aspects of textual criticism; when identifying the text type of a manuscript it is all too easy to overlook the fact that the Byzantine Imperial text and the Alexandrian Egyptian text, to take two examples that in theory are diametrically opposed to each other, actually exhibit a remarkable degree of agreement, perhaps as much as 80 percent! Textual critics themselves, and New Testament specialists

---

11. Maurice A. Robinson, William Pierpoint, *The New Testament In The Original Greek According To The Byzantine/Majority TextForm*, Atlanta, The Original Word Publishers, 1991, p. xvi. and xvii

12. Phillip Schaff, *Companion to the Greek New Testament and the English Version*, 1877, p. 177

> even more so, not to mention laypersons, tend to be fascinated by differences and to forget how many of them are due to chance or normal scribal tendencies, and how rarely significant variants occur—yielding to the common danger of failing to see the forest for the trees.[13]

This is so important to understand. Whatever manuscript tradition we use as the basis for our translation, the outcome will be basically the same because the text is basically the same. Whether one prefers to use the Byzantine text type, which is found in the greatest number of manuscripts, or the Alexandrian text type, which has fewer but older manuscripts, the final result will be more or less the same. They all tell the same story!

Textual scholar Michael Holmes concurs in this assessment. He writes.

> Indeed, in view of the attention that is rightly focused on the places where the evidence differs, it is worth noting just how much of the New Testament is well established. A survey by the Alands reveals that out of the 7,947 verses in the Greek New Testament, seven major editions are in complete agreement regarding 4,999, or 62.9% (Aland, text, p. 28-29). If one were to leave aside certain idiosyncrasies and minor differences between these editions, it may be estimated where there is substantial agreement approaches 90% of the total. To be sure, the remaining differences can be substantial and important, and fully merit the attention given to them over the centuries by the textual critics. One should not neglect, however, to keep them in perspective, especially as people unacquainted with textual matters are sometimes shocked to encounter statements to the effect that "there are over 30,000 errors in the New Testament." The statements are

13. Kurt Aland and Barbara Aland, *The Text of the New Testament*, 1987, p. 28

> uninformed and inaccurate. If one defines "error" broadly enough, to include, e.g., spelling mistakes or differences, then it is true that there are tens of thousands of "errors' among the 5000 + manuscripts of the New Testament. But this hardly affects the reliability of the New Testament itself, since wherever some MSS are in error, other have accurately preserved the original text.[14]

This is another crucial point to understand. The thousands upon thousands of variants in the New Testament manuscripts are in direct proportion to the number of manuscripts which exist. Thus, the only reason that there are so many variants is because of the enormous number of manuscripts which we have to investigate. Furthermore, though the variants do exist, there also exists a way to correct the copying mistakes through comparing the manuscripts with each other.

Therefore, we must keep the issue of the variants in the text in proper perspective. If one reads the various printed editions of the Greek New Testament, whether it be the text behind the King James Version of 1611, the so-called Textus Receptus, or the latest printed text of the New Testament from the United Bible Society, the differences are miniscule compared to the places where they agree.

NONE OF THE VARIANTS AFFECT CHRISTIAN DOCTRINE

Since the variants do not materially affect the meaning of the text, Christian doctrine is not affected by textual variations. The introduction to the Revised Standard Version of the Bible declares the following about the text.

> It will be obvious to the careful reader that still in 1946 as in 1881 and 1901, no doctrine of the Christian faith has been

---

14. Michael Holmes, *New Testament Criticism and Interpretation*, Editors David Alan Black and David S. Dockery, Zondervan, 1991, pp. 127,128, note 21

> affected by the revision, for the simple reason that, out of the thousands of variant readings in the manuscripts, none has turned up thus far that requires a revision of Christian doctrine.[15]

New Testament scholar F.F. Bruce concurs with this finding. He wrote.

> The variant readings about which any doubt remains . . . affect no material question of historic fact or of Christian faith and practice.[16]

We can rightly conclude that the variations in the different manuscripts have no affect whatsoever on the reliability of the text or upon Christian theology.

SOME OF THE DISPUTED PASSAGES IN THE NEW TESTAMENT

We mentioned there were only about fifty passages where variants really affect the meaning. We will now consider a few of these disputed passages to get an idea of the issues.

The passages where the readings are disputed can be broken down into two different categories. First, there are passages that are questionable as to whether they belong in the New Testament. Second, there are verses that everyone agrees belong, but there is a question as to exactly how the verse should be worded.

ARE THESE PASSAGES OMITTED OR ADDED?

First, there are passages that are questionable as to whether they belong in Scripture. In other words, it is not certain whether they were original

---

15. F.C. Grant, "*An Introduction to the Revised Standard Version of the New Testament,*" The New Testament, Revised Standard Version, Nashville: Thomas Nelson, 1946, p. 42

16. F.F. Bruce, *The New Testament Documents: Are They Reliable?* Grand Rapids: Eerdmans, 1954, p. 178

with the New Testament authors or that they were added later either intentionally or unintentionally. They include the following.

MATTHEW 6:13

There is the famous doxology at the end of the Lord's Prayer. It reads.

> For Yours is the kingdom and the power and the glory forever. Amen (Matthew 6:13 NKJV).

Most scholars believe this was not an original part of the Lord Prayer but rather was added later by copyists. However, there are some who do believe that these are the words of Jesus and are not a later addition to the text.

MARK 16:9-20

The last twelve verses of Mark contain an account of the appearances of Jesus after His death. Is this passage original with Mark, or was it added later? While most scholars believe that these verses are not original with Mark there are some who still argue for the authenticity of this passage.

Indeed, a recent study contends that these verses are the only part of Mark that was actually composed by Mark himself. The ancient evidence consistently says that Mark wrote down Peter's account of the life and ministry of Jesus. It is possible that what we have in Mark's gospel is the transcribing of actual speeches given by Peter in which he explained the life and ministry of Jesus. Peter's oral account ended at verse eight. The last twelve verses of Mark were actually written by Mark himself to complete the story.

JOHN 5:3-4

In John 5:3-4 there is a parenthetical explanation of why people were waiting at the pool of Bethesda to be healed. It reads as follows.

> . . . waiting for the moving of the water. For an angel went down at a certain time into the pool and stirred up the water;

> then whoever stepped in first, after the stirring of the water, was made well of whatever disease he had (John 5:3-4 NKJV).

As is true with the other passages, there are scholars who accept this reading as an original part of John's gospel while others believe it was a later addition to explain why the people were waiting at the pool to be healed.

JOHN 7:53-8:11

John 7:53-8:11 is the famous story of Jesus forgiving the woman who was caught in the act of adultery and then brought before Him. This particular passage shows up in several different places in the existing manuscripts of the New Testament. Whether or not it is original with John, almost all scholars agree that this is an actual story of a confrontation between Jesus and the religious leaders.

ACTS 8:37

There is a verse in the Book of Acts which contains the answer of Philip to the Ethiopian Eunuch after the Eunuch asked if he could be baptized.

> Then Philip said, "If you believe with all your heart, you may." And he answered and said, "I believe that Jesus Christ is the Son of God" (Acts 8:37 NKJV).

This verse seems to have been added later to the text in Acts to conform to the way the early church practiced water baptism. The person administering baptism would ask for a confession of faith in Jesus and the one being baptized would testify to his or her faith in Christ.

1 JOHN 5:7

There is also the famous Trinitarian statement of 1 John 5:7. It reads as follows.

> For there are three that bear witness in heaven: the Father, the Word, and the Holy Spirit; and these three are one (1 John 5:7 NKJV).

This passage is a clear statement of the Trinity. However, the doctrine of the Trinity—there is one God who is manifest in three distinct Persons—is not based upon this verse alone. The doctrine of the Trinity is taught throughout the entire New Testament. Of these questionable passages we have considered, this particular passage has the weakest claim to be authentic. Very few scholars would argue for its authenticity.

To sum up, these passages are not found in some important manuscripts of the New Testament. Whether or not they belong in the New Testament does not affect Christian belief. There is no Christian doctrine which stands or falls on any of these passages.

SOME DISPUTED NEW TESTAMENT READINGS

There is a second group of passages where it is certain that the verse belongs—yet the particular reading of that verse is in doubt. The following are examples of this type of variant.

JOHN 1:18

This is a notoriously difficult passage. Not only is there a question as to whether Jesus is called the "Son" or whether He is called "God" there is also the issue as how to understand the word translated "begotten" or "one and only."

The King James Version says.

> No man hath seen God at any time; the only begotten Son, which is in the bosom of the Father, he hath declared him (John 1:18 KJV).

The New International Version puts it this way.

> No one has ever seen God, but the one and only Son, who is himself God and is in closest relationship with the Father, has made him known (John 1:18 NIV).

These two translations believe "Son" is the original reading here. However, the NIV adds "who is himself God."

On the other hand, the New English Translation believes "God" is the original reading in this verse. It translates the verse as follows.

> No one has ever seen God. The only one, himself God, who is in closest fellowship with the Father, has made God known (John 1:18 NET).

Therefore, according to the New English translation, Jesus is the "only one," "himself God," and "is in closest fellowship with the Father." In other words, there are three different descriptions of Him in this passage.

JOHN 7:8

Did Jesus say, "I am not going up" or "I am not yet going up." Again, we will look at the way various versions translate this verse.

The New International Version reads

> You go to the Feast. I am not yet going up to this Feast, because for me the right time has not yet come (John 7:8 NIV).

The New King James Version says.

> You go up to this feast. I am not yet going up to this feast, for My time has not yet fully come (John 7:8 NKJV).

The question is whether Jesus said He would not go up at all to Jerusalem for the feast or that He would not go up at that time with his brothers. The existing manuscripts differ as to what He said.

1 TIMOTHY 3:16

The question in this passage concerns the reading of one word. Is it God or He?

The King James Version sees this verse as referring to the Deity of Jesus Christ. It says.

> God was manifest in the flesh (1 Timothy 3:16 KJV).

The New International Version says.

> He appeared in the flesh (1 Timothy 3:16 NIV).

Most scholars today believe that the original reading was not "God" but rather "He." In other words, it is not a confessional statement that God was manifest in the flesh. Scholars have come to this conclusion, not because they want to deny the Deity of Christ, but rather because they believe the evidence is stronger for the other reading.

However, there are some scholars who still argue for "God" as the correct reading in this passage.

This is a brief synopsis of the major variants found in the New Testament text. Again we stress, no Christian doctrine is affected by any of these passages.

OBSERVATIONS AND SUMMARY ON VARIANT READINGS

Therefore, after examining the evidence, we can summarize the evidence of the variant readings in the following manner: 80-85% of the text reads exactly the same, no matter what manuscript tradition is followed. Of the 15-20% that has any variations, 99% of these are meaningless and do not affect the translation of the text.

Thus, there are only about 400-600 places in the entire New Testament where translation is affected by a variant reading. Of these only about fifty have any real importance. Finally, no Christian doctrine is affected, one way or the other, in these fifty variants. Thus the variants have no real affect on the meaning of the text.

SUMMARY AND CONCLUSION TO THE RELIABILITY OF THE NEW TESTAMENT TEXT

After looking at the evidence for the reliability of the New Testament text, we can make the following summary statements.

1. The time span between the date of the composition of the books of the New Testament and the earliest surviving manuscripts is relatively short. Most other ancient works have a much longer gap between the time when they were written and the earliest available manuscript.

There is in existence a complete New Testament manuscript (Codex Vaticanus) which was copied within two hundred and fifty years of the time of the writing of the New Testament. In addition, we have over about fifty fragments of the New Testament that go back even earlier. These fragments contain about two thirds of the New Testament next. The classical writings (Plato, Aristotle, etc.) are viewed as having been transmitted in a reliable manner, yet, the time span, between the original and their earliest copy, is over a thousand years. The New Testament documents, if evaluated on the same basis, also must be viewed as trustworthy.

2. Not only is the interval shorter between the writings of the New Testament and the earliest existing manuscripts, the number of manuscripts (over 5,000 in Greek) is far superior to any other ancient work. Given the axiom, "The more manuscripts, the better chance to reconstruct the original," we again see that the New Testament is in much better shape than other ancient works.

3. The Greek New Testament was translated into other languages at an early date. Those versions provide further evidence in establishing the true text. The number of manuscript copies of the different versions is around 25,000 and may be as high as 30,000. Most other ancient writings were never translated into another language.

4. A further line of evidence is found in the writings of the church fathers, where verses, passages and entire books are cited. If the other sources for the New Testament were non-existent (Greek manuscripts and versions) the text still could be reconstructed through the writings of the church fathers alone. There is nothing like this for any other ancient work. There are over one million citations of the New Testament from the writings of the early Christians.

5. It should be remembered that there were different groups who carefully watched the transmission of the New Testament text. These groups were opposed to one another in various beliefs and practices. They would certainly be watching each other to make sure the text was not altered in any way.

6. The variant readings that do exist, do not affect the reliability of the text. The number of places where there are variants is relatively small and they do not affect any Christian doctrine. In fact, there are only about fifty places in the entire New Testament where they are of any consequence whatsoever.

7. Therefore, three important facts demonstrate the New Testament can be trusted. They are:

(1) The short time span between the originals and the manuscript copies

(2) The great number of manuscripts, and

(3) The lack of any substantial variation between the manuscripts.

Given the above facts, we conclude that the New Testament has been accurately transmitted throughout history. Any contrary conclusion is based either on a willful desire not to accept the evidence as it stands, or ignorance of the facts.

Sir Frederic Kenyon, former keeper of ancient manuscripts and director of the British Museum, was an authority second to none on manuscript evidence. After a lifetime of study of ancient documents, he came to the following conclusions.

> The interval between the dates of the original composition [of the New Testament] and the earliest extant [existing] evidence becomes so small as to be in fact negligible, and the last foundation for any doubt that the Scriptures have come down to us substantially as they were written has now been removed. Both the authenticity and the general integrity of the books of the New Testament may be regarded as finally established.[17]

The reliable transmission of the New Testament is absolutely necessary for establishing the case for Christianity. However, the fact that the New Testament has been reliably handed down to us does not mean that it is the Word of God. In fact, it doesn't even mean that what it says is true. It is possible for someone to accurately record the ravings of a madman.

However, to be true, and to be the Word of God, it must be accurately transmitted for us. We have established that this is the case.

Therefore, since the New Testament has showed itself to be transmitted reliably, we now move to our next issue—the history that it records.

---

17. Sir Frederic Kenyon, *The Bible and Archaeology*, New York: Harper and Row Publishers, 1940, p. 288

CHAPTER 5

The Historical Accuracy Of The New Testament: It Matches Up With Known Events

---

In our last chapter, we showed that the New Testament has been transmitted reliably to us—it says the same thing as when originally written. Therefore, we can confidently read its pages with the realization that we are reading the same words that the apostles wrote with nothing added or subtracted. This chapter is now the next logical step.

It is not enough that the text has been accurately transmitted to us, what it says must match up with known reality. In other words, the people, places and events which are mentioned in the New Testament must match up with known history if the case for Christianity is to be taken seriously.

This chapter examines this subject of the historical reliability of the New Testament. We will discover that the references contained in its page's match up with what we know about the people, places, culture, and events of that time. We will establish ten important points concerning the historical reliability of the New Testament.

We conclude our chapter with the testimony of law. We look at what is known as the "ancient documents rule." From this rule, we discover that a court of law would admit the New Testament into evidence as a trustworthy document. Therefore, if someone says that it is not true, they must bring evidence to the contrary. Consequently, the burden of proof rests with those who doubt the New Testament—not with the claims of the New Testament itself.

We emphasize that merely being historically accurate does not mean the New Testament is the Word of God. However, to be God's Word to the human race, it must be accurate in the details which it provides us. We will discover that the evidence says that it is.

Now that we know the New Testament has been accurately transmitted throughout history, we come to our next issue: Do the events, names, places, etc., that the New Testament records, match up with known history? Can we be confident that the historical references within the New Testament are accurate? This chapter will deal with the question of the historical accuracy of the New Testament.

THE IMPORTANCE OF THE HISTORICAL ACCURACY OF THE BIBLE

The historical accuracy of the Bible is of the utmost importance because the revelation of God to humankind was accomplished through His mighty words and deeds in history. The Bible is a testimony to the mighty works of God. The evidence is as follows.

1. THE OLD TESTAMENT REMINDED THE PEOPLE OF GOD'S MIGHTY DEEDS

The Lord constantly reminded Israel of His mighty power. The Old Testament called the people's attention to the past deeds of God. We read the following in the Book of Exodus.

> I am the LORD your God, who brought you out of slavery in Egypt (Exodus 20:2 God's Word).

The Lord is the One who brought His people out of the slavery in Egypt.

The nation was continually urged to remember what He had done for them in the past. In the Book of Second Kings, they were again reminded of what the Lord has done for their nation. It says.

> But you shall worship the LORD, who brought you out of the land of Egypt with great power and with an outstretched

> arm; you shall bow yourselves to him, and to him you shall sacrifice (2 Kings 17:36 NRSV).

We also read the prophet Micah calling to mind what the Lord has done. He wrote the following to the people in his day.

> O my people, remember now what King Balak of Moab devised, what Balaam son of Beor answered him, and what happened from Shittim to Gilgal, that you may know the saving acts of the Lord (Micah 6:5 NRSV).

Consequently, the Old Testament writers stress the acts of God in history. These events are assumed to have literally occurred and they testify to the great power of the God of the Bible.

2. GOD CAME TO OUR WORLD THROUGH JESUS CHRIST

The same historical importance is found in the New Testament. At a certain time in history, Jesus Christ, God the Son, came into our world. John wrote.

> And the Word became flesh and dwelt among us, and we beheld His glory, the glory as of the only begotten of the Father, full of grace and truth (John 1:14 NKJV).

The main message of the New Testament is that God became a human being in the Person of Jesus Christ.

We find the various writers of Scripture appealing time and time again to actual historical events to testify to both the existence and the power of God. God exists and He has acted in history.

3. THE BIBLE CONTAINS MANY SPECIFIC HISTORICAL REFERENCES

In fact, the entire biblical revelation centers on what God has done in history. For example, one chapter in Scripture, Genesis 10, has five times more specific geographical references of importance than the entire Koran, the holy book of Islam! In addition, there are over three hundred references in the Book of Acts alone to names, places, and events. With so much attention to detail, the historical reliability of the Scriptures is of vital importance. If the Bible is the Word of God, then it must be able to withstand the most thorough historical investigation. These events must match up with known history.

4. WE ARE TO INVESTIGATE THE NEW TESTAMENT THE SAME WAY WE INVESTIGATE OTHER DOCUMENTS

The New Testament was written in the same way as other documents in the ancient world. Consequently, it should be examined the same way as these other documents. Contrary to the claims of other religions and cults, there is no record of documents written on golden plates or discovered in some hidden cave. Neither are the writings of the New Testament brought down from heaven by angels.

To the contrary, they are the straightforward accounts of the people who walked and talked with Jesus and were observers of the things that He both said and did. The men who wrote these books made them public at the time they were written. There is no idea of hiding them in caves or burying them so as to be discovered by some later generation. Every aspect of the composition of the New Testament is the same as other historical writings of that period. Therefore, we need to investigate their claims as we would any other historical record.

5. THE NEW TESTAMENT BOOKS: FIRST HAND TESTIMONY OF THE EVENTS

As we investigate the New Testament text we observe that the writers of the books claimed to be either eyewitnesses to the events recorded, or those who gathered eyewitness testimony. The Apostle John wrote the following.

> The one who existed from the beginning is the one we have heard and seen. We saw him with our own eyes and touched him with our own hands. He is Jesus Christ, the Word of life.

> This one who is life from God was shown to us, and we have seen him. And now we testify and announce to you that he is the one who is eternal life. He was with the Father, and then he was shown to us (1 John 1:1,2 NLT).

John emphasized that he had seen Jesus, had heard Jesus teach, and touched Him. We are dealing with reality—not mythology.

As an eyewitness, Simon Peter testified to what he saw and heard. He wrote.

> We did not follow cleverly contrived myths when we made known to you the power and coming of our Lord Jesus Christ; instead, we were eyewitnesses of His majesty. For when He received honor and glory from God the Father, a voice came to Him from the Majestic glory: This is My beloved Son. I take delight in Him. And we heard this voice when it came from heaven while we were with Him on the holy mountain (2 Peter 1:16-18 HCSB).

Peter says that he and the other disciples did not follow after myths. They were there and they tell us what happened.

The fact that the New Testament writers claimed such objective, complete, and firsthand evidence concerning Jesus Christ is of the utmost importance. Their evidence is not hearsay or imaginary—it is direct and reliable.

6. THE NEW TESTAMENT WAS WRITTEN A SHORT TIME AFTER THE EVENTS

The time of the composition of the New Testament text is extremely important. If the documents were written and circulated at an early date, then the eyewitnesses would still be living. They could either verify or deny the events recorded. They could serve as a check to see if the New Testament writers were telling the truth.

The evidence shows that the four Gospels were written in a relatively short time after the death and resurrection of Jesus Christ. This can first be seen by examining the internal evidence of the New Testament itself.

In fact, we find several clues in the New Testament that suggest an early date of its composition. They are as follows.

THE CITY OF JERUSALEM AND TEMPLE WERE STILL STANDING WHEN THE NEW TESTAMENT WAS WRITTEN

The first three Gospels, and seemingly also the fourth, were apparently written while the city of Jerusalem was still standing. Each of the first three Gospels contain predictions by Jesus concerning the destruction of Jerusalem and the Temple (Matthew 24, Mark 13, Luke 21), but none records the fulfillment of the predictions.

We know that Titus the Roman destroyed the city and Temple in the year A.D. 70. Hence, the composition of the first three Gospels seemingly occurred sometime before this event. Otherwise the destruction of Jerusalem and the temple would have been recorded so as to prove that Jesus' predictions came true.

THE BOOK OF ACTS PROVIDES A CLUE TO THE DATE OF THE GOSPELS

The Book of Acts also provides us with a clue as to when the gospels were written. Acts records the highlights in the life and the ministry of the Apostle Paul. The book concludes with Paul at Rome awaiting trial before Caesar. The inference is that Acts was written while Paul was still alive, seeing his death is not recorded. Since there is good evidence that Paul died in the Neronian persecution about A.D. 67, the Book of Acts can be dated approximately A.D. 62.

ACTS IS THE SECOND PART OF LUKE'S WRITINGS

If Acts were written about A.D. 62, then this helps us date the gospels, since the Book of Acts is the second half of a treatise written by Luke to a man named Theophilus. Because we know that the Gospel of Luke was written before the Book of Acts, we can then date the Gospel of Luke sometime around A.D. 60 or before.

THE BROTHER WHO WAS WELL-KNOWN MAY HAVE BEEN LUKE

There may be further evidence for an early date for Luke's gospel. Paul wrote of a brother who was well-known among the churches for the gospel. He said.

> With him we are sending the brother who is famous among all the churches for his proclaiming the good news (2 Corinthians 8:18 NRSV).

There is ancient testimony that this refers to Luke and his written gospel. If this is speaking of Luke and the gospel he composed, then we have it as being well-known in the mid-fifties of the first century.

MARK WAS POSSIBLY USED AS A SOURCE FOR LUKE

There may be a reference in the writings of Luke that he used Mark as a written source. John Mark is called a "minister" by Luke in Acts 13:5 (the Greek word *huparetas*). In 1:2, Luke says he derived the information for his gospel from those who were "eyewitnesses" and "ministers" of the word. The term translated "minister" is the same Greek word *huparetas* that Luke uses to describe Mark in the Book of Acts. It is possible that this could be a reference to Mark as one of his written sources.

MARK MAY HAVE BEEN WRITTEN BEFORE LUKE

Furthermore, modern scholarship has generally assumed that the Gospel of Mark was written before Luke. If this is the case, then this book was composed somewhere in the fifties of the first century A.D.

Since Jesus' death and resurrection likely occurred in the year A.D. 33, these two gospels were written during the time when eyewitnesses, both friendly and unfriendly, were still alive. These eyewitnesses could either verify or falsify the information contained in the gospels.

MATTHEW WAS THE FIRST GOSPEL WRITTEN

We now go a step further by considering Matthew's gospel. According to the unanimous testimony of the early church Matthew was the first gospel written. The church father Eusebius places the date of Matthew's gospel in A.D. 41. If this is true, then we have a third independent source about the life of Christ that was written during the eyewitness period.

JOHN WAS AN EYEWITNESS TO THE EVENTS

The Gospel of John is usually assumed to have been the last of the four gospels composed. John testified that he was an eyewitness to the events that he recorded. He wrote.

> Now Jesus did many other signs in the presence of his disciples, which are not written in this book. But these are written so that you may come to believe that Jesus is the Messiah, the Son of God, and that through believing you may have life in his name (John (20:30:31 NRSV).

He also wrote.

> This disciple is the one who testifies to these events and has recorded them here. And we know that his account of these things is accurate (John 21:24 NIV).

His testimony is true. He was there!

THERE IS INTERNAL EVIDENCE FOR AN EARLY DATE FOR JOHN'S GOSPEL

There is also internal evidence that John himself wrote before A.D. 70. We read the following in the Gospel of John.

> Now in Jerusalem by the Sheep Gate there is a pool, called in Hebrew Beth-zatha, which has five porticoes (John 5:2 NRSV).

John describes the sheep gate as still standing at the time he wrote. The sheep gate was destroyed in the year A.D. 70, along with the rest of the city of Jerusalem. This could very well be an indication that John wrote his gospel while the city of Jerusalem was still standing. Greek scholar Daniel Wallace writes the following concerning this verse.

> The present tense should be used as indicating present time from the viewpoint of the speaker. The implication seems to be that this gospel was written before the destruction of Jerusalem in 70 CE. Although many may object to a pre-70 date for John's gospel, they must, in support of their view, reckon with this text.[1]

The late John A.T. Robinson, a liberal scholar, in his book *Redating The New Testament*, concluded there is sufficient evidence for believing that every New Testament book was composed before the fall of Jerusalem in A.D. 70.

THERE IS AN EARLY DATE FOR THE ENTIRE NEW TESTAMENT

When all the historical and textual evidence is amassed, it becomes clear that the New Testament was composed at a very early date either by eyewitnesses or those who recorded eyewitness testimony. The eminent archaeologist William F. Albright concluded the following.

> In my opinion, every book of the New Testament was written by a baptized Jew between the forties and the eighties of the first century A.D. (very probably sometime between A.D. 50 and 75).[2]

---

1. Daniel Wallace, *Greek Grammar Beyond The Basics*, Zondervan, Grand Rapids, 1997, p. 531

2. Interview with Christianity Today, January 18, 1963

Albright also stated.

> Thanks to the Qumran discoveries, the New Testament proves to be what it was formerly believed to be: the teaching of Christ and his immediate followers between cir. 24 and cir. 80 A.D.[3]

Again, we have expert testimony of the early composition of the gospels.

Scholar John Wenham writes the following concerning the available evidence we have to date the New Testament.

1. Luke knew Mark's Gospel.

2. The dates should be reckoned working back from Acts, the natural date of which is A.D. 62.

3. Luke's gospel was apparently well known in the mid-50's.

4. According to tradition, Mark's gospel gives Peter's teaching in Rome.

5. Peter's first visit to Rome was probably 42-44 and Mark's gospel was probably written about 45.

6. The universal tradition of the early church puts Matthew first, which means a date around 40.[4]

Legal expert, Simon Greenleaf, makes a sensible conclusion concerning the dating of the four gospels.

> The earlier date, however, is argued with greater force, for the improbability that the Christians would be left for several years without a general and authentic history of our Savior's ministry.[5]

---

3. W.F. Albright, *From Stone Age to Christianity*, Baltimore, MD: Johns Hopkins Press, 1963, p. 29

4. John Wenham, *Redating Matthew, Mark, And Luke*, Downers Grove, Illinois; IVP, 1992, p. 243

5. Simon Greenleaf, *The Testimony of the Evangelists*, Kregel, 1995, p. 19

This makes complete sense. We know that the early Christian leaders did indeed write authoritative letters to other believers. Acts chapter fifteen records an example of this. This being the case, we have every reason to believe that the gospels were written at an early date.

The Unwitting Testimony Of Unbelievers To The New Testament

We add to this the testimony of unbelievers. Unwittingly, they have given testimony to the early composition of the New Testament. Speaking of Celsus, a man living in the second century who hated Christianity, Bishop Fallows writes the following.

> This unbeliever, although he caused great annoyance to the believers in Christ living in his day, and seemed to be disturbing the foundations of the Christian faith, rendered more real service to Christianity than any father of undisputed orthodoxy in the Church. He admits all the grand facts and doctrines of the gospel, as they were preached by the Apostles, and contained in the acknowledged writings, for the sake of opposing. He makes in his attacks eighty quotations from the New Testament, and appeals to it as containing the sacred writings of Christians, universally received by them as credible and Divine.
>
> He is, therefore, the very best witness we can summon to prove that the New Testament was not written hundreds of years after the Apostles were dust; but in less than a century and a half had been received by the Christian Church all over the world. He expressly quotes both the synoptic Gospels, as they were termed (the first three Gospels), and the Gospel of St. John.[6]

Therefore, we even have the testimony of unbelievers as to the identity of the gospel writers.

---

6. Bishop Fallows, *Mistakes of Ingersoll and His Answers*, pp. 91,92

7. INTERNAL EVIDENCE FROM THE NEW TESTAMENT THAT IT WAS ALREADY CONSIDERED SCRIPTURE

There is internal evidence from the New Testament itself that parts of it were already considered to be Scripture. Peter had the following to say about Paul's writings.

> And remember, the Lord is waiting so that people have time to be saved. This is just as our beloved brother Paul wrote to you with the wisdom God gave him—speaking of these things in all of his letters. Some of his comments are hard to understand, and those who are ignorant and unstable have twisted his letters around to mean something quite different from what he meant, just as they do the other parts of Scripture—and the result is disaster for them (2 Peter 3:15-16 NLT).

Peter puts Paul's writings on the same level as the rest of the Scripture. They were considered to be authoritative writings.

PAUL QUOTES LUKE AS SCRIPTURE

In addition, Paul quotes Luke's gospel and calls it Scripture. He wrote the following to Timothy.

> For the scripture says, "You shall not muzzle an ox while it is treading out the grain," and, "The laborer deserves to be paid" (1 Timothy 5:18 NRSV).

This quotation is from Luke 10:7. When Paul wrote First Timothy, it seems Luke's gospel had already been accepted as Scripture.

8. THE COMPLETED NEW TESTAMENT WAS RECOGNIZED EARLY

The completed New Testament was recognized early in the history of the church. Tertullian, writing in the first two decades of the third century, was the first known person to call the Christian Scriptures the "New Testament."

Consequently, when all the evidence is in, it shows that not only the New Testament documents were written soon after the events they recorded — they were also recognized at an early date to be authoritative by those who read them.

9. THE AUTHORS OF THE FOUR GOSPELS CAN BE IDENTIFIED

The life of Christ has been recorded for us by four separate works known as gospels. The traditional authorship is credited to Matthew, Mark, Luke, and John.

There are three basic reasons why we believe the four gospels were written by the men bearing their names. They are as follows.

THERE IS UNANIMOUS TRADITION AS TO AUTHORSHIP

The four gospels are unanimously attributed to Matthew, Mark, Luke and John—there are no other candidates. Scholar Craig Keener convincingly makes the point that the authorship of these works would not have been forgotten. He writes.

> Authorship would be the last thing forgotten. That this Gospel [Matthew] originally circulated without oral reports of authorship is unlikely; as an anonymous work it would not have quickly commanded the wide acceptance it received, and authors of biographies of this length normally were named.[7]

Thus, we have every reason to believe this unanimous testimony to the authorship of the four gospels.

THREE OF THE FOUR ARE UNLIKELY AUTHORS

The authors of our four gospels would not have been the obvious choices to write the accounts of the life of Christ. Only one of these

7. Craig Keener, *Matthew*, Downers Grove, Illinois, IVP, 1997, p. 32

four men (John) was a prominent character in the New Testament. Why attribute a book to the others if they were not the authors? The unanimous attestation of these unlikely authors is another strong reason for accepting the traditional view that they penned their respective gospels. There is no other reason to attribute to these men the authorship of the gospels had they not written them.

THE IDENTIFICATION OF THE DOCUMENT WAS MADE ON ITS OUTSIDE

The early preservation of the name of the author is another consideration. It was a common literary practice during the time of Christ to preserve the name of the author of a written record. Scrolls with written text on both sides had tags glued to them (called a *sittybos* in Greek) which insured the preservation of the author's name. They were attached in such a way that a person could see who authored the scroll without unrolling it. This is similar to the function of the spine on our modern books—one does not have to open the book to find out who wrote it.

With four different written gospels circulating, there needed to be a way to distinguish them from each other. The term "gospel" would not be enough, seeing that there was more than one gospel circulating. Therefore, the church had to preserve the name of each gospel writer at an early date. The tag on the outside of the scroll would accomplish that purpose. It would read in Greek, "Gospel of Matthew" or "Gospel of Mark."

THERE ARE NO VARIATIONS IN THE TITLES

The fact that this happened is clear in that there are no variations in the titles of the gospels. Every source is unanimous that Matthew wrote Matthew, Mark wrote Mark, Luke penned his gospel, and John wrote his.

These three reasons—the unanimous testimony of the church, the unlikely authorship of these men, and the early identification of the document, all present a strong case for the traditional authorship of the gospels.

THE GOSPEL WRITERS HAVE EXCELLENT CREDENTIALS

The four gospel writers also had excellent credentials to be in a position to know the facts about Jesus' ministry and to record them correctly. The evidence is as follows.

MATTHEW

The writer of the first gospel originally bore the name Levi but was also named, or possibly renamed, Matthew (gift of God). We know that he was the son of Alphaeus. The Bible says.

> As he was walking along, he saw Levi son of Alphaeus sitting at the tax booth, and he said to him, "Follow me." And he got up and followed him (Mark 2:14 NRSV).

His job was that of a tax collector, a customs official. This position would have made him an ideal candidate for writing this gospel for the following reasons.

1. A tax collector would be fluent in Greek.

2. He would also be literate.

3. He would be used to keeping records.

4. He most likely would be able to write in short-hand. Therefore, he could have been a note-taker at Jesus teachings.

5. If Levi was a tribal name, he would have known about scribal traditions and be familiar with temple practices.

6. He would have been a well-educated scribe in the secular sense.

There is something else about the tax collector position that would make Matthew a particularly good candidate to be a writer of one of the accounts of the life of Jesus. Simon Greenleaf makes this brilliant observation.

> And if the men of that day were, as in truth they appear to have been, as much disposed as those of the present time, to evade the payment of public taxes and duties, and to elude, by all possible means, the vigilance of the revenue officers, Matthew must have been familiar with a great variety of forms of fraud, imposture, cunning, and deception, and must have become habitually distrustful, scrutinizing, and cautious; and, of course, much less likely to have been deceived in regard to many of the facts in our Lord's ministry, extraordinary as they were, which fell under his observation. This circumstance shows both the sincerity and the wisdom of Jesus in selecting him for an eye-witness of his conduct, and adds great weigh to the value of the testimony of this evangelist.[8]

What a great choice Matthew was! This customs official would certainly be skeptical of the things he saw and heard. Consequently, his background adds greater credibility to his written account of the life and ministry of Jesus.

MARK

Mark was also in a unique position to write about Jesus. His gospel contained the preaching of Simon Peter—one of the Jesus' twelve disciples. Therefore, we have Mark relating to us the things Simon Peter said about the life and ministry of Jesus. There is hardly any incident related in Mark's gospel where Simon Peter was not present and the recording of minute detail shows that we have the testimony of an eyewitness.

---

8. Simon Greenleaf, *The Testimony Of The Evangelists*, Kregel, 1995, p. 21

LUKE

Luke, the writer of the third gospel, stated the purpose of his account in the preface. He wrote.

> Many have undertaken to compile a narrative about the events that have been fulfilled among us, just as the original eyewitnesses and servants of the word handed them down to us. It also seemed good to me, since I have carefully investigated everything from the very first, to write to you in an orderly sequence, most honorable Theophilus, so that you may know the certainty of the things about which you have been instructed (Luke 1:1-4 HCSB).

This statement of Luke tells us, at least, the following.

1. Luke may not have been an eyewitness to the events he recorded.

2. But he, like those before him, made careful use of the eyewitness accounts.

3. Luke had access to other narratives, possibly written documents like his own.

4. Luke felt the need for a further account.

5. His account is orderly.

6. He had full knowledge of the events he recorded.

7. His ultimate aim is truth.

Simon Greenleaf, the legal expert, declared that Luke's use of firsthand sources would make them admissible in a court of law. He wrote.

> It would possess every legal attribute of an inquisition [deposition], and, as such, would be legally admissible in evidence, in a court of justice.[9]

---

9. Simon Greenleaf, *The Testimony of The Evangelists*, Kregel, 1995, p. 25

Luke deposed the witnesses. Their authentic testimony is contained in his account.

JOHN

The author of the fourth gospel, John, was one of the twelve—an eyewitness to the events in the life of Christ. At the end of the Gospel of John we find these words.

> This is the disciple who testifies of these things, and wrote these things; and we know that his testimony is true (John 21:24 NKJV).

As an eyewitness he would certainly be in a position to correctly state the facts about the life and ministry of Jesus.

CONCLUSION: THE WRITERS OF THE FOUR GOSPELS WERE QUALIFIED

The evidence shows that each of the four gospel writers were in an excellent position to write an accurate account of the life of Jesus Christ. Two of the writers (Matthew and John) were among Jesus' inner circle while another (Mark) recorded the teachings of Peter—the most prominent disciple. Luke put his account together through the eyewitness testimony of those who were with Jesus.

THE WRITERS COULD BE CROSS-EXAMINED

Another important point to consider is that the disciples were able to be cross-examined by their contemporaries. For example, they preached the message that Jesus had risen from the dead in the very city in which He was crucified and buried. If their testimony were not true, the unbelieving enemies of Christ could easily have refuted their contention. It is crucial to appreciate the fact that the disciples of Jesus did not immediately go off to Athens or Rome to proclaim the truth of the gospel, but rather preached it in the city of Jerusalem—where the events transpired.

THE BOOK OF ACTS RECORDS MIRACLES OF THE APOSTLES

The Book of Acts records some of the major events in the early church—including miracles performed by the apostles. These events took place in Jerusalem, in front of the same people who put Jesus to death. We note what was said about one of the miracles they were confronted with. Scriptures says.

> But when they had ordered them to go outside the council, they began to confer with one another, saying, "What should we do with these men? For it is plain to all who live in Jerusalem that a notable miraculous sign has come about through them, and we cannot deny it" (Acts 4:15,16 NET).

The fact of this miracle was of such a nature that even the enemies of Christ could not deny it. They had to admit that this miracle actually took place.

THE TESTIMONY OF PAUL TO CHRIST

Though the gospels were written a relatively short time after the death and resurrection of Christ what about the letters of the Apostle Paul? When were they composed? How do they help with the reliability of the New Testament?

SOME OF PAUL'S LETTERS WERE POSSIBLY WRITTEN EARLIER THAN THE GOSPELS

Some of the letters of the Apostle Paul may actually have been written earlier than the gospels. For example, First Thessalonians was written approximately A.D. 51, while the first letter to the Corinthians was penned about A.D. 56. Obviously, all of his letters were written before A.D. 67, when he died.

PAUL CONFIRMED SOME OF THE MATERIAL IN THE GOSPELS

The testimony of the Apostle Paul confirms the evidence presented in the gospel accounts concerning Jesus Christ. We will state a few examples.

JESUS WAS THE CREATOR OF THE UNIVERSE

John tells us that Jesus was the Creator of the universe. He wrote.

> All things came into being through him, and without him not one thing came into being. What has come into being (John 1:3 NRSV).

Paul also testified that Jesus was the Creator of the universe. He said the following to the Colossians.

> For everything was created by Him, in heaven and on earth, the visible and the invisible, whether thrones or dominions or rulers or authorities — all things have been created through Him and for Him (Colossians 1:16 HCSB).

Jesus is the One who created all things. He is the active agent of creation.

JESUS LIVED A SINLESS LIFE

Jesus was always obedient to the law of God. He asked if anyone had ever seen Him sin. John records Jesus saying the following.

> Can any of you convict me of committing a sin? If I'm telling the truth, why don't you believe me? (John 8:46 God's Word).

No one could give an example—because He did not sin.

In speaking of Christ, Paul wrote the following to the Corinthians.

> God made the one who did not know sin to be sin for us, so that in him we would become the righteousness of God (2 Corinthians 5:21 NET).

Jesus lived a life without sin.

JESUS WAS BETRAYED

All four gospels record the fact that Judas Iscariot betrayed Jesus. The Apostle Paul also spoke of Jesus having been betrayed. He wrote.

> For I received from the Lord what I also handed on to you, that the Lord Jesus on the night when he was betrayed took a loaf of bread (1 Corinthians 11:23 NRSV).

Paul confirmed the report that was given in all four gospels—Jesus had been betrayed.

JESUS WAS CRUCIFIED

All four gospels are consistent that Jesus died by means of crucifixion. Paul mentions Jesus' death by crucifixion as the cornerstone of his message. He wrote the following to the Corinthians.

> But we preach Christ crucified (1 Corinthians 1:23 KJV).

This was central to his message. Jesus Christ died on a cross for the sins of the world in the city of Jerusalem.

JESUS ROSE FROM THE DEAD

Again, all four gospels testify that Jesus rose from the dead. Paul also confirmed that Christ rose from the dead. He wrote to the Corinthians.

> For I delivered to you first of all that which I also received: that Christ died for our sins according to the Scriptures, and that He was buried, and that He rose again the third day according to the Scriptures (1 Corinthians 15:3,4 NKJV).

Jesus died according to the Scriptures and then rose again according to the Scriptures.

THERE ARE IMPORTANT POINTS ABOUT PAUL'S TESTIMONY

Three points must be emphasized concerning the testimony of the Apostle Paul. They are as follows.

HE WAS A CONTEMPORARY OF THE DISCIPLES

The Apostle Paul, though not an eyewitness to the events of the life of Christ, was living at the same time as the disciples who were eyewitnesses. Therefore, he was their contemporary.

HE WROTE WITHIN THIRTY YEARS OF THE EVENTS

All of Paul's letters were composed within thirty years of the events of the life and ministry of Jesus. This is far too short of a time for him to have radically changed the message of Jesus without receiving criticism from both believing and non-believing eyewitnesses of the events.

For example, First Thessalonians is probably the earliest letter that Paul wrote. It can be dated around the year A.D. 51—less than twenty years after the death and resurrection of Jesus.

HE CHALLENGED HIS READERS TO INVESTIGATE THE EVIDENCE

Paul challenged his readers to investigate for themselves the evidence concerning the resurrection of Jesus Christ. He wrote to the Corinthians.

> After that, he was seen by more than five hundred of his followers at one time, most of whom are still alive, though some have died by now (1 Corinthians 15:6 NLT).

Many eyewitnesses to Jesus' resurrection were still alive when Paul wrote to the church at Corinth. Anyone doubting the fact of the resurrection could check out their testimony.

CONCLUSION TO PAUL'S TESTIMONY

We conclude that the testimony of the Apostle Paul adds further evidence to the trustworthiness of the gospel's picture of Jesus.

THE NEW TESTAMENT BOOKS WERE READ ALOUD IN THE CHURCHES AND CIRCULATED

We know that the New Testament books were read aloud in the churches. We have examples from the gospels, Paul's letters, and the Book of Revelation. In Paul's earliest letter, he wrote the following.

> I command you in the name of the Lord to read this letter to all the brothers and sisters (1 Thessalonians 5:27 NLT).

The Gospel of Matthew also assumes that someone will be reading it aloud. It says.

> So when you see the abomination of desolation spoken of by the prophet Daniel, standing in the holy place (let the reader understand) (Matthew 24:15 ESV).

When Paul wrote to the Colossians, he ordered his letter to be read publicly. We read.

> And when this letter has been read among you, have it read also in the church of the Laodiceans; and see that you read also the letter from Laodicea (Colossians 4:16 NRSV).

The people of this church were to read and circulate Paul's letter.

THE PUBLIC READING OF THE SCRIPTURE WAS COMMANDED BY PAUL

A very important passage is found in First Timothy. Here Paul commanded the public reading of the Scriptures. He said.

> Until I arrive, give attention to the public reading of scripture, to exhorting, to teaching (1 Timothy 4:13 NRSV).

The Scripture would include all of the New Testament that had been written until that time. Since First Timothy was one of the last New Testament books to have been written, this command probably referred to most of the twenty-seven documents that now make up the New Testament.

THERE WAS A SPECIAL BLESSING FOR THOSE WHO READ AND OBEYED THE MESSAGE

Finally, John promised a special blessing to the person who read the book out loud as well as those who heard it being read. They would receive a blessing if they obeyed the things written in the book. He wrote.

> Blessed is the one who reads aloud the words of the prophecy, and blessed are those who hear and who keep what is written in it; for the time is near (Revelation 1:3 NRSV).

Therefore, the message of Jesus went out publicly, before both believers and unbelievers. It was there for all to freely investigate.

THE EVENTS DO MATCH UP WITH KNOWN HISTORY

The evidence shows that New Testament was written at an early date by eyewitnesses, or by those who recorded eyewitness testimony. Consequently, these writers were in a position to accurately record the life and ministry of Jesus.

This brings us to the real issue: Do their writings actually reflect known history? Put another way, does secular history confirm the references to people, places, and events which are found in the New Testament? The answer is a resounding, "Yes." We will cite only a few examples.

THE PEOPLE ACTUALLY EXISTED

The people that the four gospels mention were historical figures. For example, Pontius Pilate, Herod the Great, Herod Antipas, and Tiberius

Caesar are known to have existed. Consequently, we are dealing with real people.

PONTIUS PILATE WAS PREFECT OF JUDEA

For many years there were questions about the existence and the actual title of Pontius Pilate—the Roman governor who presided over the trial of Jesus. In later Roman writers, as well as in almost all Bible reference works, Pilate is referred to as the "procurator" of Judea. According to the New Testament, he is called a "governor," not a procurator.

In 1961, on the coast of Israel in the town of Caesarea, the discovery was made of a two by three-foot stone that had a Latin inscription written upon it. The translation of the inscription reads as follows.

PONTIUS PILATE, PREFECT OF JUDEA, HAS PRESENTED THE TIBERIEUM TO THE CAESAREANS

This is the first archaeological evidence for the existence of Pilate. What is interesting about the inscription is the title that he is given—Prefect of Judea. We now know that the title "Procurator" was not used at the time for the Roman governors. This title only came into usage at a later time. During the reign of the emperor Claudius, A.D. 41-54 the title of the Roman governors shifted from Prefect to Procurator. Although the later Roman writers gave Pilate the incorrect title, the New Testament did not. It calls him a governor—not a Procurator.

THE TWO HERODS WERE HISTORICAL CHARACTERS

The gospels mention two people by the name of Herod—Herod the Great and Herod the Tetrarch.

Herod the Great was the ruler of Judea at the time of the birth of Christ. Matthew writes.

> Jesus was born in the town of Bethlehem in Judea, during the reign of King Herod. About that time some wise men from

> eastern lands arrived in Jerusalem, asking, "Where is the newborn king of the Jews? We have seen his star as it arose, and we have come to worship him" (Matthew 2:1,2 NLT)

From a number of sources, we know that Herod the Great existed. First century writer Flavius Josephus tells us much of Herod's history. Also coins have been discovered that have the inscription "Herod the King." At the site of Masada, where hundreds of Jews went to their deaths in defiance of the Roman army, a potsherd has been found that says Herod, King of the Jews. Consequently, his existence is unquestionably confirmed.

During Jesus' public ministry, some thirty years later, another Herod is mentioned—Herod the tetrarch. We read about this in Matthew. It says.

> At that time Herod the tetrarch heard the report about Jesus (Matthew 14:1 HCSB).

Again, we are dealing with genuine history. We know that Herod the Tetrarch existed because of the writings of first century Jewish historian Flavius Josephus, as well as coins that were minted that have inscribed "Herod the tetrarch."

These are a few of the many examples that could be given of extra biblical confirmation of New Testament characters.

THE CITIES EXISTED WHERE THE GOSPELS SAY THEY DID

The gospels also record various places where the ministry of the Lord Jesus took place. We find that the cities that are mentioned in the four gospels are known to have existed in the first century. The exact location of almost all of them has now been firmly established. This includes such cities as Nazareth, Cana, Bethlehem, Capernaum, Chorazin, Bethsaida, and Tiberius. In other words, we are dealing with real places.

THE WRITERS KNEW THE LOCAL CUSTOMS OF THE TIMES

The customs that were practiced in the first-century are consistent with that which is recorded in the four gospels. In fact, we find that the customs are related in a way that is minutely accurate. For example, in the Gospel of Luke we read the following account.

> Soon afterward Jesus went to a town called Nain, and his disciples and a large crowd went with him. As he approached the town gate, a man who had died was being carried out, the only son of his mother (who was a widow), and a large crowd from the town was with her. When the Lord saw her, he had compassion for her and said to her, "Do not weep." Then he came up and touched the bier, and those who carried it stood still. He said, "Young man, I say to you, get up!" So the dead man sat up and began to speak, and Jesus gave him back to his mother (Luke 7:11-15 NET).

At the time of Christ, there were different customs with respect to women walking in a funeral procession. In Judea, the area around Jerusalem, the custom was for the women to walk behind the funeral procession. However, in the Galilee region, the custom was reversed. The women walked in front of the funeral procession. The description given by Luke demonstrates the minute accuracy of his account. Jesus began to talk to the mother of the dead child, and then touched the coffin of the dead man. At that time the funeral procession stopped—because it was following behind her and the coffin. This would have only been true in the Galilee region. If this story would have been placed in Judea, then it would not have happened this way—the women would have followed the procession. The fact that Luke incidentally notes that the procession stopped when Jesus touched the coffin shows the minute accuracy of his account.

CONCLUSION: THE GOSPELS FIT THE HISTORICAL EVIDENCE

Therefore, when all the evidence is considered, we find that the gospels match up with the known history of that time. The people were real people, the cities existed, the customs were exactly as stated, and the events, actually occurred. Scholar Craig Evans sums it up perfectly.

> There is also a very important argument in favor of the general reliability of the New Testament Gospels, and that concerns what is called verisimilitude; that is, what the gospels describe matches the way things really were in the early first-century Jewish Palestine. The New Testament gospels and Acts exhibit a great deal of verisimilitude. They speak of real people (such as Pontius Pilate, Herod Antipas, Annas, Caiaphas, Herod Agrippa I and II, Felix and Festus) and real events (deaths of John the Baptist and Agrippa I). They speak of real places (villages, cities, roads, lakes and mountains) that are clarified and corroborated by other historical sources and by archaeology. They speak of real customs (Passover, purity, Sabbath, divorce law), institutions (synagogue, temple), offices/officers (priests, tax collectors Roman governors, Roman centurions) and beliefs (of Pharisees and Sadducees; interpretation of Scripture). Jesus' engagement with his contemporaries, both supporters and opponents, reflects an understanding of Scripture and theology that we now know, thanks to the Dead Sea Scrolls and related literature, to have been current in pre-70 Jewish Palestine.[10]

The evidence supports the biblical claim that the New Testament writers wrote during the first century and were either eyewitnesses of the events they described, or had carefully checked the facts and evidence with eyewitnesses. As far as we are able to tell, the New Testament writers were historically accurate.

---

10. Craig Evans, *Jesus and His World: The Archaeological Evidence*, Westminster, John Knox Press, Louisville, Kentucky, 2012, p. 9

THE TESTIMONY OF LAW–THE ANCIENT DOCUMENTS RULE

Given the above evidence for the historical reliability of the New Testament, we now look to the testimony of law on this matter. The 19th century legal authority, Simon Greenleaf, explains what is known as the, "ancient documents" rule. He wrote.

> Every document, apparently ancient, coming from the proper repository or custody, and bearing on its face no evident marks of forgery, the law presumes to be genuine, and devolves on the opposing party the burden proving it to be otherwise.[11]

Therefore, the "ancient documents rule" states the following.

(1) If a document is discovered that claims to be ancient

(2) and it comes from where we would expect to find it

(3) and there is no evidence of forgery

(4) and the text shows no sign that it has been changed

(5) and it does not contain obvious contradictions or demonstrable errors, then we are to assume it to be true until evidence can be brought forward to the contrary.

Since the New Testament meets all these criteria, it should be given a fair hearing.

THE BENEFIT OF THE DOUBT IS TO BE GIVEN TO THE NEW TESTAMENT

Furthermore, any benefit of the doubt, therefore, is to be given to the document, not to the critic. Consequently, the burden of proof is on those who deny what the work says.

---

11. Simon Greenleaf, *The Testimony of The Evangelists*, Kregel, 1995 reprint, p. 16

Applied to the New Testament, any criticism of its contents must be based in reality, not in supposition or theory. Since the New Testament has proven itself, over and over again, to be a trustworthy guide to past events, it should be given the benefit of the doubt when covering things that have no independent corroboration. Therefore, the Christian should not feel obligated to have every minute detail verified before they can believe what the New Testament says.

THERE IS SUFFICIENT EVIDENCE TO TRUST THE GOSPELS

After examining what leading lawyers had to say about the evidence for the trustworthiness of the four Gospels, Australian lawyer/theologian Ross Clifford, made the following conclusion.

> We have seen how lawyers affirm that the Gospels of Matthew, Mark, Luke and John are trustworthy historical documents. They reach their findings applying general legal principles that obtain to documents and the testimony of witnesses. These show that the gospels are a solid foundation on which to build one's faith. We could rest our case here.[12]

Indeed, we could rest our case here. However, we will look at further evidence.

SUMMARY AND CONCLUSION

After looking at the question of the New Testament's historical accuracy we can arrive at the following conclusions.

1. The question of the Bible's historical accuracy is of utmost importance because God has revealed Himself by means of historical events. This is especially true in the New Testament when God became a human.

---

12. Ross Clifford, *The Case For The Empty Tomb*, Albatross Books, Sutherland, New South Wales, Australia, 1991, p. 136

2. Those who wrote about Jesus were either eyewitnesses to the events in His life or recorded eyewitness testimony. They were there.

3. The New Testament was written soon after the death and resurrection of Jesus Christ. There was not enough time for the message to be altered.

4. The traditional view of the authorship of the gospels (Matthew, Mark, Luke, John) is supported by the facts.

5. Each of the authors was in an excellent position to give us credible evidence as to the life and ministry of Jesus.

6. The disciples were able to be cross-examined by their contemporaries about the events they proclaimed. They preached their message in the very city where many of the events took place.

7. Paul's letters were written during the eyewitness period. They confirmed many of the main facts of the gospel.

8. We know that the New Testament books were read aloud in the churches. The message was open for all to hear and evaluate.

9. The evidence concerning the events, places, and names mentioned in the New Testament conclusively affirms the basic historical reliability of the text. We know that the people actually existed, the events occurred, and the places were real. As far as we are able to determine, the historical evidence contained in the New Testament matches up with that of secular history.

10. Therefore, the testimony of law comes into play. Since the document has come down to us where we would expect to find it, without any tampering and that it contains no obvious errors or contradictions, it should be given the benefit of the doubt in matters where there is no independent evidence to confirm or deny its teachings. Therefore, we should rightly assume that the New Testament is a reliable historical document.

We now move to the content of the New Testament. Who is the main character of the story? What is the book trying to tell us? These and other related questions will be addressed in our next chapter.

CHAPTER 6

The Main Character Of The New Testament Jesus Christ: The Claims Made About Him

---

Thus far we have learned that the New Testament is a reliable document in its text and in its historical references. This being the case, we now need to go to the New Testament itself to look at the specific claims in which it makes. This chapter will examine these claims.

We find that the main character of the New Testament is Jesus Christ. The Old Testament looked forward to His coming, the gospels record His arrival, the Book of Acts chronicles the spreading of His message, the New Testament letters explain His two comings, and the Book of Revelation records the consummation of all things in Christ. The Bible is truly all about Him.

This being the case, we want to find out what specific claims it makes about Him. We find that Jesus made certain claims about Himself and others also made claims about Him.

From these claims, we will discover that there is only one God who exists and there is only one way to reach the one God—through the Person of Jesus Christ. The New Testament is clear on both of these matters.

This chapter will deal with the specific claims that the New Testament makes about Jesus Christ. Since the New Testament has been transmitted accurately, and its history matches up with known events, then we must take seriously the claims that it makes. This section examines some of those specific claims which are found in the New Testament.

WHAT IS THE INTENTION OF THE NEW TESTAMENT WRITERS?

Whenever we read any book, our goal should be to discover the intention or purpose of the author. As far as the New Testament is concerned, the main character is Jesus Christ—it is all about Him. In addition, the New Testament was written to create belief in Him. This is the claim that it makes for itself. John wrote the following.

> Jesus performed many other signs in the presence of His disciples that are not written in this book. But these are written so that you may believe Jesus is the Messiah, the Son of God, and by believing you may have life in His name (John 20:30,31 HCSB).

These verses are highly instructive. John's purpose in writing was to create in his readers, belief in Jesus. He tells us that he was selective in the signs that he recorded about the life and ministry of Jesus, but that the signs that were given were meant to cause the reader to believe. This is his stated purpose.

The remainder of the New Testament echoes that same purpose—it was written to create belief in Jesus as the Messiah or the Christ.

THE ENTIRE BIBLE IS ALL ABOUT JESUS CHRIST

Actually, the entire Bible is all about the Lord Jesus. Jesus Himself made this clear. He said the following to the religious leaders of His day.

> You pore over the scriptures, because you think you have eternal life in them, yet they testify about Me... For if you believed Moses you would believe Me, because he wrote about Me (John 5:39, 46 HCSB).

According to Jesus, the Scriptures spoke of Him. He is the main theme of the Word of God. Again, it must be remembered that this was His own claim.

On the day of His resurrection, He said the following to two disciples walking with Him on the road to Emmaus.

> So he said to them, "You foolish people—how slow of heart to believe all that the prophets have spoken! Wasn't it necessary for the Christ to suffer these things and enter into his glory?" Then beginning with Moses and all the prophets, he interpreted to them the things written about himself in all the scriptures (Luke 24:25-27 NET).

According to Jesus, the Law and the prophets spoke about Him. Now, let us look at the evidence.

THE OLD TESTAMENT—THE PREPARATION FOR THE CHRIST

The Old Testament was preparing the way for kingdom of God to come to the earth in the Person of the King, the Messiah. Isaiah the prophet wrote about the coming of the Lord. He said.

> A voice cries out, "In the wilderness clear a way for the Lord; construct in the desert a road for our God" (Isaiah 40:3 NET).

The entire Old Testament was looking forward to the coming of the Messiah, the Christ. Everything was pointing toward Him.

THE GOSPELS—THE MANIFESTATION OF THE CHRIST

He came as promised. Indeed, the four Gospels record the manifestation of the long-awaited Messiah. We find that John the Baptist acknowledged Jesus as the one whom the Old Testament spoke of. The Bible says.

> The next day John saw Jesus coming toward him and said, "Here is the Lamb of God, who takes away the sin of the world" (John 1:29 NET).

In another episode in the Gospel of John, we have the testimony to Jesus' identity by a man named Philip. Scripture says.

> Philip found Nathanael and told him, "We have found the one Moses wrote about in the law, and the prophets also wrote about—Jesus of Nazareth, the son of Joseph" (John 1:45 NET).

Jesus, the Messiah, arrived as predicted. However, He was rejected by His own people and crucified. Yet, He did not stay dead! Three days after His death Jesus Christ rose from the dead.

ACTS—THE PROPAGATION OF THE MESSAGE OF THE CHRIST

After His resurrection, Christ met with His disciples, on and off, for some forty days. As the Lord was about to leave the earth and ascend into heaven, He gave His disciples a command—they were to spread the message about Him to the entire world.

This key verse in the Book of Acts records the following words of Jesus to His disciples.

> But the Holy Spirit will come upon you and give you power. Then you will tell everyone about me in Jerusalem, in all Judea, in Samaria, and everywhere in the world (Acts 1:8 CEV).

The Book of Acts records the propagation of the message of Jesus Christ that was to go out to the entire world. Acts records the "good news" about Jesus going from Jerusalem to the city of Rome.

THE NEW TESTAMENT LETTERS—THE EXPLANATION OF THE TWO COMINGS OF CHRIST

The Jews in Jesus' day were expecting only one coming of the Messiah. Indeed, they were not looking for His death or His resurrection. However, Christ said that He would "come again" to the world.

The two comings of Christ are then explained in the New Testament letters. Paul wrote about the mystery or sacred secret that had been hidden. He said.

> God wanted to make known to those among the Gentiles the glorious wealth of this mystery, which is Christ in you, the hope of glory (Colossians 1:27 HCSB).

Christ's first coming was a "mystery" or "sacred secret" that was not explained to the Old Testament reader. The New Testament letters provide us with the explanation about His two comings.

REVELATION—THE CONSUMMATION OF ALL THINGS IN CHRIST

Finally, all things will be consummated at the Second Coming of Jesus Christ. John the evangelist wrote the following.

> Behold, he is coming with the clouds, and every eye will see him, even those who pierced him, and all tribes of the earth will wail on account of him. Even so. Amen (Revelation 1:7 ESV).

All things will be consummated, or fulfilled, when Christ comes again.

SUMMARY ON THE MAIN CHARACTER OF SCRIPTURE: JESUS CHRIST

Therefore, we can sum up the evidence as follows.

1. The Old Testament records the preparation for the Christ.

2. The Gospels record the manifestation of the Christ.

3. The Book of Acts gives us the propagation of the message of the Christ.

4. The New Testament letters provide the explanation of the two comings of Christ.

5. The Book of Revelation documents the consummation of all things in Christ.

Therefore, the entire Bible is truly about Him!

THE CLAIMS MADE ABOUT JESUS

Now that we understand that Jesus is the main character of Scripture and that the New Testament was written to cause belief in Him, we now come to our next point—the specific claims that are made about Jesus.

GOD THE SON CAME TO EARTH TO SHOW US WHAT GOD IS LIKE

The main message of the New Testament is that God the Son became a human being in the Person of Jesus Christ. We read the following in the Gospel of John.

> Now the Word became flesh and took up residence among us. We saw his glory—the glory of the one and only, full of grace and truth, who came from the Father (John 1:14 NET).

In fact, God came to earth to show us what He is like. John also wrote these words about Jesus.

> No one has ever seen God. The only one, himself God, who is in closest fellowship with the Father, has made God known (John 1:18 NET).

We do not have to be ignorant with respect to God. Indeed, God the Son has made Him known!

THERE IS ONE GOD AND ONE WAY TO THE ONE GOD

When God the Son came to earth in the Person of Jesus Christ, He made a variety of claims about Himself. Among other things, Jesus claimed was that He Himself was the only possible way that a person could have a relationship with the one true God.

There are many who do not like this assertion because it seems so narrow-minded. Others try to deny that Jesus said or meant this. But the record is clear, and whether a person likes it or not, Jesus made the colossal claim that nobody could know the living God except by means of Him.

For example, Jesus told the religious leaders of His day.

> I told you that you would die in your sins, for you will die in your sins unless you believe that I am he (John 8:24 NRSV).

Unless they accepted Him as the Messiah they would die in their sins. They had to make a choice. Indeed, they were either for Him or against Him.

To His disciples in the upper room, He said the following.

> I am the way, the truth and the life. No one goes to the Father except through me (John 14:6 God's Word).

This could not be any clearer. Jesus is the one way in which a person can know the one, true God. There is no other way.

At another time, He said.

> Very truly, I tell you, anyone who hears my word and believes him who sent me has eternal life, and does not come under judgment, but has passed from death to life. Very truly, I tell you, the hour is coming, and is now here, when the dead will hear the voice of the Son of God, and those who hear will live (John 5:24,25 NRSV).

Jesus alone gives eternal life. Furthermore, there will come a day when His voice will raise the dead!

Elsewhere in the Gospel of John, we are told that belief in Jesus leads to eternal life while rejection of Him leads to eternal punishment. It says.

> And anyone who believes in God's Son has eternal life. Anyone who doesn't obey the Son will never experience eternal life but remains under God's angry judgment (John 3:36 NLT).

The evidence from the New Testament is clear. There is only one way to reach the one God and that is through the Person of Jesus Christ.

THESE CLAIMS WERE NOT INVENTED BY THE CHURCH

The claim that Jesus is the only way to get to God was not a later invention by the church. In fact, it was central to His message.

Whether a person believes it or not, the record is clear—Jesus Himself believed and taught that only through Him could a person have their sins forgiven and come to know the living God.

THE CLAIMS OF THE BOOK OF ACTS

The Book of Acts also makes the claim that Jesus is the only way to reach the one true God. The Apostle Peter said the following to the people in his day.

> And there is salvation in no one else, for there is no other name under heaven given among men by which we must be saved (Acts 4:12 ESV).

Note well his claim. There is no salvation outside of the person of Jesus Christ. He is the only way by which a person can be saved.

THE CLAIMS OF THE APOSTLE PAUL

The Apostle Paul echoes this thought. He also stated that Jesus was the only way to get to God. He wrote the following to Timothy.

> For there is one God and one intermediary between God and humanity, Christ Jesus, himself human (1 Timothy 2:5 NET).

There is only one God who exists, and one go-between, or intermediary, between God and humanity—Jesus Christ. According to Scripture, there is no other way! This is the consistent message of the New Testament.

CONCLUSION TO THE CLAIMS ABOUT JESUS

Our look at what the New Testament claims about Jesus Christ reveals the following.

1. The stated purpose of the New Testament is to create belief in the reader that Jesus is the Christ, the Son of God. Those who believe this message will have life through His name.

2. In addition, the message of the entire Bible is about Jesus. The Old Testament looked forward to His coming, the Gospels record His appearance, the Book of Acts relates the propagation of His message, the New Testament letters explain His two comings, and finally the Book of Revelation reveals all things consummated in Christ.

3. The specific claim of the New Testament is there is only God who exists and only one way to get to the one God—through Jesus Christ. All others are pretenders. There is no salvation outside of the Person of Jesus Christ. This is their claim, not something the church later invented. It is the claim of Jesus as well as the claim of the writers of the New Testament.

Our next section will consider our various options as we look at His claims.

CHAPTER 7

The Claims Of Jesus Christ Considered: A Look At The Options

We have come to the place in our study where the various claims that Jesus Christ makes, as well as the claims others made about Him, must be dealt with. As we will discover in this chapter, there are four possible ways in which to view the claims about Jesus.

One point of view says that He never made the claims—they were legendary. The claims found in the New Testament were not made by Jesus Himself but rather by His disciples who exaggerated His words and deeds. We will find that this is not really an option. Jesus made the claims and these claims must be dealt with.

Next, we will look at the option that He made the claims, and they were not true, and Jesus knew they were not true. This would make Him a liar. We will discover that there is no evidence whatsoever that Jesus lied about anything.

The next option is that Jesus was a lunatic. That is, He made the claims about Himself which are recorded in the New Testament, thought His claims were true, but they were not. Again, we will discover there is no evidence whatsoever that Jesus was insane.

This will bring us to our last option—He is Lord. That is, Jesus actually made the claims that are recorded in the New Testament and His claims are true. This is the only position which makes sense.

However, more is needed. Though believing Jesus is the Lord may be the only sensible way in which to deal with His claims, there has to be some evidence to back up these claims. The next three chapters will document some of that evidence.

The New Testament makes it clear that Jesus Christ claimed to be the only way in which a person can know God. In addition, it says He was God in human flesh who came to earth to show us what God is like, and to die for the sins of the world. Those claims must be dealt with.

As we have seen, the New Testament has been transmitted to us in an accurate manner and the historical events contained in it match up with known reality. Consequently, the New Testament should be considered trustworthy until evidence to the contrary is brought forward. Therefore, when we consider the claims of the New Testament with respect to Christ's identity, we have three possible ways in which we can interpret these claims. They are as follows.

OPTION 1: THE CLAIMS ARE LEGENDARY

This point of view says that Jesus never personally made the claims about Himself that are recorded in the New Testament. His own disciples, who wrote the New Testament long after His death, exaggerated His words. This would make the claims of Christ legendary.

OPTION 2: HE MADE THE CLAIMS BUT THEY ARE NOT TRUE

Another possibility is that Jesus did make the claims recorded in the New Testament but His claims were not true. There are two potential options for those who hold this view.

He knew the claims were not true, yet He made them anyway. This would make Him a liar.

He made the claims truly believing He was God. This would make Him a lunatic.

OPTION 3: HE MADE THE CLAIMS AND THEY ARE TRUE

Jesus actually did make the claims about Himself that are recorded in the New Testament, and He was whom He claimed to be—the Lord of the universe.

We shall now consider each of these possibilities.

POSSIBILITY 1: LEGEND: HE NEVER MADE THE CLAIMS THAT ARE RECORDED IN THE NEW TESTAMENT

For modern humankind, the favorite way of dealing with the claims of the New Testament regarding Jesus Christ is simply to believe that He never made them. It is asserted that His followers made the claims after many years of their teaching and preaching about Him. Jesus, they argue, was a simple man who had a tremendous impact on His followers.

After His death, stories about Him were told and retold. By the time these stories had been committed to writing, Jesus was transformed from a simple Galilean teacher into a miracle worker, the Son of God, and the Savior of the world. Those who believe Jesus never claimed any of these things assert that His well-meaning disciples got caught up in all the excitement around His character, and exaggerated His claims and deeds.

RESPONSE TO THE LEGEND HYPOTHESIS

The accusation that Jesus never made the claims about Himself that are recorded in the New Testament, does not square with the facts. We can make the following observations.

OBSERVATION 1: THERE WAS NOT ENOUGH TIME FOR LEGENDS TO GROW

This first point is essential for us to understand. We are not dealing with generations but rather with a short period of time between the actual occurrence of the events and their recording. There is strong evidence that three of the four gospels were written within twenty years of the death and resurrection of Jesus. In addition, the earliest letter of the Apostle Paul, First Thessalonians, was also written within twenty years of the death, resurrection, and ascension of Jesus. This is far too short of a time for the claims about Jesus to have been exaggerated to the point where they did not accurately reflect what He actually said and did.

OBSERVATION 2: THE NEW TESTAMENT WRITERS UNDERSTOOD THE IMPORTANCE OF FIRSTHAND EVIDENCE

The importance of eyewitness testimony was not lost on the New Testament writers who repeatedly appealed to first-hand evidence to substantiate their assertions. For example, one of Jesus' disciples, John, wrote the following.

> We proclaim to you the one who existed from the beginning, whom we have heard and seen. We saw him with our own eyes and touched him with our own hands. He is the Word of life. This one who is life itself was revealed to us, and we have seen him. And now we testify and proclaim to you that he is the one who is eternal life. He was with the Father, and then he was revealed to us (1 John 1:1-2 NLT).

They testified to what they knew was true—because they were there!

OBSERVATION 3: THERE WERE UNFRIENDLY EYEWITNESSES AROUND

It must be emphasized that not all of the eyewitnesses to the events in the life of Christ were believers. If the disciples tended to distort the facts, the unbelieving eyewitnesses would have immediately objected to their distortion. Yet we find no such objections.

OBSERVATION 4: THE NUMBER OF EYEWITNESSES WAS SUFFICIENT

Not only do we have eyewitnesses, the number of eyewitnesses to the events in the life of Christ also argues for their truthfulness. The

Apostle Paul said that one of the appearances of Christ after His death was witnessed by over five hundred people. He wrote the following to the Corinthians.

> After that, he was seen by more than five hundred of his followers at one time, most of whom are still alive, though some have died by now (1 Corinthians 15:6 NLT).

Multitudes of people witnessed the miracles of Jesus as well as heard His teachings. They were not isolated events seen only by a select few.

OBSERVATION 5: THEY LIVED IN A MEMORY CULTURE

In addition, the people that lived in the first century relied more upon memory than we do today. Lawyer/theologian John Warwick Montgomery makes an appropriate comment.

> We know from the Mishna that it was Jewish custom to memorize a Rabbi's teaching, for a good pupil was like 'a plastered cistern that loses not a drop' [Mishna Aboth II.8]. And we can be sure that the early Church, impressed as it was with Jesus governed itself by this ideal.[1]

The memorization of Jesus' teachings, as well as His mighty deeds, would be expected from His audience. They were used to committing to memory the important sayings and deeds of famous teachers.

OBSERVATION 6: JESUS MADE A LASTING IMPRESSION

The extraordinary events of the life of Christ would have made a lasting impression upon all of the people who witnessed them. Miracles were not something they were used to seeing. After Jesus healed a paralyzed man, the Bible records the reaction of the people.

---

1. John Warwick Montgomery, *History and Christianity*, Downers Grove, Ill.: Intervarsity Press, 1964, pp. 37,38

> Immediately he arose, took up the bed, and went out in the presence of them all, so that all were amazed and glorified God, saying, "We never saw anything like this!" (Mark 2:12 NKJV).

We note that they had never seen anything like this event. This miracle of Jesus astounded them. Such a deed would not be soon forgotten.

OBSERVATION 7: THERE WAS NO EXAGGERATION IN THEIR DESCRIPTIONS OF JESUS

These reasons refute the idea that the disciples exaggerated Jesus' claims. The New Testament was composed in such a short time after the events occurred that it would be folly to assume that the writers' memories were so faulty that neither they, nor the unbelievers, could remember the actual events of the life of Christ—especially because of the miraculous nature of the deeds.

OBSERVATION 8: THE WRITERS HAD A BIOGRAPHICAL INTEREST IN CHRIST'S LIFE

It is also evident that the early church had a biographical interest in the life of Jesus Christ. The gospel accounts are filled with specific historical details or allusions to events in Jesus' ministry. Matthew, for example, records Jesus' genealogy (chapter 1), and the visit of the Magi to Herod and the slaughter of the innocents (chapter 2). He also gives the events associated with the trial and death of Jesus (chapters 26-27).

In the writings of Luke, we also find many historical references. He wrote.

> In the fifteenth year of the reign of Emperor Tiberius, when Pontius Pilate was governor of Judea, and Herod was ruler of Galilee, and his brother Philip ruler of the region of Ituraea and Trachonitis, and Lysanias ruler of Abilene,

> during the high priesthood of Annas and Caiaphas, the word of God came to John son of Zechariah in the wilderness (Luke 3:1,2 NRSV).

In this passage seven different people, and their governmental positions, are listed in order to indicate the time that God's Word came to John the Baptist. This testifies that the gospel writers were interested in the biographical and historical details of the life of Jesus.

OBSERVATION 9: THERE WAS CONSISTENT TESTIMONY BY THE DISCIPLES

Furthermore, the testimony of the various gospel writers is consistent. They do not disagree among themselves on the fact that Jesus was the Messiah, the Son of God. Their testimony remained consistent throughout their lives.

Theologian John Gerstner makes an appropriate observation.

> We note, in the first place, that they had the best possible jury to test their competency—their own contemporaries among whom the events related were said to have taken place. If the writers had been palpably contradicted by the facts, the people to whom they related the facts would have been the very ones to expose them. If they had been misguided zealots the nonzealots to whom they spoke could have spotted in a moment and repudiated it as quickly. If they had garbled the actual events, eyewitnesses in quantity could have testified to the contrary . . . As a matter of fact, their record went unchallenged. No man called them liars; none controverted their story. Those who did not believe in Jesus did not dispute the claims to his supernatural power. The apostles were imprisoned for speaking about the resurrection of Christ, not, however, on the ground of what they said was untrue, but that it was unsettling the people. They were accused of being heretical, deluded, illegal, un-Jewish, but they were

> not accused of being inaccurate. And that would have been by far the easiest to prove if it had been thought to be true.[2]

If their testimony could have been challenged, it would have been. However, they were never accused of lying concerning what they said about Jesus.

OBSERVATION 10: THE DISCIPLES WERE MARTYRED FOR THEIR TESTIMONY

The final evidence of the truthfulness of the disciples' testimony is that they were martyred for their beliefs. The disciples signed their testimony in their own blood. Certainly, a person might lie for someone else, but will not die for that person or a cause if he believes it to be false. They obviously believed Jesus' story to be true.

CONCLUSION: THE GOSPELS CAN BE TRUSTED

These reasons are sufficient to trust the gospel portrait of Jesus as given by the New Testament writers. Because of the early dates of the composition and the circulation of the New Testament books, and the evidential and substantiated nature of those books, it is impossible that Jesus never made the unique claims for which Christianity stands—His sacrifice on the cross, His forgiveness of sin, His resurrection from the dead, and His Second Coming.

Thus, if we assume that Jesus truly made the claims attributed to Him in the New Testament, then we are left with two choices—His claims were not true or they were true.

POSSIBILITY 2: LIAR OR LUNATIC: HE MADE THE CLAIMS BUT THEY WERE NOT TRUE

It is possible that Jesus actually made the claims attributed to Him in the New Testament yet His claims were not true. If this is the case, then there are two possibilities. The first is that He knew He was not the Son

---

2. John Gerstner, *Reasons For Faith*, Grand Rapids: Baker Book House, 1953, p. 98

of God yet He lied about His identity. The second option is that Jesus thought He was the Son of God but was deluded.

HE KNEW THE CLAIMS WERE NOT TRUE: JESUS WOULD HAVE BEEN A LIAR

This first option identifies Jesus as a liar. As we have seen, Jesus made some fantastic claims about whom He was. He made Himself out to be the eternal God, the Creator of the universe and humankind's only Savior. He consistently made these claims during His time here on earth. The question arises, "Is there any evidence that He lied about who He was?"

THERE IS NO EVIDENCE THAT JESUS LIED ABOUT ANYTHING

While it is theoretically possible that Jesus lied about who He was, there is certainly no evidence to suggest it. Everything we know about the character of Jesus testifies that He always told the truth. He underscored the fact that His words were truthful. John records the following.

> The Pharisees replied, "You are making false claims about yourself!" Jesus told them, "These claims are valid even though I make them about myself. For I know where I came from and where I am going, but you don't know this about me. I am one witness, and my Father who sent me is the other" (John 8:13,14,18 NLT).

Jesus Himself clearly said.

> I am the way, the truth, and the life (John 14:6 KJV).

The centurion who presided over His crucifixion testified to Jesus' character. Mark writes.

> When the Roman officer who stood facing him saw how he had died, he exclaimed, "This man truly was the Son of God" (Mark 15:39 NLT).

The evidence is that Jesus always told the truth.

JESUS TOLD THE SAME STORY UNTIL THE END

If He were a liar, then He was a consistent liar up until the end. He confessed to being the Messiah before His accusers. When Jesus made His confession, He did it while He was under oath. Matthew records.

> But Jesus was silent. Then the high priest said to him, "I put you under oath before the living God, tell us if you are the Messiah, the Son of God." Jesus said to him, "You have said so. But I tell you, From now on you will see the Son of Man seated at the right hand of Power and coming on the clouds of heaven" (Matthew 26:63,64 NRSV).

This statement caused the Jews to bring Jesus to Pilate to be crucified. We read in John's gospel.

> The Jews answered him, "We have a law, and according to our law He ought to die, because He made Himself the Son of God" (John 19:7 NKJV).

Even when Jesus went to His death, He never changed His testimony as to His identity.

THERE WAS NO MOTIVATION FOR JESUS TO LIE

Furthermore, if one contends that Jesus lied about whom He was, a motive needs to be found for His lying. People lie to gain some advantage but one becomes hard-pressed to see any advantage in Jesus' lying. What advantage was there to being pressured night and day by the multitudes to perform acts of healing and forgive sin? What advantage was there to being a traveling preacher who had no place to call home? What advantage was there to being put to death for claiming to be the Son of God, if He knew His claims were not true? He could have been released if He had only denied being the Christ. Why not simply admit that He was not?

CONCLUSION

Thus the evidence indicates that Jesus Christ did not deliberately lie about who He was or why He came. He consistently told the truth.

HE MADE THE CLAIMS AND THOUGHT HIS CLAIMS WERE TRUE: HE WAS A LUNATIC

It is clear that Jesus made astounding claims about Himself. It is also clear that the evidence leads us to believe that He believed His claims were true. There are some who contend that Jesus made the claims and believed them to be true because He was mentally unbalanced.

RESPONSE TO THE IDEA THAT JESUS WAS DERANGED

We respond to this accusation as follows.

JESUS DID NOT ACT INSANE

From someone deluded or insane, we would expect them to act consistent with insanity. That is, someone insane would do and say insane things. When we look at the life and teachings of Jesus we see anything but insanity.

After Jesus delivered the Sermon on the Mount the crowd was awed by His teachings. Matthew writes.

> After Jesus finished speaking, the crowds were amazed at his teaching, for he taught as one who had real authority—quite unlike the teachers of religious law (Matthew 7:28,29 NLT).

On one occasion, the Pharisees sent some of their men to apprehend Jesus. John records what happened.

> Some of them wanted to seize Him, but no one laid hands on Him. Then the temple police came to the chief priests and Pharisees, who asked them, "Why haven't you brought

> Him?" The police answered, "No man ever spoke like this!" (John 7:44-46 HCSB).

The words of Jesus rang clear and true.

JESUS WAS ALWAYS IN CONTROL IN EVERY SITUATION

Moreover, Jesus handled Himself as one always in control. When He was betrayed in the Garden of Gethsemane, He demonstrated self-control and mastery over the situation. He said.

> Don't you realize that I could ask my Father for thousands of angels to protect us, and he would send them instantly? But if I did, how would the Scriptures be fulfilled that describe what must happen now? Then Jesus said to the crowd, "Am I some dangerous criminal, that you have come armed with swords and clubs to arrest me? Why didn't you arrest me in the Temple? I was there teaching every day. But this is all happening to fulfill the words of the prophets as recorded in the Scriptures." At that point, all the disciples deserted him and fled (Matthew 26:53-56 NLT).

Jesus was the Master of every situation.

HIS TEACHINGS WERE NOT THAT OF A LUNATIC

As we search the Scriptures, we find there is nothing in the character of Jesus to cause us to believe Him to be insane. On the contrary, the depth of His teaching and His masterful character testify that He was indeed the Son of God.

Secular psychiatrist, J. T. Fisher, explains it this way.

> If you were to take the sum total of all authoritative articles ever written by the most qualified of psychologists and psychiatrists on the subject of mental hygiene—if you were to combine them and refine them and cleave out all the excess

> verbiage . . . and if you were to have these unadulterated bits of pure scientific knowledge concisely expressed by the most capable of living poets, you would have an awkward and incomplete summation of the Sermon on the Mount. And it would suffer immeasurably through comparison. For nearly two thousand years the Christian world has been holding in its hands the complete answer to its restless and fruitless yearnings. Here . . . rests the blueprint for successful human life with optimism, mental health, and contentment.[3]

The same Jesus, whom some claim was insane when He talked about His identity, is also lauded the world over for His practical teaching concerning mental and spiritual health. Thus this accusation does not make sense.

The well-respected church historian Philip Schaff remarked.

> Is such an intellect—clear as the sky, bracing as the mountain air, sharp and penetrating as a sword, thoroughly healthy and vigorous, always ready and always self-possessed—liable to a radical and most serious delusion concerning His own character and mission? Preposterous imagination!.[4]

It is indeed preposterous imagination to think that Jesus was somehow deluded.

WAS JESUS MERELY A GREAT PROPHET?

If Jesus actually made the claims attributed to Him in Scripture, then what are we to make of them? There are those who attempt to sidestep the issue of Jesus' claims. They contend that He was not God,

---

3. J. T. Fisher and L. S. Hawley, *A Few Buttons Missing*, Philadelphia: Lippincott, 1951, p. 273

4. Philip Schaff, *The Person of Christ*, New York, NY: American Tract Society, 1913, p. 97, 98

but neither was He lying or deranged. They usually place Him in the category of a great teacher, perhaps the greatest teacher who ever lived. Some go as far as calling Him a prophet. But they deny He was anything more. They deny He is God.

IT IS NOT POSSIBLE THAT JESUS WAS ONLY A GREAT PROPHET

The possibility that Jesus was only a great teacher, or a great prophet, does not exist. He clearly claimed to be more than that. Jesus said to the religious leaders.

> Jesus answered them, "Many good works I have shown you from My Father. For which of those works do you stone Me?" The Jews answered Him, saying, "For a good work we do not stone You, but for blasphemy, and because You, being a Man, make Yourself God" (John 10:32,33 NKJV).

The religious leaders understood the claims Jesus made about Himself.

At the grave of a friend Jesus said.

> I am the resurrection and the life. Those who believe in me, even though they die, will live, and everyone who lives and believes in me will never die. Do you believe this? (John 11:25,26 NRSV).

If He were the one whom He claimed to be, then He should be worshiped as God and His teaching diligently followed.

THE CHOICES THAT PEOPLE HAVE

C.S. Lewis pointed out the choices that Jesus has given us. He wrote.

> I am trying to prevent anyone saying the really foolish thing that people often say about Him. 'I'm ready to accept Jesus as a great moral teacher, but I don't accept His claim to be God.' This is the one thing we must not say. A man who was

> merely a man and said the sort of things Jesus said would not be a great moral teacher. He would either be a lunatic—on a level with the man who says he is a poached egg—or else he would be the Devil of Hell. You must make your choice. Either this man was, and is, the Son of God: or else a madman or something worse.[5]

Jesus clearly claimed to be both God and Savior. If He was not whom He claimed to be, then He was either a liar or a madman.

POSSIBILITY 3: HE IS LORD: HIS CLAIMS WERE TRUE

There is one final possibility—Jesus made these claims about Himself and His claims were true—He is, therefore, God Almighty. If this be the case, then each human being, created in His image, must judge and decide either:

(1) To accept Him as Savior and Lord, or

(2) To reject Jesus and His gift of eternal life and peace with God.

The issue is clear: Jesus is not merely another religious figure who gave the world some memorable teachings—He is much more than that.

CONCLUSION

When the claims of Jesus are considered we are left with three possibilities. Again, they are as follows.

HE NEVER MADE THE CLAIMS-LEGEND

This view does not take into account all the facts surrounding the life and ministry of Jesus. There was too short a period of time for legends about Jesus to arise to the place where all the New Testament writers believed them.

---

5. C.S. Lewis, *Mere Christianity*, New York: Macmillan Company, 1962, pp. 40,41

HE MADE THE CLAIMS AND THEY WERE NOT TRUE—LIAR OR LUNATIC

This option has Jesus actually making the claims attributed to Him but His claims were not true.

HE COULD HAVE BEEN A LIAR

While this is theoretically possible, as we have seen, there is no evidence to support it.

HE MAY HAVE BEEN A LUNATIC

Again, this is possible in theory, but the facts speak otherwise.

He Made The Claims And They Are True–He is Lord

Of the three options this is the only one that makes sense.

Jesus Christ is either Lord of all or not Lord at all! If He is Lord of all then we should expect to find some evidence to back up these claims. Our next chapter begins to examine some of that evidence.

CHAPTER 8

The Miracles Of Jesus Christ: He Demonstrated Authority Over Every Realm

Jesus' claims were backed up by three lines of evidence—His miraculous deeds, prophecies made about Him which He fulfilled, and His resurrection from the dead. This chapter looks at His miracles.

The first section deals with the biblical definition of a miracle. We will discover that Scripture uses the term miracle in two distinct ways—a natural event where the miracle is in the timing, and a purely supernatural event which has no natural explanation.

Our next section gives twenty-two reasons as to why the miracles of Jesus should be believed. This gives extensive evidence as to why the accounts of Jesus' miracles did indeed occur.

Our final section lists some common objections to Jesus' miracles. We will discover that all the objections to miracles can easily be dealt with.

We will conclude that the miracles attributed to Jesus did indeed happen and they demonstrate that He had the right to make the claims which He made. No other explanation fits all the facts.

The first line of evidence that we will examine, to determine if Jesus is the One whom He claimed to be, is His miraculous deeds. Jesus Himself appealed to miracles as a testimony to His Divine character. When John the Baptist was in prison, he sent messengers to Jesus to ask if He were the Christ. The Bible says.

> John the Baptist, who was now in prison, heard about all the things the Messiah was doing. So he sent his disciples to ask Jesus, "Are you really the Messiah we've been waiting for, or should we keep looking for someone else?" Jesus told them, "Go back to John and tell him about what you have heard and seen—the blind see, the lame walk, the lepers are cured, the deaf hear, the dead are raised to life, and the Good News is being preached to the poor" (Matthew 11:2-5 NLT).

This would remind them of various Old Testament passages—including Isaiah 35:5,6. This passage reads as follows.

> Then blind eyes will open, deaf ears will hear. Then the lame will leap like a deer, the mute tongue will shout for joy; for water will flow in the desert, streams in the wilderness (Isaiah 35:5,6 NET).

Jesus, therefore, appealed to His miracles to back up His claims.

On another occasion, He said to His disciples.

> Believe me that I am in the Father and the Father is in me; but if you do not, then believe me because of the works themselves (John 14:11 NRSV).

Therefore, miracles are an important part of the case for Christianity seeing that it is Jesus' specific claim to substantiate His identity—it is not our claim.

THE WORD MIRACLE IS USED IN TWO WAYS: MIRACLES OF TIMING AND THE PURELY SUPERNATURAL

What is a miracle? The word miracle is used in two different ways in Scripture. In the first instance, it is used to describe an unusual or natural event that occurs at a precise time. This is usually in answer to prayer. The miracle is in the timing—not in the event itself.

The second way in which the word miracle is used in the Bible concerns events that are purely supernatural—there is no natural explanation for them.

EXAMPLES OF MIRACLES OF TIMING

There are examples of this type of miracle in the gospels. They include the following.

THE MIRACULOUS CATCH OF FISH IS A MIRACLE OF TIMING

On two separate occasions, the gospels record Jesus being involved in a miraculous catch of fish. Luke records one of these incidents.

> When he had finished speaking, he said to Simon, 'Put out into deep water and let down your nets for a catch.' Simon answered, 'Master, we were hard at work all night and caught nothing; but if you say so, I will let down the nets.' They did so and made such a huge catch of fish that their nets began to split. So they signaled to their partners in the other boat to come and help them. They came and loaded both boats to the point of sinking (Luke 5:4-7 REB).

There is nothing remarkable about fishermen putting out their nets and bringing in a huge catch of fish. However, the miracle here is in the timing of the event.

After Jesus' resurrection, John reports an incident between Jesus and several of His disciples on the Sea of Galilee. The Bible says.

> When it was already very early morning, Jesus stood on the beach, but the disciples did not know that it was Jesus. So Jesus said to them, "Children, you don't have any fish, do you?" They replied, "No." He told them, "Throw your net on the right side of the boat, and you will find some." So they threw the net, and were not able to pull it in because of the large number of fish (John 21:4-6 NET).

Again, there is nothing miraculous about throwing a net into the water and having it filled with fish. This event, however, was a miracle because they had been fishing all night and had not caught a thing. However, when Jesus told them where to put their net, it immediately became full.

THE MIRACLE OF THE COIN IN THE MOUTH OF THE FISH

Another natural event, that is a miracle of timing, is the episode of the coin found in the mouth of the fish to pay the temple tax. Jesus told Peter to do the following.

> However, so that we do not give offense to them, go to the sea and cast a hook; take the first fish that comes up; and when you open its mouth, you will find a coin; take that and give it to them for you and me (Matthew 17:27 NRSV).

Again, the miracle is not in the event itself, but rather in the timing of the event.

THE MIRACLE OF THE PIGS RUNNING INTO THE SEA

The account of the pigs running into the sea could also be considered a natural event. Matthew records it this way.

> And He [Jesus] said to them, "Go." So when they had come out, they went into the herd of swine. And suddenly the whole herd of swine ran violently down the steep place into the sea, and perished in the water (Matthew 8:32 NKJV).

It is possible for a herd of pigs to rush into the sea and drown because of some natural cause, or causes. However, this herd did so immediately after the command of Jesus.

THE SERVANT HEALED AT A DISTANCE BY JESUS

John's gospel tells us of Jesus healing a man's son at a distance. The account reads as follows.

> Jesus then said, "Your son will live. Go on home to him." The man believed Jesus and started back home. Some of the official's servants met him along the road and told him, "Your son is better!" He asked them when the boy got better, and they answered, "The fever left him yesterday at one o'clock." The boy's father realized that at one o'clock the day before, Jesus had told him, "Your son will live!" So the man and everyone in his family put their faith in Jesus (John 4:50-53 CEV).

We have another example of a miracle of timing. The fact that the fever broke was not miraculous in-and-of itself. The miracle is that it broke at the exact time Jesus told the man that his son was healed.

THE EARTHQUAKE AT JESUS' DEATH

The Bible says that an earthquake occurred at Jesus' death. Matthew writes.

> And Jesus cried out again with a loud voice, and yielded up His spirit. Then, behold, the veil of the temple was torn in two from top to bottom; and the earth quaked, and the rocks were split (Matthew 27:50-51 NKJV).

The miracle is that the timing of the earthquake coincided with Jesus' death.

Events like these are not contrary to the laws of science—nonetheless, they are miracles of timing and place. Other New Testament events that could fall into this category include the cessation of the storm on the Sea of Galilee, and the withering of the fig tree. They are natural events that were supernaturally timed to show Jesus' authority.

THE OLD TESTAMENT CONTAINS THESE TYPES OF MIRACLES

These types of miraculous events occurred in the Old Testament as well. Some of them include: Elijah being fed by the ravens, the storm stopping the moment Jonah hit the water, and the rivers of the Jordan rolling back when the children of Israel entered the Promised Land. Again, we have natural events that are miracles due to their timing.

THERE ARE EVENTS THAT ARE BEYOND NATURAL LAW: THE PURELY SUPERNATURAL

The Bible also speaks of a second type of miracle performed by God. This kind of miracle cannot be explained in terms of normal cause and effect.

JESUS WALKING ON WATER–THERE IS NO NATURAL EXPLANATION POSSIBLE

Jesus walking on the water is an example of this type of totally supernatural miracle. Matthew writes.

> About three o'clock in the morning Jesus came to them, walking on the water (Matthew 14:25 NLT).

The normal laws of science cannot explain this miracle because it is physically impossible for people to walk on water.

THE MIRACULOUS FEEDING OF THE FIVE THOUSAND

Another example of this kind of miracle is Jesus feeding the five thousand. When a multitude of people who had followed Jesus became hungry, Jesus took the food that was available—five loaves and two fish—and He miraculously turned it into enough food to feed the great crowd. The Bible says.

> They all ate and were satisfied, and they picked up the broken pieces left over, twelve baskets full. Not counting women and children, there were about five thousand men who ate (Matthew 14:20,21 NET).

Not only did everyone eat, they all were satisfied. The disciples then gathered twelve baskets full of leftovers from the miracle. The normal laws of cause and effect cannot explain this event.

THE RAISING OF LAZARUS WHO WAS DEAD FOR FOUR DAYS

Another example of a miracle that is purely supernatural is the raising of Lazarus. Lazarus had been dead for four days when Jesus brought him back to life. Scripture says.

> "Roll the stone aside," Jesus told them. But Martha, the dead man's sister, said, "Lord, by now the smell will be terrible because he has been dead for four days." Jesus responded, "Didn't I tell you that you will see God's glory if you believe?" So they rolled the stone aside. Then Jesus looked up to heaven and said, "Father, thank you for hearing me. You always hear me, but I said it out loud for the sake of all these people standing here, so they will believe you sent me." Then Jesus shouted, "Lazarus, come out!" And Lazarus came out, bound in graveclothes, his face wrapped in a headcloth. Jesus told them, "Unwrap him and let him go!" (John 11:39-44 NLT).

In the life of Jesus, we see both of these types of miracles performed. The miracles were either unusual events that occurred at God's precise timing, or events beyond the normal laws of nature and science. In either case, the miracles are convincing evidence of God's great power and His control over the laws He established when He created the entire universe.

THE PURPOSE OF JESUS' MIRACLES

What was the purpose of Jesus' miracles? The word, translated miracle, can also mean, "sign." The Apostle John testified why he recorded Jesus' miracles.

> Now Jesus did many other signs in the presence of his disciples, which are not written in this book. But these are written so that you may come to believe that Jesus is the Messiah, the Son of God, and that through believing you may have life in his name (John 20:30,31 NRSV).

The miracles were done as a testimony to the identity of Jesus—that He was the promised Messiah. They were meant to create belief in Him. These signs that Jesus performed convinced many that He was the Messiah. John wrote.

> When he [Jesus] was in Jerusalem during the Passover festival, many believed in his name because they saw the signs that he was doing (John 2:23 NRSV).

The signs Jesus performed convinced many people that He was the Christ.

SOME DOUBTED JESUS' MIRACLES

Yet even with all these miraculous signs, there were some who doubted. When Jesus was speaking to the multitude, He said.

> "Father, glorify your name." Then a voice came from heaven, "I have glorified it, and I will glorify it again." The crowd standing there heard it and said that it was thunder. Others said, "An angel has spoken to him" (John 12:28,29 NRSV).

Though it was the voice of the Father who spoke, many believed they only heard thunder.

After Jesus' resurrection there were still some who did not believe. Matthew writes.

> When they saw him, they worshiped him—but some of them still doubted! (Matthew 28:17 NLT).

Therefore, the miracles of the New Testament were performed as signs to testify to Jesus' identity. And although the signs convinced many, there were still some who doubted.

PART 2
WHY SHOULD ANYONE BELIEVE IN THE MIRACLES OF JESUS?

Since the time of Christ, there have been many people who have denied His miracles. For whatever reason, they have not believed the New Testament's account of His supernatural works. The people in Jesus' day, however, had a chance to witness firsthand whether or not Jesus performed miraculous deeds. They had a lot to say on the matter.

1. JESUS DID A SUFFICIENT NUMBER OF MIRACLES

First, the number of miracles Jesus performed was sufficient for honest inquirers to believe in them. The four gospels record Jesus performing about thirty-five separate miracles. Most of the miracles that Jesus performed are recorded in more than one gospel. Two of His miracles, the feeding of the five thousand and the resurrection, are found in all four gospels.

JESUS DID MANY MORE MIRACLES THAN ARE RECORDED IN THE GOSPELS

In addition, each gospel writer says that Jesus performed many more miracles than they recorded. Matthew wrote.

> Jesus went throughout Galilee, teaching in their synagogues and proclaiming the good news of the kingdom and curing every disease and every sickness among the people (Matthew 4:23 NRSV).

Mark wrote.

> Wherever He entered into villages, cities, or in the country, they laid the sick in the marketplaces, and begged Him that they might just touch the hem of His garment. And as many as touched Him were made well (Mark 6:56 NKJV).

Luke stated it this way.

> The whole crowd was trying to touch Him, because power was coming out from Him and healing them all (Luke 6:19 HCSB).

John declared the following.

> And many other signs truly did Jesus in the presence of his disciples, which are not written in this book (John 20:30 KJV).

The vast number of miracles in which Jesus performed demonstrates that they were a regular part of His ministry.

2. THERE WAS A SUFFICIENT VARIETY OF JESUS' MIRACLES

The miracles of Jesus were also of a sufficient variety to show that He had supernatural power. Of the specific miracles recorded in the four gospels, we find the following: seventeen were bodily cures, six were healing of demonic possession, nine were miracles of nature, and there were three occasions where He raised someone from the dead.

Of the seventeen specific healing miracles that are recorded, there is a variety of different illnesses that Jesus healed. These include: leprosy, paralysis, fever, shriveled limbs, an amputated ear, blindness, deafness, muteness, and blood hemorrhaging.

HE HAS ULTIMATE AUTHORITY

Jesus also had the authority over life and death. The Bible records three specific cases of Jesus resurrecting someone from the dead: Jairus' daughter who had just died (Matthew 9:18-26), the widow of Nain's son who was in the coffin (Luke 7:11-15), and Lazarus who had been in the tomb for four days (John 11). Consequently, Jesus showed His control over the three stages of death—those who had just died, those who were going to be buried, and those who were already in the tomb.

3. HIS MIRACLES COVERED ALL AREAS OF AUTHORITY

As the Son of God, Jesus exercised authority over all realms. The Gospel of Matthew, in the eighth and ninth chapter, relates many different areas over which Jesus demonstrated His authority. The point of recording these various miracles is to show that Jesus is Lord of every realm imaginable—He is Lord of all!

JESUS HEALED INCURABLE DISEASE

After delivering the Sermon on the Mount, Jesus came down from the mountain and reached out to the most repulsive of people—a man with leprosy. At that time there was no known cure for the disease. Therefore, a leper was considered one of the living dead. Jesus had compassion on this particular man and healed him instantaneously. Matthew says.

> And behold, a leper came and worshiped Him, saying, "Lord, if You are willing, You can make me clean." Then Jesus put out His hand and touched him, saying, "I am willing; be cleansed" Immediately his leprosy was cleansed (Matthew 8:2,3 NKJV).

Here Jesus demonstrated authority over the realm of incurable disease.

JESUS HEALED FROM A DISTANCE

Jesus also had the ability to heal someone without being physically present. A centurion approached Jesus on behalf of his paralyzed servant. The centurion's faith was such that he believed the servant would be healed if Jesus just gave the word—there was no need for His actual presence. Jesus marveled at the man's faith. Matthew writes.

> When Jesus heard it, He marveled, and said to those who followed, "Assuredly, I say to you, I have not found such great faith, not even in Israel!" . . . Then Jesus said to the centurion, "Go your way; and as you have believed, so let it be

> done for you." And his servant was healed that same hour" (Matthew 8:10,13 NKJV).

Jesus exhibited power to heal when He was not present—He was not even near the afflicted person. This demonstrates that He is Lord of space and time.

JESUS IS THE LORD OVER NATURE

Jesus is not only the Lord over disease¬—He is also the Lord over nature. A great storm arose on the Sea of Galilee covering their boat with waves.

> And they went and woke him, saying, "Save us, Lord; we are perishing." And he said to them, "Why are you afraid, O you of little faith?" Then he rose and rebuked the winds and the sea, and there was a great calm. And the men marveled, saying, "What sort of man is this, that even winds and sea obey him (Matthew 8:25-27 ESV).

When He calmed the storm, Jesus displayed authority over nature—the realm of the visible world.

JESUS IS THE LORD OVER THE SUPERNATURAL REALM

Jesus also had authority over the supernatural realm. Jesus met two demon-possessed men who were terrorizing the countryside. When Jesus approached they cried out. Matthew writes.

> And suddenly they cried out, saying, "What have we to do with You, Jesus, You Son of God? Have You come here to torment us before the time?" (Matthew 8:29 NKJV).

Jesus cast out demons into a herd of swine and the two men returned to normal. By doing this Jesus showed His authority in the area of the supernatural—the invisible realm. Therefore, in one short boat trip on the Sea of Galilee, Jesus showed His authority over both the visible and invisible realm.

JESUS HAS AUTHORITY TO FORGIVE SINS

This account is found in Matthew 9:1-8. In the episode of healing a paralyzed man at Capernaum, Jesus showed that His authority extended to the forgiveness of sins.

JESUS HAS AUTHORITY OVER LIFE AND DEATH

Furthermore, Jesus demonstrated His authority was over life and death. We read the following account.

> As He was telling them these things, suddenly one of the leaders came and knelt down before Him, saying, "My daughter is near death, but come and lay Your hand on her, and she will live." . . . When Jesus came to the leader's house, He saw the flute players and a crowd lamenting loudly. "Leave," He said, "because the girl isn't dead, but sleeping." And they started laughing at Him. But when the crowd had been put outside, He went in and took her by the hand, and the girl got up (Matthew 9:18,23-25 HCSB).

Even death was subject to His authority.

HE IS LORD OVER THE NATURAL AND THE SUPERNATURAL AT THE SAME TIME

The last miracle consists of a man who had problems in both the natural and supernatural realm. Matthew records the following event.

> After they had gone away, a demoniac who was mute was brought to him. And when the demon had been cast out, the one who had been mute spoke; and the crowds were amazed and said, "Never has anything like this been seen in Israel." But the Pharisees said, "By the ruler of the demons he casts out the demons" (Matthew 9:32-34 NRSV).

This man was demon-possessed and mute at the same time. Jesus had no problem dealing with both realms simultaneously.

Therefore, Jesus' miracles consisted of the following.

1. Authority over incurable disease.

2. Being able to heal without being physically present.

3. Authority over nature.

4. Authority over the supernatural realm.

5. Authority over sins.

6. Authority over life and death.

7. Authority over the natural and supernatural realm at the same time.

These various types of miracles prove that Jesus is Lord of all!

4. THE MIRACLES WERE DONE PUBLICLY

Another important fact concerning the miracles of Jesus is that they were done publicly. The Apostle Paul said.

> I am not out of my mind, most excellent Festus, but I am speaking the sober truth. Indeed, the king knows about these things, and to him I speak freely; for I am certain that none of these things has escaped his notice, for this was not done in a corner (Acts 26:25,26 NRSV).

The facts concerning the miracles of Christ were obviously well-known. If not, Paul could not make such a statement.

EVERYONE KNEW JESUS WORKED MIRACLES

When Jesus rose on Easter Sunday He walked, unrecognized, with two disciples on the road to Emmaus. When Jesus asked them what they were talking about, He received the following response.

> Then the one whose name was Cleopas answered and said to Him, "Are You the only stranger in Jerusalem, and have You not known the things which happened there in these days?" (Luke 24:18 NKJV).

Cleopas could not believe that this stranger would even ask the question. There is only one subject that everyone was talking about—Jesus. This clearly demonstrates that the ministry of Jesus was known to everyone.

5. THE MIRACLES WERE DONE IN A STRATEGIC LOCATION

Furthermore, the land of Israel was a strategic place in the Roman Empire. In fact, it was in the middle of great crossroads. A large amount of travel occurred through the Holy Land. This is the spot where Jesus performed His miraculous deeds—not on some barren fringe of the empire where no one could observe them. He performed His miracles where the maximum number of people could see for themselves if they were genuine supernatural events.

6. THE MIRACLES WERE PERFORMED BEFORE LARGE CROWDS

When Jesus performed His miracles, it was often done in the presence of the crowds. Some passages emphasize that multitudes and even entire cities saw the miracles of Jesus (Matthew 15:30,31; 19:1,2; Mark 1:32-34; 6:53-56; Luke 6:17-19).

7. THERE WAS NO SPECIAL PLACE WHERE JESUS DID HIS MIRACLES

The ability of Jesus to perform miracles went with Him wherever He went. Whether it be on the Sea of Galilee, in the city of Jerusalem, or in the town of Jericho, the miracle power went with Him. There was no staging area where Jesus brought those who needed healing. Consequently, there was no way in which His followers could control the event or the outcome.

8. THERE WAS NO SPECIAL TIME WHEN JESUS PERFORMED MIRACLES

His miraculous deeds were performed at all times of the day—morning, noon, and night and all seasons of the year—fall, winter, spring, and summer There was nothing hindering the miracle power of Jesus. We find Jesus walking on the water in the early morning, healing the servant's ear in the Garden of Gethsemane at night, and healing the infirmed in the temple during the day.

9. JESUS PERFORMED MIRACLES IN FRONT OF GENTILES AS WELL AS JEWS

The miracles of Jesus were not limited to His countrymen the Jews, we also find Jesus doing miracles for Gentiles as well (Mark 7:24-30; John 4:46-53).

10. JESUS WORKED MIRACLES WITHOUT PROPS

Jesus' miracles were performed without any props. There were no devices, no magic wands, that helped Him when He performed His miraculous deeds. He simply spoke and then the miracle occurred.

11. HIS MIRACLES WERE DONE WITH RESTRAINT

Whenever Jesus performed a miracle, it was always done for a specific purpose. The miracles were performed for two basic reasons—as signs to testify to God's existence and power, or to meet a specific need. They were never performed as a sideshow or to merely attract attention.

For example, when Jesus was being tempted by the devil, He refused to use His miraculous powers to show off. The devil wanted Jesus to throw Himself down from the pinnacle of the temple and let the angels miraculously save Him, but Jesus would not stoop to this type of supernatural sideshow.

12. JESUS DID ONLY BENEFICIAL MIRACLES TOWARD HUMANS

With only two exceptions, the cursing of the fig tree and the demons sent into swine, the miracles of Jesus were curative in nature. Every miracle that involved humans was beneficial—never destructive. They were done to help people, not to curse His enemies. When two of Jesus' disciples wanted Him to destroy a Samaritan village by fire, they were rebuked. The Bible says.

> When his disciples James and John saw it, they said, "Lord, do you want us to command fire to come down from heaven and consume them?" But he turned and rebuked them (Luke 9:54,55 NRSV).

The miraculous power of Jesus was never done vindictively or in reaction to what someone said or did.

13. THE MIRACLES WERE NOT FOR HIS OWN ADVANTAGE

In addition, Jesus' miracles were not done in His own interest but in the interest of others. For example, He would not turn stones into bread for Himself to eat, but He multiplied the fish and bread for the five thousand when they were hungry.

When Peter tried to stop Jesus' arrest in Gethsemane, Jesus corrected His well-intentioned sword play. He also told Peter that it was well within His capability to perform a miracle if necessary.

> Then Jesus said to him, "Put your sword back into its place; for all who take the sword will perish by the sword. Do you think that I cannot appeal to my Father, and he will at once send me more than twelve legions of angels?" (Matthew 26:52,53 NRSV).

Jesus certainly had the ability to stop His arrest if He so desired.

14. JESUS MIRACLES MET REAL HUMAN NEEDS

Jesus performed miracles to meet real human needs, not to draw a crowd. For example, when people were in a desert place and needed food, Jesus miraculously provided the food. The miracle met the particular need of the people at that time.

15. HIS MIRACLES WERE IN CONTRAST TO THE MIRACLES IN THE APOCRYPHAL GOSPELS

After the New Testament was completed, a number of accounts about the life of Jesus were composed. Some of these filled in the gaps of Jesus' missing years. When they are read in comparison to the four gospels, the differences become immediately obvious. One of these stories has Jesus making birds out of clay and then making them fly. Another account of the boyhood of Jesus has Him turning the shell of a snail on the Sea of Galilee into the size of Mt. Tabor! Then suddenly the snail went back to its original form. Some of these later stories paint Jesus as vindictive—one who uses His miraculous power to turn His friends into stones or animals.

In contrast, the four gospels never contain any of this type of nonsensical material. Consequently, we never find the type of miracles that are grotesque or childish. Nothing in the miracles of Jesus leads us to think of the absurd or the bizarre.

16. HIS MIRACLES WERE DONE WITH GREAT EASE

The miracles of Jesus were performed without ceremony or ostentatious behavior—they were done with great ease. There was no strain on Jesus' behalf to bring forth the miracle. He simply spoke and it was done. In almost all of the cases, the miracles occurred immediately after His simple word or gesture. They were so much a part of His ministry that He could easily move into the area of the miraculous without going through any outward display.

17. THE MIRACLES OF JESUS WERE RECORDED BY EYEWITNESSES

We will emphasize again that the accounts given to us in the four Gospels are from eyewitnesses. The writers Matthew and John were observers of the miracles and reported what they saw occur. Mark and Luke recorded the eyewitness testimony that was reported to them. Therefore, the miracles of Jesus are well substantiated by people who were there. John the evangelist wrote.

> That which was from the beginning, which we have heard, which we have seen with our eyes, which we have looked upon, and our hands have handled, concerning the Word of life (1 John 1:1 NKJV).

The miracles were well-attested.

18. THE REACTION TO JESUS' MIRACLES IS WHAT WE WOULD EXPECT

Our next point is extremely important! If the miracles occurred as reported, the reaction to Jesus' miracles from those who observed them is exactly what we would expect. Those who witnessed the miracles of Jesus were not gullible people expecting miraculous deeds. It must be recognized that the people living at the time of Jesus were as skeptical of the miraculous as modern humanity. One need only look at the responses by the people to the miracles of Jesus to see that this is the case.

HIS DISCIPLES WERE THE FIRST UNBELIEVERS OF HIS RESURRECTION

For example, the disciples were the first unbelievers of Jesus' resurrection. When certain women returned from the tomb and told them Jesus had risen. His disciples responded as follows.

> But the story sounded like nonsense, so they didn't believe it (Luke 24:11 NLT).

When Jesus healed a man who had been blind from birth, the response was amazement. The crowd said.

> Never since the world began has it been heard that anyone opened the eyes of a person born blind (John 9:32 NRSV).

They were not used to seeing something like this. The deed was something extraordinary to them.

NO ONE HAD EVER HAD SEEN ANYTHING SIMILAR

On another occasion, Jesus healed a man who had been lame. When He performed this miracle the people reacted as we would expect anyone to act who witnessed a similar thing. Mark records the following.

> Immediately he arose, took up the bed, and went out in the presence of them all, so that all were amazed and glorified God, saying, "We never saw anything like this!" (Mark 2:12 NKJV).

On the Sea of Galilee, Jesus performed another miracle like no one had ever seen. Luke records the event.

> On the way across, Jesus lay down for a nap, and while he was sleeping the wind began to rise. A fierce storm developed that threatened to swamp them, and they were in real danger. The disciples woke him up, shouting, "Master, Master, we're going to drown!" So Jesus rebuked the wind and the raging waves. The storm stopped and all was calm! Then he asked them, "Where is your faith?" And they were filled with awe and amazement. They said to one another, "Who is this man, that even the winds and waves obey him?" (Luke 8:23-25 NLT).

These accounts illustrate that first-century humanity was just as amazed and puzzled as modern human beings would be when it comes to viewing the miraculous first hand.

19. HIS MIRACLES WERE NEVER DENIED BY HIS CONTEMPORARIES

But we see that these same people, even though they were not used to seeing miracles, could not deny these deeds. The religious rulers, who were enemies of Jesus, sought to discredit Him. Instead of denying His miracles, they attributed them to the power of the devil. Matthew writes.

> Then some people brought Jesus a man possessed by a demon. The demon made the man blind and unable to talk. Jesus cured him so that he could talk and see. The crowds were all amazed and said, "Can this man be the Son of David?" When the Pharisees heard this, they said, "This man can force demons out of people only with the help of Beelzebul, the ruler of demons" (Matthew 12:22-24 God's Word).

The religious leaders, by arguing that Christ's miracles were a work of Satan, were acknowledging the fact that Jesus was a miracle worker. If they could have denied them, they would have.

However, the lack of denial on their part, from an unfriendly source, shows that the miracles attributed to Jesus did indeed occur.

EVERYONE KNEW THAT JESUS PERFORMED MIRACLES

On the Day of Pentecost, after the death, resurrection and ascension of Jesus, Simon Peter, in testifying to Christ's resurrection, appealed to the knowledge of his hearers. He said the following to the crowd that had gathered.

> Men of Israel, hear these words: Jesus of Nazareth, a Man attested by God to you by miracles, wonders, and signs which God did through Him in your midst, as you yourselves also know (Acts 2:22 NKJV).

He stated to that large audience that the miracles of Jesus were something that they themselves knew about. The fact that Peter was not immediately shouted down by the crowd demonstrates that the people knew he was telling the truth.

Multitudes had seen Jesus perform many miracles. The certainty that Jesus performed miracles was never in question. The question was, "How did He do it?"

ALL REPORTS AGREE THAT JESUS DID MIRACLES

Another important point is this: for the first five centuries of the Christian era, every account of Jesus, whether coming from a believer or a non-believer, has Jesus performing miracles. No friend or foe, in the early centuries, ever denied His miraculous power.

20. THE TESTIMONY ABOUT JESUS MIRACLES IS FROM A NUMBER OF DIFFERENT GROUPS

The testimony of Christ's miracles comes from several different groups of witnesses. They include the following.

THOSE WHO BENEFITED FROM THE MIRACLES GAVE TESTIMONY

The first group that gives testimony are those who directly benefited from Jesus' deeds. They give first-hand testimony with respect to what Jesus did for them.

THOSE WHO OBSERVED THE MIRACLES GAVE THEIR TESTIMONY

Next, we have those who were not direct beneficiaries of the miracles but who saw them occur. This would include Jesus' disciples.

THOSE WHO WERE UNBELIEVERS AND SKEPTICS TESTIFIED TO JESUS' MIRACLES

Not only were the miracles of Jesus done publicly with the multitudes present, they were also performed in front of unbelievers. Among those who watched Jesus perform healings were the unbelieving religious leaders (Matthew 12). They were there to find fault, not to believe. Jesus, therefore, was not just preaching to the converted.

21. MIRACLES WERE AN ESSENTIAL PART OF HIS MINISTRY

Miracles were not something that was an afterthought in the ministry of Jesus. They are interlocked with everything that He said or did. Certain teachings of Jesus would be meaningless without the miracle connected to it.

For example, the discourse in John's gospel about Jesus being the bread of life makes no sense whatsoever without the miracle that explains it. Apart from the miracle of the feeding of the five thousand, this discourse is unexplainable (John 5,6).

22. THERE IS CIRCUMSTANTIAL EVIDENCE FOR JESUS' MIRACLES

Apart from the four gospels, we also have circumstantial evidence for the miracles of Jesus that is found elsewhere in the New Testament.

THE BOOK OF ACTS GIVES TESTIMONY TO JESUS' MIRACLES

We find that the Book of Acts testifies to His miraculous deeds. On the Day of Pentecost, Peter said.

> Men of Israel, hear these words: Jesus of Nazareth, a Man attested by God to you by miracles, wonders, and signs which God did through Him in your midst, as you yourselves also know (Acts 2:22 NKJV).

Peter said that the crowd themselves were aware that Jesus had performed miracles.

PAUL EMPHASIZED JESUS' RESURRECTION

The Apostle Paul emphasized that the miracle of the resurrection proved Jesus was whom He claimed to be. He wrote to the Romans.

> This letter is from Paul, Jesus Christ's slave, chosen by God to be an apostle and sent out to preach his Good News. This Good News was promised long ago by God through his prophets in the holy Scriptures. It is the Good News about his Son, Jesus, who came as a man, born into King David's royal family line. And Jesus Christ our Lord was shown to be the Son of God when God powerfully raised him from the dead by means of the Holy Spirit (Romans 1:1-4 NLT).

The resurrection shows Jesus to be the One whom He claimed to be.

THE APOSTLES HAD THE POWER TO WORK MIRACLES

In addition, His miracle power was also given to His apostles. The Book of Acts records some of their miracles done through the authority of Jesus. When Peter saw a lame man at the temple he said.

> I have no silver or gold, but what I do have I give you. In the name of Jesus Christ the Nazarene, stand up and walk!" Then Peter took hold of him by the right hand and raised him up, and at once the man's feet and ankles were made strong. He jumped up, stood and began walking around, and he entered the temple courts with them, walking and leaping and praising God (Acts 3:6-8 NET).

After Peter healed this man, the religious leaders made the following admission.

> "What should we do with these men?" they asked each other. "We can't deny they have done a miraculous sign, and everybody in Jerusalem knows about it" (Acts 4:16 NLT).

Even the miracles of the apostles were undeniable.

SUMMARY

To sum up we can say the following about Jesus miracles.

1. There were a sufficient number of them.

2. They were of a sufficient variety.

3. They covered all possible areas of authority.

4. They were done publicly.

5. They were done in a strategic location.

6. They were performed before large crowds.

7. There was no special place in which the miracles occurred.

8. There was no special time when they were performed.

9. They were performed in front of Gentiles as well as Jews.

10. They were done without props.

11. They were done with restraint.

12. The miracles were beneficial to humanity.

13. They were not done for Jesus' own advantage.

14. They met real needs.

15. They are in contrast to the miracles in the apocryphal gospels.

16. They were done with great ease.

17. They were recorded by eyewitnesses.

18. Those who observed them had same reaction as we would have.

19. The miracles of Jesus were never denied by His contemporaries.

20. There was sufficient testimony to them by believers and unbelievers alike.

21. His miracles were an essential part of His ministry.

22. There is also circumstantial evidence that Jesus performed miracles.

We conclude that the reports of Jesus' miracles, as contained in the New Testament, are accurate—Jesus was indeed a miracle worker!

PART 3
OBJECTIONS TO THE MIRACLES OF JESUS

Historically, there have been many objections to Jesus' miracles. They include the following.

OBJECTION 1: MIRACLES, BY DEFINITION, ARE IMPOSSIBLE

One of the popular ways to deny miracles is simply to define them out the realm of possibility. Many people state as a fact that the idea of a miracle is something which is impossible. End of discussion.

Of course, the problem with that position is that only God could know whether miracles are possible or not. Only someone with all knowledge of every event that has ever taken place would be able to deny miracles had ever occurred. Therefore, the denial of the possibility of miracles is something beyond the ability of humans.

THE ILLUSTRATION OF THE PLATYPUS

When explorers first came to eastern Australia they came across a creature that should not have existed. It was a furry, semi-aquatic, egg-laying mammal with a duck's bill and webbed feet. It was named the platypus. The characteristics of this little rabbit-sized creature were so strange that some people in England considered it a hoax when the skin of a dead platypus was first brought to London.

The reason the existence of the platypus was doubted had nothing to do with the evidence—for the evidence, strange as it was, pointed to the existence of this egg-laying mammal. The rejection came because it did not fit the scientist's particular view of the world of nature. Since no mammal was known to have laid eggs, zoologists were certain this creature could not exist. Eventually scientists came around to believe the platypus did exist with all its bizarre characteristics.

IT IS THE SAME MISCONCEPTION WITH RESPECT TO MIRACLES

Since no one had ever seen a creature like this before, people assumed that it could not exist. This is the same misconception of many of those who reject miracles—because they have never seen a miracle they assume it cannot happen. No amount of evidence would convince them to change their mind. Yet the platypus does exist and miracles did happen— this is what the evidence testifies.

OBJECTION 2: THE MIRACLES HAPPENED IN A PRE-SCIENTIFIC AGE

It is alleged that since the miracles recorded in Scripture occurred from two thousand to four thousand years ago they should not be believed. Supposedly they took place before the age of modern science when people were ignorant about the way the universe functioned.

Granted, the miracles were recorded before modern times, yet the testimony to their truthfulness remains. The eyewitnesses were just as skeptical as modern humankind and their reaction to the miraculous was the same as ours would have been if we had seen the same events.

OBJECTION 3: THE MIRACLES WERE SELF-INDUCED

There are those who argue that the healing miracles recorded in the New Testament could have been self-induced. In the first century, before the advent of modern medicine, there was much ignorance regarding disease. Could not one easily argue that the healings of Jesus were self-induced because the illnesses were psychological rather than physical?

MANY MIRACLES ARE BEYOND NATURAL EXPLANATION

A study of the Gospel accounts will put that question to rest. The healing miracles of Jesus were of such a nature as to be beyond any natural explanation. For example, Jesus healed a man who was paralyzed (Mark 2:3-12) and another who was blind from birth (John 9:1-7). Lazarus was dead four days when Jesus brought him back to life (John 11). A young girl who was dead was brought back to life by Jesus (Luke 8:51-56). He healed ten lepers at once (Luke 17:11-19) and Jesus healed a man who was a deaf mute (Mark 7:31-37).

It stretches beyond the bounds of imagination to think that all these people, including the ones who had been dead, could only be ill in their minds and not in their bodies. Furthermore, we are never told of Jesus ever refusing to heal a person because of lack of ability. Unless one would want to argue that no legitimate disease was present in the first century, it seems clear that His healings were often and varied enough to prove valid.

OBJECTION 4: WHY AREN'T THEY HAPPENING TODAY?

Another objection, which is similar to an earlier one, is that if miracles occurred long ago, we should expect them to occur today, if indeed they really did occur. In answering this objection, we first note that it ignores the fact that miracles are found in clusters in Scripture, not on every page. But even if they were found everywhere in the Bible the answer is, "So what?" The issue is, "Did they happen as the eyewitnesses testify?" This is the real issue.

OBJECTION 5: THERE IS THE POSSIBILITY OF MISINTERPRETING THE EVENT

This objection deals with the frailty of us as humans. We all know that it is possible to watch an event and describe it in such a way as to misinterpret what actually happened. Since humans sometimes poorly report what they have seen, why should we believe the biblical account of miracles?

If we took this objection to its logical fulfillment, then there could be no accurate reporting of any event. All reports would be suspect and nothing could be believed. Yet experience tells us that humans can accurately report on events they witness. The evidence has to be weighed and evaluated for each incident.

OBJECTION 6: THERE ARE CONTRADICTIONS BETWEEN THE ACCOUNTS

Often it is alleged that the biblical accounts of the miraculous are so hopelessly contradictory that they should not be believed. Yet this is not the case. The fact that there are minor differences in detail between the accounts only shows that they are independent of one another. There is agreement between them on the major points.

OBJECTION 7: THERE ARE MIRACLE REPORTS IN OTHER RELIGIONS

What about the miracles in other religions? Since there are other religions who also report miraculous deeds occurring among them, why should they be rejected and the biblical miracles believed? Three things should be considered when answering this question.

THERE ARE NOT THAT MANY MIRACLE REPORTS IN OTHER RELIGIONS

First, there are not as many miracles in the world religions as some people assume. Miracles are very rare in the accounts of the major religions of the world. The exception, of course, is the biblical account, where miracles are an important part of the message.

THE MIRACLES IN OTHER RELIGIONS WERE NOT DONE PUBLICLY

The public demonstration of Jesus with respect to His miracles is in contrast to other so-called miracle workers who did their work in private. For example, almost all the miracles that are attributed to Muhammad in the Koran occurred in private—where there was no way either to prove or disprove the testimony.

THERE IS NO REAL PURPOSE FOR THE MIRACLES IN NON-CHRISTIAN RELIGIONS

The miracles attributed to other religions are not backed up by eyewitness testimony. Furthermore, they are all too often performed as a sideshow with no direct purpose in mind. The so-called miracles of other religions do not touch humanity at its basic needs as do the miracles recorded in the Bible. This, and the lack of corroborative testimony to their actually occurring, causes them to be rejected.

OBJECTION 8: THE MIRACLES WERE RECORDED LONG AFTER THE FACT

Often it is objected that the miracles of the New Testament were written long after the events transpired. Supposedly this makes them untrue. Again, as we have seen, those who were actually present recorded the miracles in Scripture—they were eyewitnesses to the events. Their accounts did not grow larger and larger with time.

IF GOD EXISTS, THEN MIRACLES ARE POSSIBLE

Our last point about miracles is an obvious one. If an all-powerful God truly exists, then miracles are possible. He would have the ability to perform miraculous deeds if He so chooses. Therefore, the idea that the God of Scripture, who claims to be the only God who exists, would perform miracles to testify to His existence and power, is certainly something that is reasonable.

SUMMARY TO THE MIRACLES OF JESUS CHRIST

All of the evidence points to the fact that Jesus Christ did indeed work miracles. Both believers and unbelievers testified this to. No one doubted His ability to perform supernatural deeds. The question asked of Jesus was not if He performed miracles but rather how did He do these supernatural works. The truth of His miracle working ability was beyond all doubt.

Therefore, miracles are a strong line of evidence to support Jesus' claims but they are not the only line of evidence. Next we will move on to an even stronger line of evidence—fulfilled prophecy.

CHAPTER 9

Predictive Prophecy: Jesus Fulfilled Prophecy And Made Predictions That Have Come True

One of the most powerful lines of evidence for the truthfulness of the Christian faith is predictive prophecy. In this chapter, we will discover two incredible truths: first, Jesus miraculously fulfilled prophecy when He came to the earth the first time, and second, He Himself made predictions that were fulfilled.

Therefore, the evidence from predictive prophecy shows that Jesus fulfilled the Old Testament prophecies regarding the coming Messiah as well as making predictions which have come true.

This chapter is divided into three basic sections. First, we look at the subject of predictive prophecy. We find the requirements the Bible gives for someone to be called a prophet of God.

Next, we look at predictions Jesus fulfilled at His first coming. We discover that He was born in the right family line, in the right city, and at the right time in history. The evidence reveals Jesus to be the promised Messiah.

Finally, we look at a number of predictions which He made which we accurately fulfilled. He has made predictions that have come true.

Since only God knows the future, and only He can predict what will occur, fulfilled prophecy gives us evidence of His existence as well as His control of history. This is a comforting truth for the believer.

The first line of evidence for the truthfulness of the Christian faith consists of the miracles which Jesus performed. These miraculous signs demonstrated Jesus' authority over every conceivable area.

The second line of evidence for the truthfulness of Jesus' claims is one of the strongest anyone can imagine—predictive prophecy. As we shall see, this line of evidence sets Jesus apart from any other religious leader who has ever lived.

WHAT IS A BIBLICAL PROPHET?

First, we must understand what we mean by the word "prophet." The word translated "prophet" occurs over three hundred times in the Old Testament and over one hundred times in the New Testament. It comes from two Greek words—*pro* meaning "before," or "in place of" and *fayme* meaning "to speak." A prophet, therefore, is someone who speaks in the place of someone else. The Bible says Aaron was a prophet to Moses.

> Then the Lord said to Moses . . . your brother Aaron will be your prophet (Exodus 7:1 NIV).

Moses told God that his lack of eloquence prevented him from being His spokesman. God then told Moses that his brother Aaron could accompany him and be his spokesman, or prophet, to the people.

A BIBLICAL PROPHET WAS A SPOKESMAN FOR GOD

In the Bible, a prophet is a spokesman for God. God sent and commissioned the prophet so that the words of the prophet are the words of God. As the priest represented the people to God, the prophet was God's representative to the people. The Bible is clear that the words of the prophet were not the product of his own spirit, but came from a higher source—the One True God.

THE BIBLICAL PROPHET PROCLAIMED GOD'S WORD

The prophet's message was the proclamation of the Word of God to the people. He was essentially a preacher and a teacher—a person who relays a message from God to humanity. The prophet Jeremiah recorded his prophetic calling. He wrote.

> "Don't say that," the LORD replied, "for you must go wherever I send you and say whatever I tell you" . . . "Get up and get dressed. Go out, and tell them whatever I tell you to say. Do not be afraid of them, or I will make you look foolish in front of them" (Jeremiah 1:7,17 NLT).

Jeremiah the prophet was commissioned to speak the truth—no matter what the response of the people.

THERE IS ALSO A PREDICTIVE ELEMENT IN BIBLICAL PROPHECY

There is also the predictive element in Bible prophecy. If the people did not receive the message of the prophet, then the prophet would predict future events. This would often involve judgment upon the nation Israel for their refusal to listen to the Lord.

THE BIBLICAL PROPHET SPOKE OF THINGS TO COME

Jesus said one of the ministries of the Holy Spirit was to show believers "things to come." We read in John's gospel the following words of Jesus.

> When the Spirit of truth comes, he will guide you into all the truth, for he will not speak on his own authority, but whatever he hears he will speak, and he will declare to you the things that are to come (John 16:13 ESV).

Bible prophecy, therefore, has both a local and future application. A biblical prophet was both a forth teller of local issues and foreteller of the future.

THE PURPOSE OF BIBLE PROPHECY

Bible prophecy teaches us that there is a God who exists, and this God is in control of history. The purpose of prophecy is given to us in Scripture. We read the following in the Book of Isaiah.

> Remember the former things of old, For I am God, and there is no other; I am God, and there is none like Me, Declaring the end from the beginning, And from ancient times things that are not yet done, Saying, 'My counsel shall stand, And I will do all My pleasure' (Isaiah 46:9,10 NKJV).

In another passage, the Lord said the following.

> I announced events beforehand, I issued the decrees and made the predictions; suddenly I acted and they came to pass. I did this because I know how stubborn you are. Your neck muscles are like iron and your forehead like bronze. I announced them to you beforehand; before they happened, I predicted them for you, so you could never say, 'My image did these things, my idol, my cast image, decreed them.' You have heard; now look at all the evidence! Will you not admit that what I say is true? (Isaiah 48:3-6 NET).

From these passages we learn the following about Bible prophecy.

1. There is only one God who exists.

2. No creature anywhere in the universe is like God.

3. The God of the Bible knows everything that will take place in the future.

4. The one God also tells us about certain events which will happen before they occur.

5. Predictive Prophecy is given to fulfill His promises to His people.

6. We can know that God exists, that He knows the future, and is in control of the future, when His predictions come to pass.

7. Consequently, when one honestly examines the evidence they must admit that everything which the Lord has said about Himself, as well as future events, is true.

According to Scripture, these are the various reasons for Bible prophecy.

THE PROPHETS GAVE EVIDENCE OF AUTHENTICITY

A practical question arises, "How would the people know if a prophet was sent by God? Could not anyone claim to be a spokesman for God?"

God provided a simple method so that the people would know if this person was actually speaking for the Lord—the prophecies he gave must come to pass.

> I will raise up for them a prophet like you from among their brothers; I will put my words in his mouth, and he will tell them everything I command him. If anyone does not listen to my words that the prophet speaks in my name, I myself will call him to account. But a prophet who presumes to speak in my name anything I have not commanded him to say, or a prophet who speaks in the name of other gods, must be put to death. You may say to yourselves, "How can we know when a message has not been spoken by the LORD?" If what a prophet proclaims in the name of the LORD does not take place or come true, that is a message the LORD has not spoken. That prophet has spoken presumptuously. Do not be afraid of him (Deuteronomy 18:18-22 NIV).

The prophet had to give evidence of his prophetic calling.

THE BIBLICAL PROPHET ENCOURAGED PEOPLE TO FOLLOW THE LORD

From this passage we see that a prophet of God must speak in the name of the Lord. He shall not encourage the people to follow after false gods. No matter how correct a prophet may seem to be, if he does not encourage people to follow the Lord then he cannot be considered a prophet of God. Merely getting some future events correct is not enough to be considered a prophet of God.

THE BIBLICAL PROPHET WAS ALWAYS 100% RIGHT

This is the biblical test for a true prophet. The person must be 100% right 100% of the time. A prophet of God could not even make one mistake. But what if someone predicted events that would only happen in the distant future? Everyone would be dead before it was known whether or not that person was a true prophet. How could the people immediately know if that person who claimed to be a prophet was, in actuality, sent from God?

THE PROPHET HAD TO PREDICT SOMETHING IN THEIR OWN LIFETIME

God gave a simple test: his authenticity as a genuine prophet would be demonstrated by predicting something to happen in his own lifetime. Before he could be received as God's prophet, he had to give clear evidence of his supernatural calling.

ISAIAH WAS A GENUINE PROPHET

For example, Isaiah the prophet spoke to King Hezekiah about the possible attack of the Assyrian army. He said the following.

> Therefore, thus says the LORD concerning the king of Assyria: He shall not come into this city, shoot an arrow there, come before it with a shield, or cast up a siege ramp against it (Isaiah 37:33 NRSV).

The prophecy was clear. Although the city of Jerusalem was surrounded by the Assyrian army, there would be no destruction whatsoever. Furthermore, there would not even be one arrow shot into the city by the enemy. This prophecy was literally fulfilled as Isaiah records.

> Then the angel of the LORD set out and struck down one hundred eighty-five thousand in the camp of the Assyrians; when morning dawned, they were all dead bodies (Isaiah 37:36 NRSV).

As Isaiah the prophet predicted there was not even one arrow shot into the city. Therefore, we have an immediate fulfillment in the lifetime of Isaiah that demonstrates that he was speaking for God.

JEREMIAH GAVE EVIDENCE HE WAS A GENUINE PROPHET

We also have an example from the life of Jeremiah. During his lifetime, there was a false prophet named Hananiah. Jeremiah pronounced judgment upon him. It is recorded as follows.

> Then Jeremiah the prophet said to Hananiah, "Listen, Hananiah! The LORD has not sent you, but the people believe your lies. Therefore, the LORD says you must die. Your life will end this very year because you have rebelled against the LORD." Two months later, Hananiah died (Jeremiah 28:15-17 NLT).

Again, we have a prediction fulfilled in the lifetime of the prophet Jeremiah. The same test held true for other biblical prophets.

SUMMARY TO BIBLE PROPHECY

We can summarize Bible prophecy in the following manner.

1. A biblical prophet is a person who spoke for God to the people.

2. The main idea behind Bible prophecy is proclamation of His Word.

3. There is a difference between prophecy and predictive prophecy.

4. If the message of the prophet was not received by the people, then judgment was often predicted upon them.

5. Prophecy testifies that God not only exists, He is also in control of history.

6. A prophet must give evidence in his own lifetime that he is a genuine prophet.

This summarizes what the Scripture says about Bible prophecy.

PART 2
PROPHECIES FULFILLED BY JESUS SOME PREDICTIONS FULFILLED AT HIS FIRST COMING

One of the major themes of the Old Testament is that God would send a Deliverer or Messiah (the Christ) to come into the world. He would eventually rule as king over Israel as well as rule over all the nations of the earth. A practical question arises, "How would the people know the identity of this promised Messiah when He arrived?" Theoretically, anyone could claim to be God's anointed one.

This, however, was not the case. God narrowed it down in such a way that whoever claimed to be the Messiah would have to fulfill some very specific predictions. We will look at three specific areas that had to be fulfilled by anyone claiming to be the promised Messiah.

THE FAMILY LINE OF THE MESSIAH WAS PREDICTED

The first set of predictions, which we will consider, has to do with the Messiah's genealogy, or family line. God narrowed down the family line of the Messiah in such a way that eliminated most of the people who have ever been born.

PREDICTION: HE WILL COME FROM THE FAMILY OF SHEM

The Bible says that the Messiah will be a descendant of one of Noah's sons—Shem. We read about this in the Book of Genesis. It says.

> Then Noah said, "May Shem be blessed by the LORD my God; and may Canaan be his servant. May God enlarge the territory of Japheth, and may he share the prosperity of Shem; and let Canaan be his servant" (Genesis 9:26,27 NLT).

Noah had three sons, Shem, Ham and Japheth. God eliminated two thirds of humanity when He said the Messiah would come through the line of Shem.

THE FULFILLMENT RECORDED

Luke lists the genealogy of Jesus in which he records Jesus was a descendant of Shem. It says.

> Son of Cainan, son of Arphaxad, son of Shem (Luke 3:36 HCSB).

Thus, Jesus was a descendant of Shem.

PREDICTION: THE CHRIST WILL BE A DESCENDANT OF ABRAHAM

The Bible says that the Messiah will descend from Abraham. We read in the Book of Genesis the Lord saying the following.

> Now the Lord said to Abram, "Go from your country and your kindred and your father's house to the land that I will show you. And I will make of you a great nation, and I will bless you and make your name great, so that you will be a blessing. I will bless those who bless you, and him who dishonors you I will curse, and in you all the families of the earth shall be blessed" (Genesis 12:1-3 ESV).

Now God eliminates all the families of the earth but one—the family of Abraham. Whoever claims to be the Messiah has to be a descendant of Abraham for God told Abraham that one of his descendants will bless all the families of the earth.

THE FULFILLMENT RECORDED

In the first verse of Matthew's gospel, he states that Jesus descended from Abraham. We read.

> This is the list of ancestors of Jesus Christ, descendant of David and Abraham (Matthew 1:1 God's Word).

Jesus descended from Abraham. The promise to Abraham was literally fulfilled.

THE TESTIMONY OF PAUL

The Apostle Paul, in the New Testament, also emphasized that God specified one from Abraham's line would be the Christ. He wrote to the Galatians.

> God gave the promise to Abraham and his child. And notice that it doesn't say the promise was to his children, as if it meant many descendants. But the promise was to his child—and that, of course, means Christ (Galatians 3:16 NLT).

The Apostle Paul says that God uses the singular rather than the plural to emphasize it will be one particular descendant of Abraham who will bless the world—this one descendant was Jesus.

PREDICTION: HE WILL BE A DESCENDANT OF ISAAC

Abraham had two sons, Isaac and Ishmael. God promised Isaac that the Messiah would be through his family line. We also read about this in Genesis.

> Stay in this land for a while, and I will be with you and will bless you. For to you and your descendants I will give all these lands and will confirm the oath I swore to your father Abraham. I will make your descendants as numerous as the stars in the sky and will give them all these lands, and through your offspring all nations on earth will be blessed (Genesis 26:3,4 NIV).

Therefore, the Messiah would be born through the line of Isaac, not Ishmael, the other son of Abraham.

THE FULFILLMENT RECORDED

According to Matthew, Jesus was from Isaac's line. He stated.

> The book of the genealogy of Jesus Christ, the son of David, the son of Abraham. Abraham was the father of Isaac, and Isaac the father of Jacob, and Jacob the father of Judah and his brothers (Matthew 1:1,2 NIV).

The promise to Isaac was fulfilled.

PREDICTION: THE MESSIAH WILL COME FROM THE FAMILY OF JACOB

Isaac had two sons, Jacob and Esau. Scripture says that the chosen line was through Jacob. This continues to narrow the possible candidates for the Messiah. It says in the Book of Genesis.

> And God said to him, "I am God Almighty; be fruitful and increase in number. A nation and a community of nations will come from you, and kings will come from your body. The land I gave to Abraham and Isaac I also give to you, and I will give this land to your descendants after you" (Genesis 35:11,12 NIV).

Jacob, not Esau, would have the Messiah come through his line.

THE FULFILLMENT RECORDED

Jesus was also from the line of Jacob. Matthew records it as follows.

> An account of the genealogy of Jesus the Messiah, the son of David, the son of Abraham. Abraham was the father of Isaac, and Isaac was the father of Jacob (Matthew 1:1,2 NRSV).

The promise to Jacob was fulfilled.

PREDICTION: HE WILL COME FROM TRIBE OF JUDAH

Jacob had twelve sons. God eliminated 11/12 of the line of Jacob by saying the Messiah would come from the tribe of Judah.

> The scepter shall not depart from Judah, nor the ruler's staff from between his feet, until tribute comes to him; and the obedience of the peoples is his (Genesis 49:10 NRSV).

Therefore, the line of the Messiah is narrowed even further.

THE FULFILLMENT RECORDED

Jesus descended from the line of Judah. Matthew records the following.

> This is a record of the ancestors of Jesus the Messiah, a descendant of King David and of Abraham: Abraham was the father of Isaac. Isaac was the father of Jacob. Jacob was the father of Judah (Matthew 1:1,2 NLT).

The promise that the Lord made to Judah was literally fulfilled.

PREDICTION: THE MESSIAH WILL BE FROM FAMILY LINE OF JESSE

There were many family lines in the tribe of Judah, but only through the family line of Jesse could the Messiah come. He is the Branch that will bear fruit according to the prophet Isaiah. He wrote.

> Then a shoot will grow from the stump of Jesse, and a branch from his roots will bear fruit (Isaiah 11:1 HCSB).

The Bible says that Jesse would have a descendant who would be the Messiah.

THE FULFILLMENT RECORDED

Jesus was a descendant of Jesse. Matthew writes.

> This is the list of ancestors of Jesus Christ, descendant of David and Abraham. . . Boaz and Ruth were the

> father and mother of Obed. Obed was the father of Jesse (Matthew 1:1,5 God's Word).

Again, we find that God's promise is fulfilled.

PREDICTION: HE WILL DESCEND FROM THE HOUSE OF DAVID

God told David that the Messiah would be from His line. We read about this promise in Second Samuel. It says.

> When your days are fulfilled and you lie down with your ancestors, I will raise up your offspring after you, who shall come forth from your body, and I will establish his kingdom (2 Samuel 7:12 NRSV).

Jesse had at least eight sons. God eliminated 7/8 of the sons of Jesse when He said the Messiah would be through the line of David. Again, the list of potential candidates gets narrower and narrower.

THE FULFILLMENT RECORDED

The Bible records the fulfillment as follows.

> This is a record of the ancestors of Jesus the Messiah, a descendant of King David and of Abraham (Matthew 1:1 NLT).

The very first verse of the New Testament records the fulfillment of this prophecy.

When the angel appeared to Mary announcing Jesus' birth he confirmed that Mary's child would be a descendant of David. Luke writes.

> And now, you will conceive in your womb and bear a son, and you will name him Jesus. He will be great, and will be called the Son of the Most High, and the Lord God will give to him the throne of his ancestor David (Luke 1:31,32 NRSV).

The Bible says that Jesus descended from David. Again, the promises of God come true.

SUMMARY TO THE GENEALOGY OF THE MESSIAH

Whoever the promised Messiah would be, He would have to be a male physical descendant of David the king. All other individuals would not qualify. Therefore, from the predictions with respect to the genealogy of the Messiah, the great majority of the people who have ever been born are eliminated from contention.

Jesus, however, fulfilled the Old Testament prophecies about the family line of the Messiah by being a descendant of David.

THE PLACE OF THE MESSIAH'S COMING WAS PREDICTED

In addition, the exact place of His birth was predicted.

PREDICTION: HE WILL BORN IN BETHLEHEM

God predicted, through the prophet Micah, the exact city where the Messiah would be born. He said the following.

> But you, Bethlehem Ephrathah, though you are small among the clans of Judah, out of you will come for me one who will be ruler over Israel, whose origins are from of old, from ancient times (Micah 5:2 NIV).

Every city in the world was eliminated but one—Bethlehem of Judah or Judea. Thus if someone was a descendant of King David, yet was born in any other city than Bethlehem of Judea, he would not qualify as the promised Messiah.

What is interesting is that there was another city named Bethlehem in Israel at that time. However, this Bethlehem was not in the land of Judah. Thus, to fulfill the prophecy, the Messiah had to be born in Bethlehem of Judea, or Judah, not the other Bethlehem.

THE FULFILLMENT RECORDED

Jesus was not only born in the right family—He was also born at the right place—Bethlehem of Judea. Matthew records the following.

> Jesus was born in the town of Bethlehem in Judea, during the reign of King Herod. About that time some wise men from eastern lands arrived in Jerusalem (Matthew 2:1 NLT).

Matthew records that Jesus was indeed born in the predicted city—the city of Bethlehem of Judea.

3. THE TIME OF THE MESSIAH'S COMING WAS PREDICTED

Finally, we have the prediction with respect to the time in history of the Messiah's coming.

PREDICTION: HE WILL BE KILLED BEFORE THE TEMPLE AND THE CITY OF JERUSALEM ARE DESTROYED

The Old Testament predicts the death of the Messiah. This is found in the Book of Daniel. It reads.

> After the sixty-two weeks, an anointed one shall be cut off and shall have nothing, and the troops of the prince who is to come shall destroy the city and the sanctuary. Its end shall come with a flood, and to the end there shall be war. Desolations are decreed (Daniel 9:26 NRSV).

The New International Version puts it this way.

> After the sixty-two 'sevens,' the Anointed One will be cut off and will have nothing. The people of the ruler who will come will destroy the city and the sanctuary. The end will come like a flood: War will continue until the end, and desolations have been decreed (Daniel 9:26 NIV)

We learn three things from this verse.

1. The Messiah will come on the scene of history.

2. He will be killed.

3. After His death, the city of Jerusalem and the temple will be destroyed.

THE FULFILLMENT RECORDED

When Jesus came to the earth, the city of Jerusalem, and the temple, had not yet been destroyed. Teaching at the temple was an important part of Jesus' ministry. The temple was destroyed in the year A.D. 70, along with the city of Jerusalem. This was about forty years after His death and resurrection. Again, the predictions were literally fulfilled.

SUMMARY TO THE PROPHECIES CONCERNING THE MESSIAH

Therefore, Jesus fulfilled certain prophecies about the coming Messiah. They include.

1. He was born in the right family line—David's.

2. He was born at the right place—Bethlehem of Judea.

3. He was born at the right time in history—before the city of Jerusalem and the temple were destroyed

THERE ARE TWO IMPORTANT POINTS TO CONSIDER

These three areas of prophecy we have looked at reveal two startling things. They are as follows.

First, the prophecies were fulfilled literally—exactly as they were written. Jesus was literally a descendant of King David, He was literally born in the city of Bethlehem, and He literally came upon the scene of history and was killed before the city of Jerusalem and the temple were destroyed. In other words, the prophecies were fulfilled exactly as they were written.

THERE WAS NO HUMAN MANIPULATION IN THE FULFILLMENT

Second, these three lines of prophecy were all fulfilled without any human manipulation. There is no way Jesus could have deliberately fulfilled them, seeing they were all fulfilled by His birth. Before He gave any sermons, before He did anything miraculous, Jesus supernaturally fulfilled these prophecies. He was born in the right family, at the right place, and at the right time in history. Humanly speaking, there is no way Jesus could control these factors. Therefore, we find in the birth of Jesus Christ, miraculous fulfillment of Bible prophecy.

PART 3
PROPHECIES JESUS MADE THAT HAVE BEEN FULFILLED
A LOOK AT JESUS THE PROPHET

Jesus not only fulfilled prophecy in His own life, He Himself predicted events that were to come to pass some time in the future. One of the ministries of Jesus was that of a prophet. As has been true with the prophecies fulfilled in His own life, His prophetic words have been literally and marvelously fulfilled.

We are going to look at ten specific predictions that Jesus made as well as their fulfillment. They include the following.

PREDICTION 1: HIS WORDS WOULD BE EVERLASTING

Jesus made the astounding prediction that heaven and earth would pass away but that His words would not pass away. He said.

> Heaven and earth will pass away, but my words will not pass away (Matthew 24:35 ESV).

He predicted that His words would be everlasting. We need to appreciate the amazing nature of this prophecy. Here was a man who lived in the first century A.D. with only a small group of followers, and His country was subject to the bondage of Rome. There was no modern means of mass communication or storage of the words of a person.

Yet Jesus made the statement that His words would be eternal—they will never pass away. Although it seemed improbable at the time, it has occurred exactly as He predicted. The words of Jesus are still with us today. They are read and believed by untold millions as they have been for the last two thousand years. It has happened just as He said.

PREDICTION 2: THE STORY OF MARY OF BETHANY WILL BE CONTINUALLY TOLD

Mary of Bethany poured ointment on the body of Jesus in anticipation of His coming death. The disciples rebuked her for wasting it, but Jesus said she had done a good thing. Matthew records the following words of Jesus.

> For you always have the poor with you, but you will not always have me. In pouring this ointment on my body, she has done it to prepare me for burial. Truly, I say to you, wherever this gospel is proclaimed in the whole world, what she has done will also be told in memory of her (Matthew 26:11-13 ESV).

Jesus predicted that her story would be told wherever the gospel was preached. As He predicted, the story of Mary of Bethany, and her anointing of Jesus before His death, is still told today wherever the gospel is preached. The fact that you are reading about it right now continues to fulfill Jesus' prophecy.

PREDICTION 3: JESUS GAVE SPECIFIC DETAILS OF HIS OWN BETRAYAL AND DEATH

The Bible says that Jesus predicted the circumstances surrounding His death. He said the following to His disciples.

> From that time Jesus began to show to His disciples that He must go to Jerusalem, and suffer many things from the elders and chief priests and scribes, and be killed, and be raised the third day (Matthew 16:21 NKJV).

Jesus also predicted His death would occur during the Passover celebration, and it would be by means of crucifixion. He said.

> You know that the Passover takes place after two days, and the Son of Man will be handed over to be crucified (Matthew 26:2 HCSB).

He also predicted that He would be betrayed by one of His own disciples. Matthew also writes.

> While they were eating, He said, "I assure you: One of you will betray Me." Deeply distressed, each one began to say to Him, "Surely not I, Lord?" (Matthew 26:21,22 HCSB).

This occurred as predicted. Judas Iscariot betrayed Jesus. Christ suffered at the hands of the religious rulers and was crucified in the city of Jerusalem during the Passover. All these events occurred just as He had said.

The following points were literally fulfilled with respect to these predictions by Jesus.

1. He suffered as a result of the religious rulers.

2. He was betrayed by one of His own disciples.

3. He died in Jerusalem.

4. He died during the Passover celebration.

5. He died by means of crucifixion.

Therefore, He fulfilled at least five specific predictions with respect to His betrayal and death.

PREDICTION 4: HIS OWN RESURRECTION FROM THE DEAD THREE DAYS AFTER HIS DEATH

Jesus also predicted His resurrection from the dead. He said it would happen exactly three days after His death. We read in Matthew.

> The next day, that is, after the day of Preparation, the chief priests and the Pharisees gathered before Pilate and said, "Sir, we remember what that impostor said while he was still alive, 'After three days I will rise again'" (Matthew 27:62,63 NRSV).

The chief priests, and the teachers of the law, were the ones who arrested Jesus and brought Him to Pilate for execution. Yet, three days after His crucifixion, Jesus was alive again. The angel at His tomb on that first Easter made it clear to those who arrived.

> He isn't here! He has been raised from the dead, just as he said would happen. Come, see where his body was lying (Matthew 28:6 NLT).

Jesus was crucified on Good Friday and came back from the dead on Easter Sunday morning—three days by Jewish reckoning. Again, His predictions were literally fulfilled.

PREDICTION 5: THE DESTRUCTION OF THE CITY OF JERUSALEM

After Jesus was rejected by His people, the Lord pronounced judgment upon them. Jesus predicted that the city of Jerusalem would be destroyed. Forty years before it occurred, Jesus gave specifics to its destruction.

> For the days will come upon you when your enemies will build an embankment against you, surround you, and hem

> you in on every side. They will crush you and your children within you to the ground, and they will not leave one stone on another in you, because you did not recognize the time of your visitation (Luke 19:43, 44 HCSB).

Jesus also said.

> When you see Jerusalem surrounded by armies, then know that its desolation has come near (Luke 21:20 NRSV).

In A.D. 70, as Jesus had predicted, the city of Jerusalem was surrounded and destroyed by the armies of Titus the Roman. The reason Jesus gave for the fall of the city was the peoples' rejection of Him as Messiah, "because you did not know the time of your visitation."

PREDICTION 6: THE TEMPLE IN JERUSALEM WOULD BE DESTROYED

Another prediction of Jesus that was literally fulfilled concerns the destruction of the temple in Jerusalem. Jesus specified the manner of its destruction. Matthew writes

> As Jesus was leaving the Temple grounds, his disciples pointed out to him the various Temple buildings. But he told them, "Do you see all these buildings? I assure you, they will be so completely demolished that not one stone will be left on top of another!" (Matthew 24:1,2 NLT).

This happened exactly as predicted. When Titus the Roman destroyed the city of Jerusalem in A.D. 70, the temple was also destroyed.

PREDICTION 7: THE JEWISH PEOPLE WOULD BE SCATTERED

When Jesus predicted the destruction of the city of Jerusalem and the temple, He made clear the fate that awaited the Jewish people. They will be scattered from their land and taken captive by other nations. He said.

> They will fall by the edge of the sword and be led captive among all nations, and Jerusalem will be trampled underfoot by the Gentiles, until the times of the Gentiles are fulfilled (Luke 21:24 ESV).

This occurred just as He had predicted. When the city and temple were destroyed, the people were scattered to the ends of the earth. Those who were not killed when the city was captured, were sold into slavery.

PREDICTION 8: THE HOLY LAND WOULD BE RULED BY GENTILES

Jesus also predicted the nation Israel would be dominated for a long period of time by the Gentile (or non-Jewish) peoples.

> And they will fall by the edge of the sword, and be led away captive into all nations. And Jerusalem will be trampled by Gentiles until the times of the Gentiles are fulfilled (Luke 21:24 NKJV).

The land remained under Gentile domination for two thousand years. Except for a few short years in the second century the Jews had no rule over Jerusalem from A.D. 70 until 1967. The prediction that the nation would be subject to Gentile rule has been literally fulfilled.

PREDICTION 9: THE JEWISH PEOPLE WOULD BE PERSECUTED

The people would not only be scattered, Jesus also predicted that the Jewish race would be persecuted. On His way to the cross He said.

> Daughters of Jerusalem, don't weep for me, but weep for yourselves and for your children. For the days are coming when they will say, 'Fortunate indeed are the women who are childless, the wombs that have not borne a child and the breasts that have never nursed.' People will beg the mountains to fall on them and the hills to bury them (Luke 23:28-30 NLT).

History records that the Jewish people have gone through terrible persecution as Jesus predicted. From the ghettos of the Middle Ages, to the Holocaust of World War II, the Jews have been a persecuted race, like no other people in history.

PREDICTION 10: THOUGH PERSECUTED, THE JEWISH NATION WILL SURVIVE

Though scattered and persecuted, Jesus also predicted the Jewish people would not perish. Though the nation was to suffer terribly, Jesus made it clear they would still survive. Again, we read the prediction in Luke's gospel.

> They will fall by the sword and will be taken as prisoners to all the nations. Jerusalem will be trampled on by the Gentiles until the times of the Gentiles are fulfilled (Luke 21:24 NIV).

They would be persecuted until the times of the Gentiles would be fulfilled. Once this period of Gentile rule was over, the Jews would again have self-rule. This has only begun to be fulfilled in modern times. On May 14, 1948, the modern state of Israel was reborn. Again, the words of Jesus have been literally fulfilled.

SUMMARY TO PREDICTIONS MADE BY JESUS

From the examples given, it is clear that Jesus had the ability to predict what was going to occur in the future. The historical evidence establishes that Jesus was a reliable prophet. The predictions of Jesus that have been fulfilled include the following.

1. The words of Jesus would be everlasting.

2. The story of Mary of Bethany would be continually told.

3. He would be betrayed by one of His disciples, suffer at the hands of the religious rulers, and die on the cross in the city of Jerusalem during the Passover.

4. He would come back from the dead exactly three days later.

5. The city of Jerusalem would be destroyed because they did not receive Him as their Messiah.

6. The temple would also be destroyed because the people refused to accept Him as their Savior.

7. The Jewish people would be scattered from their land.

8. The Holy Land would be dominated by Gentile nations.

9. The Jews would suffer terrible persecution.

10. Though persecuted, the nation would survive.

These are merely some of the predictions that Jesus has made that have been fulfilled and continue to be fulfilled—there are many more than we have listed. Thus we have Jesus fulfilling prophecies in His own life as well as predicting things in the future that have come to pass.

So far we have seen two impressive lines of evidence for the claims of Jesus—miracles and fulfilled prophecy. We now move to our third line of evidence—the resurrection of Jesus Christ from the dead.

CHAPTER 10

The Resurrection Of Jesus Christ: He Is The Only One Who Has Conquered Death

The cornerstone of the Christian is the resurrection of Jesus Christ from the dead. This chapter looks at this crucial subject in some detail.

Our first section looks at the importance of the resurrection. We will discover that without the resurrection, there is no Christianity. According to Scripture, the truth of the Christian faith stands or fall on the resurrection of Jesus.

After we determine that the resurrection is central to the Christian faith, we then weigh the direct evidence for it. We will find that the main reason the people believed that Jesus came back from the dead is that He appeared to them after His crucifixion and burial.

Our next section looks at some of the indirect, or circumstantial, evidence for the resurrection. There are about ten lines of circumstantial evidence which give further testimony to the resurrection of Christ.

We then move on to answering some common objections which are made about the resurrection. In doing so, we will discover that it takes much more faith to believe in these alternative theories than to believe in the resurrection itself.

Our last section looks at the meaning of the resurrection to the individual. If Jesus did come back from the dead, then what does it mean to us as individuals as well as to the human race? We will find that it means everything.

This section concludes our evidence for the truth of Jesus' claims. When all the facts are weighed and evaluated the verdict becomes clear—Jesus is the One whom He claimed to be.

The big question, that sooner or later every human being has to face, was asked long ago by a man named Job. He said.

> If mortals die, can they live again? (Job 14:14 NLT).

This same question remains to this day, "Is this life all that there is? Or is there life beyond the grave? Is it possible for anyone to know the answer to this question?"

Our third line of evidence is the Christian's answer to Job's question—the resurrection of Jesus Christ from the dead.

PART 1: THE IMPORTANCE OF THE RESURRECTION OF JESUS CHRIST: WHAT IT MEANS TO THE CHRISTIAN FAITH

The message of the early Christians, and the focal point of the New Testament, was stated in this simple truth by the Apostle Paul.

> Remember Jesus Christ, risen from the dead, the offspring of David, as preached in my gospel (2 Timothy 2:8 ESV).

This is the central truth of the Christian faith. The importance of the resurrection of Jesus Christ cannot be overemphasized. Without the resurrection there is no Christianity.

WHY THE RESURRECTION IS IMPORTANT

Why is the resurrection of Jesus Christ so important? The Apostle Paul wrote to the church in Corinth and declared the following.

> Now if Christ is preached as raised from the dead, how can some of you say, "There is no resurrection of the dead"? But if there is no resurrection of the dead, then Christ has not been raised; and if Christ has not been raised, then our preaching is without foundation, and so is your faith. In addition, we are found to be false witnesses about God, because we have testified about God that He raised up Christ—whom He did not raise up if in fact the dead are not raised. For if the dead are not raised, Christ has not been raised. And if Christ has not been raised, your faith is worthless; you are still in your sins. Therefore, those who have fallen asleep in Christ have also perished. If we have placed our hope in Christ for this life only, we should be pitied more than anyone (1 Corinthians 15:12-19 HCSB).

Notice how clearly Paul stated the matter—no resurrection, no Christianity. According to Paul, if Christ has not been raised, then the following things would be true.

A. Christian preaching is empty and so in anyone's faith because the object of the faith, Jesus Christ, is not whom He said He was.

B. The apostles are liars for testifying to a resurrection that did not occur.

C. No forgiveness has been granted for anybody's sin.

D. Those who have died believing in Christ have no hope.

If hope in Christ is limited to this life, Christians are to be pitied above all people.

CHRISTIANITY HAS NO MEANING FOR HUMANITY WITHOUT A RESURRECTION

Without the resurrection, Christianity has no meaning for humanity—its founder would have been a liar and a failure, and its followers are men and women who have no hope. Thus the importance of the resurrection to the Christian faith cannot be overestimated.

There are those who say that even without the resurrection, Christianity has significance. They hold that Christ's teachings provide ethical guidelines for humanity. The New Testament, however, testifies that this is not the case. Without the resurrection there is no meaningful Christianity.

THERE ARE OTHER AREAS OF IMPORTANCE

We add further areas of importance of Christ's resurrection—to His identity, ministry and message.

THE RESURRECTION IS IMPORTANT TO HIS IDENTITY

If Christ did not rise, then He was a liar, for He predicted He would come back from the dead (Matthew 20:19). The resurrection authenticates Him as a true prophet. Without His resurrection everything that Jesus said would be subject to doubt.

THE RESURRECTION IS IMPORTANT TO HIS MINISTRY

If Jesus did not rise, then His ministry would have ended in defeat. Believers would not have a High Priest to intercede for them to God the Father. There would be no one to the Head the church and no Holy Spirit to indwell believers and give them power to live godly lives.

THE RESURRECTION IS IMPORTANT TO HIS MESSAGE

According to the Apostle Paul, the resurrection of Jesus is one of the four pillars of the gospel message. He wrote to the Corinthians.

> For I handed on to you as of first importance what I in turn had received: that Christ died for our sins in accordance with the scriptures, and that he was buried, and that he was raised on the third day in accordance with the scriptures, and that he appeared… (1 Corinthians 15:3-5 NRSV).

These four pillars are.

1. Christ died.

2. Christ was buried

3. Christ was raised.

4. Christ appeared.

Without the resurrection there is no gospel message. Its importance to the Christian faith cannot be overestimated.

THE RESURRECTION IS UNIQUE TO CHRISTIANITY

The resurrection of Jesus Christ is unique to the Christian faith—no other religious figure has ever predicted his own resurrection, then accomplished it.

All other world religions are based upon a founder who lived in the past and whose religion is his only legacy. Muhammad died at age 61 on June 8, A.D. 632 in Medina. He is still dead. Confucius died and Buddha also died. They also remain dead—Jesus Christ is alive.

THE RESURRECTION WAS IN GOD'S ETERNAL PLAN

The death and resurrection of Christ is part of the eternal plan of God. Fifty days after Jesus' death, the Apostle Peter declared the following on the day of Pentecost.

> Men of Israel, listen to these words: This Jesus the Nazarene was a man pointed out to you by God with miracles, wonders, and signs that God did among you through Him, just as you yourselves know. Though He was delivered up according to God's determined plan and foreknowledge, you used lawless people to nail Him to a cross and kill Him. God raised Him up, ending the pains of death, because it was not possible for Him to be held by it (Acts 2:22-24 HCSB).

Peter makes it clear that the death and resurrection of Christ was by God's deliberate intention and foreknowledge. It was all part of God's plan. Indeed, it is a crucial element in God's eternal plan to save humanity from their sins. Therefore, the resurrection was not an isolated event.

THE RESURRECTION IS NOT BEYOND GOD'S POWER

The resurrection of Jesus is not greater than any other miracle recorded in Scripture. Once a person grants the possibility of God performing miracles, then the testimony for the resurrection has to be evaluated like any other miracle that is recorded. The first verse of the Bible declares.

> In the beginning God created the heavens and the earth (Genesis 1:1 KJV).

This verse is the basis of all miracles. If a person can believe the truth of this verse—that God spoke and the universe came into existence from nothing—then what is too hard for Him to do? That is why the Apostle Paul declared.

> Why does it seem incredible to any of you that God can raise the dead? (Acts 26:8 NLT).

Nothing is too difficult for the God of the Bible. Nothing!

Other passages also testify to God's miraculous power. We read in Jeremiah.

> Behold, I am the LORD, the God of all flesh: is there any thing too hard for me? (Jeremiah 32:27 KJV).

And of course, the answer is, "No!" Indeed, there is nothing too difficult for God. Therefore, the idea that the God of the Bible has the ability to raise the dead is certainly consistent with what Scripture teaches about His mighty power.

THE RESURRECTION WAS FORETOLD BY JESUS

The resurrection was not only in the eternal plan of God; it was also predicted beforehand by Jesus. The fact that He would rise from the dead was central to Jesus' ministry and message. As we have said, the resurrection must not be seen as an isolated event in the life of Christ.

JESUS MADE MANY PREDICTIONS

As one reads the four gospels, they are struck by the fact that Jesus predicted, over and over again, His betrayal, death, and resurrection. Three years before He was raised from the dead, the following exchange between Jesus and the Jewish religious leaders occurred.

> So the Jews replied to Him, "What sign of authority will You show us for doing these things?" Jesus answered, "Destroy this sanctuary, and I will raise it up in three days." Therefore, the Jews said, "This sanctuary took 46 years to build, and will You raise it up in three days?" But He was speaking about the sanctuary of His body. So when He was raised from the dead, His disciples remembered that He had said this. And they believed the Scripture and the statement Jesus had made (John 2:18-22 HCSB).

Jesus predicted that His body would be raised from the dead.

THE RESURRECTION WAS THE SIGN THAT JESUS GAVE TO PROVE HIS IDENTITY

The resurrection was to be the sign that demonstrated Jesus as the one whom He claimed to be. When asked for a specific sign from the religious leaders Jesus said.

> An evil and adulterous generation asks for a sign, but no sign will be given to it except the sign of the prophet Jonah. For just as Jonah was three days and three nights in the belly of the sea monster, so for three days and three

> nights the Son of Man will be in the heart of the earth (Matthew 12:39-40 NRSV).

Especially during the last six months of His earthly life, Jesus emphasized the importance and necessity of His upcoming crucifixion as well as the triumph of His resurrection. Matthew records.

> From that time Jesus began to show to His disciples that He must go to Jerusalem, and suffer many things from the elders and chief priests and scribes, and be killed, and be raised the third day (Matthew 16:21 NKJV).

The resurrection would demonstrate Jesus is the One whom He claimed to be.

JESUS HAD THE ABILITY TO RAISE HIMSELF

Jesus also made the amazing claim that He had the authority to accomplish the resurrection Himself. We read the following in John's gospel.

> For this reason, the Father loves me, because I lay down my life in order to take it up again. No one takes it from me, but I lay it down of my own accord. I have power to lay it down, and I have power to take it up again. I have received this command from my Father (John 10:17, 18 NRSV).

Jesus claimed that He could bring Himself back from the dead!

JESUS' PREDICTIONS WERE COMMON KNOWLEDGE

The predictions by Jesus of His resurrection were of such common knowledge that it led the religious rulers to ask Pontius Pilate to secure the tomb. We read the following in Matthew's gospel.

> The next day, which followed the preparation day, the chief priests and the Pharisees gathered before Pilate and said, "Sir, we remember that while this deceiver was still alive, He said,

> 'After three days I will rise again.' Therefore, give orders that the tomb be made secure until the third day. Otherwise, His disciples may come, steal Him, and tell the people, 'He has been raised from the dead.' Then the last deception will be worse than the first" (Matthew 27:62-64 HCSB).

From these predictions, it can be readily seen that the resurrection was a central part of the message and ministry of Jesus.

SETTING THE SCENE BEFORE THE RESURRECTION

As we examine the events leading up to Easter Sunday, we discover that certain precautions taken by Jesus' enemies actually give circumstantial evidence to His resurrection.

THE PRECAUTIONS: A STONE, SEAL, AND GUARD

The precautions taken at the tomb consisted of three things—the large stone, the Roman seal, and the guard.

THE STONE

The Bible says that a large stone was rolled in front of the tomb of Jesus. This stone, not only sealed the tomb, it also would have made it difficult for someone to come right in and steal the body.

THE ROMAN SEAL

The Roman seal was a sign of authentication that the tomb was occupied and the power and authority of Rome stood behind the seal. Anyone breaking the Roman seal would suffer the punishment of an unpleasant death.

THE GUARD

A guard, either the Roman guard or the Jewish temple police, watched Jesus' tomb. There is a question as to which one of the two groups was watching over it. The context seems to favor the Roman guard. The Roman guard was a sixteen-man unit that was governed by some very strict rules. Each member was responsible for six square feet of space. The guard members could not sit down or lean against anything while they were on duty.

If a guard member fell asleep, he was beaten and burned with his own clothes. But he was not the only one executed. In fact, the entire sixteen-man guard unit was executed if only one of the members fell asleep while on duty.

THE RELIGIOUS LEADERS FELT SECURE

These precautions made the religious rulers feel secure that the excitement around Jesus would soon go away. Jesus lay dead in the tomb, and His frightened disciples had scattered and gone into hiding. They thought that they had won.

THE EVENT THAT CHANGED THE WORLD

But the story was not over. The Bible says that early Sunday morning certain women came to the tomb to anoint the body of Jesus. The stone had been removed, the seal had been broken, and the body was gone. An angel at the tomb asked.

> Why do you look for the living among the dead? He is not here, but has risen. Remember how he told you, while he was still in Galilee (Luke 24:5,6 NRSV).

They went back to tell the other disciples, who at first did not believe their report. Luke records.

> But these words seemed like nonsense to them, and they did not believe the women (Luke 24:11 HCSB).

However, they were persuaded to look for themselves, and they also found the tomb empty. This caused them confusion. The confusion vanished as the resurrected Christ first appeared to Mary Magdalene, then to some other women, and finally to the disciples. After being with the disciples for forty days, Jesus ascended into heaven. Ten days later, the disciples publicly proclaimed to all Jerusalem, and to all of the world, the fact that Jesus Christ had risen from the dead.

THE CASE FOR THE RESURRECTION WEIGHING THE EVIDENCE

We will now begin with our presentation of the case for the resurrection. The evidence will be weighed and evaluated.

THINGS WE KNOW FOR CERTAIN

As we begin to look at the case for the resurrection, we will start by examining certain undisputed facts that both believers and unbelievers can agree upon. They include the following.

JESUS EXISTED

Jesus was a historical figure who lived two thousand years ago. The primary source for His life and ministry is the New Testament, which, as we have already seen, was written by eyewitnesses, or people who recorded eyewitness testimony. There is no doubt that Jesus existed.

JESUS PERFORMED MIRACLES

Another historical fact about Jesus is that He was a miracle worker. In the first five centuries of the Christian era, every report that has come down to us about Jesus, whether from friend or foe, has Him working miracles. There is no doubt that miracles were a central part of His ministry.

THERE WAS NO DYING AND RISING REDEEMER IN FIRST CENTURY JUDAISM

Another fact beyond dispute is that the disciples of Jesus were not prepared for His death. First-century Judaism had no concept of the

Messiah dying and then coming back from the dead. The disciples were not expecting the resurrection of Jesus because they were not expecting Him to die.

JESUS DIED ON A CROSS IN JERUSALEM

Another fact that is beyond dispute is the manner of death of Jesus—He died on a cross. All four gospels make it clear that Christ was crucified in Jerusalem. The testimony of the Book of Acts concurs as do the writings of Paul. Jesus was executed by means of crucifixion in the city of Jerusalem.

JESUS WAS BURIED IN JERUSALEM

The New Testament also states that Jesus was buried in Jerusalem after His death. All four gospels testify to this fact as well as Paul's statement. He said.

> For I delivered to you as of first importance what I also received: that Christ died for our sins in accordance with the Scriptures, that he was buried, that he was raised on the third day in accordance with the Scriptures (1 Corinthians 15:3,4 ESV).

After His death, Jesus was buried.

THE TOMB WAS EMPTY ON EASTER SUNDAY

A further fact is that the tomb of Jesus was empty on Easter Sunday morning. Had the body of Jesus remained in the tomb it would have been a simple thing for the authorities to remove the stone and produce it.

The Sanhedrin itself testifies that the tomb was empty. They concocted a story in which they commanded the soldiers to repeat thereafter to explain how the tomb became empty—the body was stolen by the disciples.

JESUS WAS REPORTED TO HAVE RISEN

The New Testament is unanimous in the fact that Jesus' disciples saw Him after His death. This was the message they brought to the world—Jesus Christ has risen from the dead!

THE MESSAGE WAS IMMEDIATELY PREACHED IN THE CITY WHERE THE EVENTS TOOK PLACE

When the account of the resurrection was first proclaimed, it occurred in Jerusalem—the same city where Jesus was buried. This took place less than two months after Jesus was crucified. The disciples did not go away to some distant place where it would have been hard to check out the facts. They began in the very city where all the events took place. If their testimony were not true, then their enemies would have promptly corrected them.

THE NEW TESTAMENT WRITERS BELIEVED JESUS HAD RISEN FROM THE DEAD

When the New Testament was committed to writing, it was from the perspective that Jesus had risen from the dead. All of the New Testament writers believed the resurrection occurred. Obviously something led them to that belief. The question, of course, is, "What made them believe?"

THESE ARE FACTS BEYOND DISPUTE

These facts, which we just mentioned, are not in dispute. Jesus existed. In addition, during His earthly ministry He reportedly worked miracles. Furthermore, His disciples were not prepared for His death and were not looking for a resurrection. We also know that Jesus was dead and buried yet the tomb was empty on Easter morning. Moreover, the disciples testified they saw Him alive after His death and then proclaimed the resurrection message in Jerusalem less than two months after Jesus' death. Finally, all the New Testament writers believed the resurrection was a reality.

WEIGHING THE EVIDENCE

We will now weigh the evidence for Christ's resurrection and see if it meets a legal standard of proof. This means we will be looking at the facts and determining what is the most likely thing that happened. Therefore, we should let the evidence speak for itself.

JESUS APPEARED ALIVE TO PEOPLE AFTER HIS DEATH

The main reason the disciples believed in the resurrection of Jesus is that they saw Him alive after He was dead. Therefore, we see them testifying, time and time again, to the fact they were eyewitnesses of His resurrection. This firsthand evidence of the disciples is a powerful argument for the resurrection of Christ. The disciples knew that He had risen because they saw Him with their own eyes.

THE VARIOUS APPEARANCES LISTED

After the resurrection many different people saw Jesus. Some of the appearances include the following.

MARY MAGDALENE

The first appearance of Jesus was to Mary Magdalene. The gospel of John puts it this way.

> As soon as Mary said this, she turned around and saw Jesus standing there. But she did not know who he was. Jesus asked her, "Why are you crying? Who are you looking for?" She thought he was the gardener and said, "Sir, if you have taken his body away, please tell me, so I can go and get him." Then Jesus said to her, "Mary!" She turned and said to him, "Rabboni." The Aramaic word "Rabboni" means "Teacher" (John 20:14-16 CEV).

This appearance was totally unexpected.

MARY THE MOTHER OF JAMES, SALOME, AND JOANNA

Jesus also appeared to these three women. This happened after the appearance to Mary Magdalene. After an angel told them Jesus had risen, they were on their way to tell Jesus' disciples when they met the risen Christ. The Bible says.

> Suddenly Jesus met them. "Greetings," he said. They came to him, clasped his feet and worshiped him (Matthew 28:9 NIV).

Again, we have another unexpected appearance. As was true with Mary Magdalene, these women touched the body of Jesus.

PETER

Peter is the first person mentioned in Paul's list of witnesses, and is the first of the apostles to see the risen Christ. This was a private appearance to reassure him, since he had recently denied his Lord. The gospels are completely silent as to the details of this meeting. Luke merely wrote.

> The Lord has really risen! He appeared to Peter! (Luke 24:34 NLT).

We only know that Jesus appeared to Peter, nothing else.

TWO DISCIPLES ON THE EMMAUS ROAD

Later on Easter Sunday, Jesus appeared to two disciples on the road to Emmaus. Luke wrote.

> Now on that same day two of them were going to a village called Emmaus, about seven miles from Jerusalem, and talking with each other about all these things that had happened. While they were talking and discussing, Jesus himself came near and went with them, but their eyes were kept from recognizing him (Luke 24:13-16 NRSV).

As was true with the women, these two disciples were not expecting Jesus to rise. In fact, they were leaving Jerusalem because they had lost hope in Him.

THE ELEVEN DISCIPLES—THOMAS ABSENT

This is the last of the five appearances of Jesus on Easter Sunday. It took place in the evening, probably in the upper room in which Jesus had instituted the Lord's Supper. It is recorded in both Luke's and John's gospel, giving us two independent accounts as to what happened. John wrote:

> That evening, on the first day of the week, the disciples were meeting behind locked doors because they were afraid of the Jewish leaders. Suddenly, Jesus was standing there among them! "Peace be with you," he said. As he spoke, he held out his hands for them to see, and he showed them his side. They were filled with joy when they saw their Lord! . . . One of the disciples, Thomas (nicknamed the Twin), was not with the others when Jesus came (John 20:19,20,24 NLT).

As we mentioned, this is the last of the five recorded appearances of Jesus on Easter Sunday.

THE ELEVEN DISCIPLES–THOMAS PRESENT

Eight days later, He appeared again—this time with Thomas present. The Bible says.

> A week later the disciples were together again. This time, Thomas was with them. Jesus came in while the doors were still locked and stood in the middle of the group. He greeted his disciples and said to Thomas, "Put your finger here and look at my hands! Put your hand into my side. Stop doubting and have faith!" Thomas replied, "You are my Lord and my God" (John 20:26-28 CEV).

On this occasion, doubting Thomas believed in the resurrected Christ.

SEVEN DISCIPLES ON THE SEA OF GALILEE

Another appearance was to seven disciples on the Sea of Galilee. John writes.

> After these things Jesus showed himself again to the disciples by the Sea of Tiberias; and he showed himself in this way. Gathered there together were Simon Peter, Thomas called the Twin, Nathanael of Cana in Galilee, the sons of Zebedee, and two others of his disciples (John 21:1,2 NRSV).

This particular appearance is described in some detail in John 21.

TO THE ELEVEN DISCIPLES ON A MOUNTAIN IN GALILEE

There is also the account of Jesus appearing before His eleven disciples in Galilee. Matthew records the following.

> Then the eleven disciples went away into Galilee, to the mountain which Jesus had appointed for them. When they saw Him, they worshiped Him; but some doubted (Matthew 28:16,17 NKJV).

Here Jesus meets His disciples in Galilee.

JESUS APPEARED TO OVER FIVE HUNDRED PEOPLE AT ONE TIME

On another occasion, Jesus appeared to over five hundred people at one time. Paul wrote.

> Then he appeared to more than five hundred brothers and sisters at one time, most of whom are still alive, though some have died (1 Corinthians 15:6 NRSV).

We know nothing about when or where this happened.

SAUL OF TARSUS

After Jesus' ascension into heaven, He appeared again—this time to Saul of Tarsus.

> Now as he went on his way, he approached Damascus, and suddenly a light from heaven shone around him. And falling to the ground he heard a voice saying to him, "Saul, Saul, why are you persecuting me?" And he said, "Who are you, Lord?" And he said, "I am Jesus, whom you are persecuting (Acts 9:3-5 ESV).

These are some the appearances of Jesus that the New Testament records. They caused His disciples to believe that He had risen from the dead.

OBSERVATIONS ABOUT THE APPEARANCES OF JESUS CHRIST

As we examine the New Testament account of the appearances of Christ after His death, we can make the following observations.

THE APPEARANCES OF JESUS WERE CONVINCING

The different appearances of Jesus convinced His disciples that He had truly risen from the dead. The first chapter of the Book of Acts makes this statement about Jesus' appearances.

> After his suffering he presented himself alive to them by many convincing proofs, appearing to them during forty days and speaking about the kingdom of God (Acts 1:3 NRSV).

When describing Jesus' appearances, Luke uses a Greek word translated as "convincing proof." This term refers to the strongest type of legal proof imaginable. The case for Jesus' resurrection would stand up in a court of law.

JESUS APPEARED TO MANY DIFFERENT PEOPLE

We note that Jesus appeared to a number of different people after His death. The multiple appearances that are recorded in the New Testament range in size from one individual, (Peter), to over five hundred people (1 Corinthians 15). These various appearances to different numbers of people testify to the fact that He did indeed come back from the dead.

JESUS APPEARED AT DIFFERENT TIMES AND PLACES

There was no specific time or place when the resurrected Jesus appeared. His appearances include: in a locked room, on the road to Emmaus, on a mountain in Galilee, at the sea of Galilee, on the Mount of Olives in Jerusalem, and at the empty tomb. Jesus was able to appear wherever He wished, He was not limited to one geographical area.

Jesus' appearances consisted of brief encounters with people (the women returning from the tomb) to long periods of time (the two disciples on the road to Emmaus).

He also appeared at different times of day—morning (to Mary Magdalene at the tomb), afternoon (the two disciples on the road to Emmaus), and night (the disciples in the locked upper room).

THE PEOPLE WERE NOT EXPECTING JESUS TO APPEAR

Jesus' followers were surprised by the events that occurred in those few short days. Beginning with His betrayal by one of their own—Judas Iscariot—to the arrest, trial and crucifixion, these rapidly occurring events shocked the disciples. They were not expecting any of this to happen. However, the one thing that surprised them most was seeing Christ alive after His death.

The women who arrived at the tomb were not expecting Jesus to have risen. Their intention was to embalm His dead body. They went to the tomb expecting to find someone there. This shows they did not expect a resurrection.

When the disciples were first told of the empty tomb, and the reports that Jesus was alive, they did not believe them. They thought the women who were making these reports were deluded.

When Thomas first heard that Jesus had risen, he did not believe it. Until he saw Jesus for himself, and touched the scars of His wounds, he would not believe.

All of these facts testify to the state of mind of the disciples—they were not looking for Him to appear.

JESUS' APPEARANCES SUDDENLY STOPPED AFTER HE ASCENDED INTO HEAVEN

The New Testament says it was for only forty days that Jesus showed Himself after His resurrection before ascending into heaven. After His ascension, Jesus did not appear any longer to His disciples—except for one episode on the isle of Patmos to John. In that instance He appeared as the glorified Christ.

THE CHARACTER OF THE WITNESSES

We also need to consider the character of the witnesses who testified that Christ had risen. The following observations need to be made concerning them.

THEY WERE IN A POSITION TO TESTIFY

The ones who saw Jesus after His death were in a position to give testimony to whether or not Jesus had risen from the dead. First, they would have been able to testify if He had died. We are told that John and certain others were there at the cross when Jesus died—they observed His death. Others saw where He was buried.

Finally, the same Jesus they had seen dead and buried appeared to them alive. They saw the scars that were on His body from the cross. They knew Jesus intimately and would not have been fooled by some impostor. Therefore, those who testified that Jesus had risen could certainly certify that Jesus had been dead, and that they saw Him again alive.

THERE WAS A SUFFICIENT NUMBER OF THEM

The number of witnesses to the resurrection was sufficient for us to believe their account. We are dealing with the twelve disciples of Jesus (minus Judas), other disciples apart from the twelve, and certain women who knew Him well. One appearance was before over five hundred people at one time. The different number of people who saw the risen Christ is sufficient to cause belief.

THEY EXHIBITED AN HONEST CHARACTER

Next, we consider the honesty of the witnesses. We are told they were not expecting Him to rise, they were all surprised by His appearance and, in the case of Jesus' disciples, they were the first unbelievers of the resurrection story. There is no effort to make the disciples into some type of "super believers." Their faults are listed—Peter denying knowing Jesus on the night of His betrayal as well as all of the other disciples fleeing the scene.

THEY HAD NO MOTIVATION FOR LYING

When all the facts are considered, we find no motivation for them to lie about what happened. There was no financial gain or greed that motivated the witnesses to tell the story that Jesus had risen. To the contrary, they suffered mightily from their fellow countrymen by proclaiming the resurrection. Their status in society was certainly not elevated for believing in Jesus—they were considered members of a sect or cult. When everything is considered, lying about Jesus' resurrection caused them no direct benefit but rather only grief.

THEIR STORY WAS ALWAYS CONSISTENT

The ones who had seen Him alive after His death consistently told the same story—Jesus had risen from the dead and they had seen Him alive. As we read through the sermons in the book of Acts, we find them always telling the same account. Their story was consistently told as long as they lived.

THEY DID NOT EMBELLISH THE STORY WITH EXCESSIVE DETAILS

The account surrounding Jesus' death and resurrection is told in a straightforward manner without excessive details. Many things we would like to know are not told us. The account is sober and restrained—something we would not expect from a made up story. There are no elements in the account that are mythical.

For example, if the account of the resurrection were legendary, we would expect some explanation of what occurred the moment Jesus rose from the dead, yet the New Testament gives us no such explanation of what happened the moment He left the tomb.

SUMMARY TO THE CHARACTER OF THE WITNESSES

The character of those who saw the resurrected Christ is sufficient for us to believe their testimony. There is nothing that would cause us to be suspicious of their account. Therefore, it is not unreasonable to accept their report that Jesus had risen.

THE NATURE OF THE RESURRECTION: IT WAS BODILY

It is very important to understand the form that the resurrected Jesus took upon Himself, for the New Testament teaches that when we are resurrected, we shall have a form similar to His. John wrote.

> Beloved, we are God's children now; what we will be has not yet been revealed. What we do know is this: when he is revealed, we will be like him, for we will see him as he is (1 John 3:2 NRSV).

The resurrected Christ had a body. Someday, we too will have a body like His.

HE WAS NOT MERELY A SPIRIT

There are some who believe that Jesus did not have a resurrected body, but was only a spirit. However, the Scripture is very clear on the issue— the resurrection of Jesus was in bodily form. Early in His ministry, Jesus predicted that He would come back from the dead in a body. The Bible says.

> Jesus answered them, "Destroy this temple, and in three days I will raise it up." The Jews then said, "It has taken forty—six years to build this temple, and will you raise it up in three days?" But he was speaking about the temple of his body. When therefore he was raised from the dead, his disciples remembered that he had said this, and they believed the Scripture and the word that Jesus had spoken (John 2:19-22 ESV).

This passage shows that Jesus predicted His bodily resurrection.

HIS PREVIOUS BODY IS LINKED WITH HIS RESURRECTED BODY

Jesus refuted the idea that He was some disembodied spirit when He appeared to His disciples after His death. The Scripture shows that Christ's resurrection body had links to His non-resurrected body.

THE SIMILARITIES TO HIS EARTHLY BODY

First, we look at the similarities between Christ's earthly body and His resurrected body. They are as follows.

PEOPLE RECOGNIZED HIM AFTER HIS RESURRECTION

Jesus was recognizable after His resurrection. John explains what happened when Jesus first appeared to His disciples.

> After he said this, he showed them his hands and his side. Then the disciples rejoiced when they saw the Lord (John 20:20 NRSV).

It was the same Jesus who had been crucified on the cross.

JESUS TALKED WITH PEOPLE

Jesus talked to people after His resurrection. Luke records the following episode.

> And as they were saying these things, He Himself stood among them. He said to them, "Peace to you!" But they were startled and terrified and thought they were seeing a ghost. "Why are you troubled?" He asked them. "And why do doubts arise in your hearts?" (Luke 24:36-38 HCSB).

The resurrected Christ could talk.

JESUS INVITED PEOPLE TO TOUCH HIM

The disciples were frightened with Jesus' appearance, since they assumed they had seen a spirit. Therefore, He invited them to touch His body to see if it were real. Scripture says.

> Look at my hands. Look at my feet. You can see that it's really me. Touch me and make sure that I am not a ghost, because ghosts don't have bodies, as you see that I do! As he spoke, he held out his hands for them to see, and he showed them his feet (Luke 24:39,40 NLT).

His body was real. Indeed, people could touch it.

JESUS SHOWED HIS SCARS

When Jesus appeared to the disciples in the upper room Thomas was not among them. Thomas told the other disciples that He would not believe in the resurrection until he could see Jesus with his own eyes and touch His wounds. The Gospel of John records what happened after that.

> Eight days later the disciples were together again, and this time Thomas was with them. The doors were locked; but suddenly,

> as before, Jesus was standing among them. "Peace be with you," he said. Then he said to Thomas, "Put your finger here, and look at my hands. Put your hand into the wound in my side. Don't be faithless any longer. Believe!" "My Lord and my God!" Thomas exclaimed (John 20:26-28 NLT).

On this occasion Thomas was challenged by Jesus to see if He were indeed real. The doubter immediately realized that Jesus had come back from the dead in a resurrected body.

JESUS ATE FOOD WITH HIS RESURRECTED BODY

He had the capacity, though not the need, to eat. Luke writes.

> But while they still did not believe for joy, and marveled, He said to them, "Have you any food here?" So they gave Him a piece of a broiled fish and some honeycomb. And He took it and ate in their presence (Luke 24:41-43 NKJV).

Simon Peter later told a group of Gentiles about how he and the other disciples ate and drank with Jesus after His resurrection from the dead.

> We are witnesses to all that he did both in Judea and in Jerusalem. They put him to death by hanging him on a tree; but God raised him on the third day and allowed him to appear, not to all the people but to us who were chosen by God as witnesses, and who ate and drank with him after he rose from the dead (Acts 10:39-41 NRSV).

He ate food in their presence, showing that His resurrection was indeed bodily.

HE WAS ABLE TO BREATHE

Scripture also records that Jesus breathed out. John records the following.

> And when He had said this, He breathed on them, and said to them, "Receive the Holy Spirit" (John 20:22 NKJV).

All of these above facts show that it was the same Jesus who was placed in the tomb that came back from the dead.

THERE WERE DIFFERENCES BETWEEN HIS BODY BEFORE AND AFTER HIS RESURRECTION

Though it was the same Jesus who was placed in the tomb on Good Friday, and rose on Easter Sunday, His resurrection body was also different in some respects.

JESUS ENTERED CLOSED ROOM

The Bible says He could enter closed rooms without opening the doors. John records the following episode.

> That Sunday evening the disciples were meeting behind locked doors because they were afraid of the Jewish leaders. Suddenly, Jesus was standing there among them! "Peace be with you," he said (John 20:19 NLT).

Jesus had the supernatural ability to enter a room when the door was closed.

HE WAS ABLE TO DISAPPEAR

He was also able to disappear. Luke explains what happened when Jesus was with two disciples on the road to Emmaus.

> It was as He reclined at the table with them that He took the bread, blessed and broke it, and gave it to them. Then their eyes were opened, and they recognized Him; but He disappeared from their sight (Luke 24:30-31 HCSB).

This is another unique ability of His resurrected body.

JESUS NEVER NEEDED REST

As far as we are able to tell, Jesus' resurrected body did not need any rest or food. Every account of Jesus after His resurrection has Him busy with ministry. We read.

> After his suffering he presented himself alive to them by many convincing proofs, appearing to them during forty days and speaking about the kingdom of God (Acts 1:3 NRSV).

During the forty days after His resurrection, but before His ascension, Jesus was busy with ministry.

JESUS ASCENDED INTO HEAVEN

Jesus' resurrected body was able to ascend into heaven. We read the following account in the Book of Acts.

> It was not long after he said this that he was taken up into the sky while they were watching, and he disappeared into a cloud. As they were straining their eyes to see him, two white-robed men suddenly stood there among them. They said, "Men of Galilee, why are you standing here staring at the sky? Jesus has been taken away from you into heaven. And someday, just as you saw him go, he will return!" (Acts 1:9-11 NLT).

Finally, Jesus left the earth by way of the ascension into heaven.

THE GLORIFIED CHRIST APPEARED TO JOHN

The most detailed description of the risen and ascended Christ is found in Revelation 1:12-16. Here John records the vision of the glorified Christ. He was like the Son of Man, which links Him to His former earthly appearance, but He also radiated glory from His eyes, feet, voice, and face. This is the way that believers will someday see Him.

SUMMARY TO JESUS' BODILY RESURRECTION

From these accounts we can see that Jesus' resurrection was bodily.

1. His own testimony made it clear that He was not a disembodied spirit.

2. He did things only a person having a body can do. Indeed, He walked, He showed them the prints of the crucifixion on His body, He breathed out (John 20:22), and ate (Luke 24:41-43).

All of these acts are possible because Jesus had a body. The body He possessed, however, though like His pre-resurrection body was, in some aspects, different. His new body was no longer subject to the laws of nature. He could suddenly appear and disappear. His new body had abilities the previous one either did not have, or did not demonstrate.

WHAT THE RESURRECTION BODY IS NOT

Now that we understand what did happen with Jesus' resurrection body, we can refute some inadequate concepts of the resurrection.

IT IS NOT REINCARNATION

Reincarnation means a human comes back in the next life as another human being. Resurrection, however, means eternal life for that individual, not reincarnation.

IT IS NOT RESUSCITATION

The biblical idea of resurrection is the raising to a new body that will never die again. Paul wrote to the church at Rome.

> Because we know that Christ, having been raised from the dead, no longer dies. Death no longer rules over Him (Romans 6:9 HCSB).

To the Corinthians he wrote.

> It is sown a natural body, it is raised a spiritual body. There is a natural body, and there is a spiritual body (1 Corinthians 15:44 NKJV).

In the New Testament there are a number of examples of resuscitations or reanimations. They include: the son of the widow at Nain, Dorcas, Eutychus, Jairus' daughter, and Lazarus. Though they were brought back to life, they all died again. This is not the same as what happened to Jesus. He was raised immortal in a new body—never to die again.

CONCLUSION: JESUS WAS RAISED IN AN ACTUAL BODY

We conclude that Jesus was raised in a genuine body—not a spirit resurrection. The bodies that believers will someday possess will be like His.

INDIRECT EVIDENCE FOR THE RESURRECTION CIRCUMSTANTIAL EVIDENCE THAT JESUS HAS RISEN

Apart from the direct evidence, there is also circumstantial testimony that Jesus has risen. This includes the following.

THE CHANGED LIVES OF THE DISCIPLES

The changed lives of the disciples give indirect testimony to Christ's resurrection. Something changed the disciples of Jesus from cowards to martyrs, from frightened individuals to bold proclaimers of the resurrection. It had to be something more powerful than a delusion or a lie. They said their lives were changed because they had seen the risen Christ.

THE ORDER OF EVENTS

We find the New Testament chronicling the events that led to the changed lives of Jesus' disciples. When Jesus was betrayed, the Bible says that His disciples scattered.

> But all this has taken place, so that the scriptures of the prophets may be fulfilled. Then all the disciples deserted him and fled (Matthew 26:56 NRSV).

Simon Peter, who had promised to die for Jesus, denied that he ever knew Him. Matthew also writes.

> Meanwhile, as Peter was sitting outside in the courtyard, a servant girl came over and said to him, "You were one of those with Jesus the Galilean." But Peter denied it in front of everyone. "I don't know what you are talking about," he said. Later, out by the gate, another servant girl noticed him and said to those standing around, "This man was with Jesus of Nazareth." Again Peter denied it, this time with an oath. "I don't even know the man," he said. A little later some other bystanders came over to him and said, "You must be one of them; we can tell by your Galilean accent." Peter said, "I swear by God, I don't know the man" And immediately the rooster crowed (Matthew 26:69-74 NLT).

At Jesus' crucifixion, His disciples were nowhere to be found. Matthew records the following.

> Many women who had followed Jesus from Galilee and given him support were also there, watching from a distance (Matthew 27:55 NET).

The picture we get of the disciples at the time of Jesus' trial and death is of a frightened band of individuals who denied their Lord and went into hiding.

THE BRAVERY OF THE DISCIPLES ON THE DAY OF PENTECOST

Some fifty days later, however, we find these same disciples standing up bravely proclaiming, in the city of Jerusalem, that Christ has risen from the dead (Acts 2). Something had immediately changed these cowards into bold preachers of Christ's resurrection.

THE DISCIPLES WERE ARRESTED FOR PREACHING JESUS

Soon thereafter the boldness of the disciples caused the religious leaders to arrest two of them. We read about this in the Book of Acts.

> While Peter and John were speaking to the people, they were confronted by the priests, the captain of the Temple guard, and some of the Sadducees. These leaders were very disturbed that Peter and John were teaching the people that through Jesus there is a resurrection of the dead. They arrested them and, since it was already evening, put them in jail until morning (Acts 4:1-3 NLT).

The religious leaders then resorted to threats. They said to one another.

> But perhaps we can stop them from spreading their propaganda. We'll warn them not to speak to anyone in Jesus' name again. So they called the apostles back in and told them never again to speak or teach about Jesus. But Peter and John replied, "Do you think God wants us to obey you rather than him? We cannot stop telling about the wonderful things we have seen and heard." The council then threatened them further, but they finally let them go because they didn't know how to punish them without starting a riot. For everyone was praising God (Acts 4:17-21 NLT).

These former cowards were now fearlessly proclaiming the resurrection of Jesus Christ. Obviously, something happened to change the lives of these men. The disciples attributed their bravery to seeing Christ risen. If Christ had not risen, then some other explanation for their changed lives must be in order.

THE CONVERSION OF SAUL OF TARSUS

A second line of indirect evidence that can be offered for the resurrection of Jesus Christ is the conversion of Saul of Tarsus to the Apostle

Paul. Saul of Tarsus, the greatest antagonist of the Christian faith, was converted and became the Apostle Paul—the greatest proclaimer of the faith. According to his own testimony, Saul persecuted the believers in Christ. He said.

> I used to believe that I ought to do everything I could to oppose the very name of Jesus the Nazarene. Indeed, I did just that in Jerusalem. Authorized by the leading priests, I caused many believers there to be sent to prison. And I cast my vote against them when they were condemned to death. Many times I had them punished in the synagogues to get them to curse Jesus. I was so violently opposed to them that I even chased them down in foreign cities (Acts 26:9-11 NLT).

Saul had believers jailed and consented to their death sentence. In doing all of this, he believed he was serving God. However, something happened to Saul to change his way of thinking. He explained it in this manner.

> Under these circumstances I was traveling to Damascus with authority and a commission from the chief priests. At midday, while on the road, O king, I saw a light from heaven brighter than the sun, shining around me and those traveling with me. When we had all fallen to the ground, I heard a voice speaking to me in the Hebrew language, 'Saul, Saul, why are you persecuting Me? It is hard for you to kick against the goads.' "But I said, 'Who are You, Lord?' And the Lord replied: 'I am Jesus, whom you are persecuting. But get up and stand on your feet. For I have appeared to you for this purpose, to appoint you as a servant and a witness of things you have seen, and of things in which I will appear to you' (Acts 26:12-16 HCSB).

Saul obeyed the heavenly vision and became the Apostle Paul—the mighty defender of the faith. He wrote a number of books that became part of the New Testament. The greatest antagonist to the faith became its greatest champion. What was it that changed this man's life? He said it was meeting the risen Christ.

SAUL WENT FROM UNBELIEVER TO BELIEVER

Here we have an example of a man who was not a believer during Jesus' earthly life, who became a believer after Christ had risen. This is in contrast to Jesus' disciples—who believed in Him during His earthly ministry. Saul's testimony is another in the line of circumstantial evidence that Christ rose from the dead.

Eighteenth century author George Lyttleton wrote the following concerning the conversion of Saul of Tarsus.

> I thought the conversion and the Apostleship of St. Paul alone, duly considered, was of itself a demonstration sufficient to prove Christianity as a Divine Revelation.[1]

Saul's conversion must have some explanation. The only explanation that fits all the facts is the one which he himself gives—he met the risen Christ on the road to Damascus.

THE RISE OF THE CHRISTIAN CHURCH

The New Testament church came into existence as a result of the resurrection faith of the believers. In every sermon, the substance of the preaching of the apostles was that Christ had risen from the dead. Multitudes soon believed their message (Acts 2:41, Acts 6:7). It is an historical fact that Christianity spread faster than any other religion or philosophy in the ancient world. By the early part of the fourth century, the Roman Empire became "Christianized." Something had to account for this unprecedented growth—something at least as compelling as a resurrected Christ.

---

1. George Lord Lyttleton, *Observations on the Conversion and Apostleship of St. Paul in a letter to Gilbert West*, London, 1814

The fact of Christianity's rapid expansion gives a further witness to the truth of its resurrection message. People embraced Christianity because they were convinced that Jesus Christ has conquered death and could offer them eternal life.

THE CHANGE IN THE DAY OF WORSHIP

A further line of circumstantial evidence for the resurrection concerns the changing of the day of worship. The Jewish worship was on the Sabbath (from Friday sundown to Saturday sundown). However, the early Christians observed Sunday as their day of worship to commemorate Jesus' resurrection. This was no small thing to the first believers who were Jews. The day of worship, the Sabbath, was something that no Jew would dare break or change.

Yet Jesus' disciples preferred to worship on the first day of the week—the day He came back from the dead (Acts 20:7; 1 Corinthians 16:1,2; Revelation 1:10). Something monumental had to happen to make them change the day of worship—something like a resurrection.

The Letter of Barnabas, an early Christian document, stated the following.

Therefore, we keep the eighth day with joyfulness, the day on which Jesus rose from the dead.

The early Christians celebrated the fact that Jesus had risen from the dead.

WOMEN TESTIFYING FIRST

According to the New Testament, the first person who saw the resurrected Christ was Mary Magdalene. She thought Jesus was the gardener. Jesus then appeared to another group of women. If one were to make up the story of Christ's resurrection, they certainly would not have Him first appearing to women. In that culture, at the time of

Christ, the witness of a woman was not as readily accepted as a man's. Their testimony would not have been admissible as legal proof except in a few specific situations.

If the story had been made up, then Jesus would have first appeared to a man—either one of His disciples or perhaps one of His enemies such as Herod, Pilate, or Caiaphas the High Priest. Yet the New Testament says that Jesus appeared first to Mary Magdalene and then to other women. This is not what one would expect in a made up story. The special privilege of seeing the risen Christ would not have been given to women. Again, this is another indication the story is reliable.

THE CHRISTIANS BURIED THEIR DEAD

Another indirect line of evidence concerns Christians burying their dead. Unbelievers cremated their dead. However, from the beginning, the Christians buried theirs in underground cemeteries and catacombs. Six hundred miles of catacombs stretch around Rome. In these catacombs about four million Christians from the first three centuries are buried. Each one of these buried believers testifies to their faith in the resurrection of Jesus and faith in their own ultimate resurrection.

THE EVENTS ON THE DAY OF PENTECOST

On the Day of Pentecost, the Holy Spirit supernaturally fell upon the disciples of Jesus. They were able to speak in languages they had not previously learned. This caused amazement to those who heard. The Bible says.

> What are we to do with these men? Everyone living in Jerusalem knows that a remarkable sign was done through them, and we cannot deny it (Acts 2:7,8 NRSV).

What caused the supernatural ability of Jesus' disciples to speak in languages they had not previously learned? Peter stood up and told them the reason for this miracle—the resurrection of Christ. Three thousand people converted to Christ on that day. The reason for their conversion, according to the Scripture, was the truth of the resurrection.

THE MIRACLES IN THE BOOK OF ACTS

The miracles in the Book of Acts give further circumstantial testimony to Jesus' resurrection. The fact that the disciples of Jesus were able to perform similar miracles, as He performed, demonstrated that Jesus' power was still working after His death, resurrection and ascension.

ACTS 3

Peter and John performed a miracle—healing a lame man at the temple. They testified that the ability to perform this miracle was granted to them by the risen Christ. They emphasized again that they were eyewitnesses of His resurrection. The Scripture says.

> But you rejected the Holy and Righteous One and asked to have a murderer given to you, and you killed the Author of life, whom God raised from the dead. To this we are witnesses (Acts 3:14,15 NRSV).

They had seen the risen Christ.

ACTS 4

When Peter spoke before the council he testified that it was the power of the risen Christ which healed this sick man. The Bible says.

> Then Peter was filled with the Holy Spirit and said to them, "Rulers of the people and elders: If we are being examined today about a good deed done to a disabled man—by what means he was healed— let it be known to all of you and to all the people of Israel, that by the name of Jesus Christ the Nazarene—whom you crucified and whom God raised from the dead—by Him this man is standing here before you healthy" (Acts 4:8-10 HCSB).

The enemies could not deny this healing. Scripture says.

> "What should we do with these men?" they asked each other. "We can't deny they have done a miraculous sign, and everybody in Jerusalem knows about it" (Acts 4:16 NLT).

This miracle was undeniable.

Therefore, the miracles of the apostles, as recorded in the Book of Acts, were all based on the power of resurrected Christ. The message of the early church was that Christ had risen from the dead and His disciples were witnesses to that event. Their testimony was evidenced by these miracles.

THE GRAVE CLOTHES WERE UNDISTURBED

Another bit of circumstantial evidence is the undisturbed and folded grave clothes. John reported.

> Then Simon Peter came, following him, and went into the tomb. He saw the linen wrappings lying there, and the cloth that had been on Jesus' head, not lying with the linen wrappings but rolled up in a place by itself (John 20:6,7 NRSV).

If the body of Jesus had been taken from the tomb by Jesus' disciples, then they certainly would not have taken the time to remove and unwind the grave clothes and then fold them again. Thus, the position of the grave clothes at Jesus' tomb is another circumstantial indication of His resurrection.

THE NAZARETH DECREE

In 1930, a Frenchman named Franz Cumont published an inscription of a text from the city of Nazareth. Though the inscription is in Greek, it is probably a translation of a Latin original. The inscription records the decree of the Emperor Claudius, who ruled from A.D. 41 to 54. This decree ordered the death penalty for anyone disturbing tombs.

The inscription reads as follows.

> It is my pleasure that sepulchers and tombs, which have been erected as solemn memorial of ancestors or children or relatives, shall remain undisturbed in perpetuity. If it be shown that anyone has either destroyed them or otherwise thrown out bodies which have been buried there or removed them with malicious intent to another place, thus committing a crime against those buried there, or removed the headstones or other stones, I command that against such person the same sentence be passed in respect to solemn memorials of men as is laid down in respect of the gods. Much rather one must pay respect to those who are buried. Let no one disturb them on any account. Otherwise it is my will that capital sentence be passed upon such person for the crime of tomb-spoilation.

Obviously something led to this decree. Why would the Roman Emperor give his attention to body snatching in this remote part of the Roman Empire? Why did Claudius institute the death penalty for robbing tombs only in this one particular geographic area—the area where Jesus came from? The decree of Claudius seems to support the early Jewish contention that the body of Jesus was stolen—which is an admission that the tomb was empty.

JESUS CHRIST CAN STILL CHANGE LIVES

The final testimony to the resurrection of Jesus Christ is that He is still in the business of changing lives. Millions of people throughout history, as well as millions today, personally testify to a changed life. This power to live a new life is based on the belief in the resurrected Christ.

SUMMARY ON CIRCUMSTANTIAL EVIDENCE

Apart from the direct testimony of the eyewitnesses to Christ's resurrection, we also have much circumstantial evidence that it actually occurred. We have listed eleven different lines of circumstantial evidence. They are as follows.

1. The changed lives of the disciples can only be explained by the risen Christ.

2. The conversion of Saul of Tarsus to the Apostle Paul makes no sense without the resurrection.

3. Some power had to have given rise to the Christian church.

4. According to the New Testament, women were the first to see the risen Jesus. This is not to be expected in a made up story.

5. The change of the day of worship from Saturday to Sunday had to have been occasioned by some great event.

6. The Christians buried their dead expecting them to eventually rise.

7. The miraculous events on the Day of Pentecost have to have some explanation.

8. The miracles in the Book of Acts testify to the resurrection power of Jesus.

9. The grave clothes were undisturbed in Jesus' tomb.

10. The Nazareth Decree testifies that the first century Jews were concerned about empty tombs.

11. Jesus Christ has changed lives and can still change lives today.

The evidence, both direct and circumstantial testifies to the fact that Jesus had risen from the dead three days after He was crucified on Calvary's cross.

OBJECTIONS TO THE RESURRECTION SOME COMMON OBJECTIONS ANSWERED

If Jesus did not come back from the dead, as the New Testament plainly says He did, then some alternative explanation must be offered to explain what happened. The problem is that other explanations take as much faith to believe as the New Testament's account. These alternative theories leave more questions unanswered than they explain.

HOW TO FALSIFY THE RESURRECTION

First, we do want to make it clear that it is theoretically possible to falsify the resurrection account. It can be done in one of two ways. They are as follows:

(1) Produce the body.

(2) Have a reasonable theory that explains all the evidence.

Since the body has not been produced, we will examine some of the major theories that attempt to explain away the New Testament account. These include.

1. The Real Story Was Suppressed.

2. The Story About Jesus Became Embellished.

3. Jesus Did Not Actually Die On The Cross.

4. The Body Was Stolen.

5. The Women Went To The Wrong Tomb On Easter Sunday.

6. The Disciples Merely Had Hallucinations About Seeing the Risen Christ.

7. Jesus Appeared To Believers Only—Those Expecting A Resurrection.

8. The Reports About His Resurrection Are Hopelessly Contradictory.

9. It Doesn't Matter What Happened.

We will now take a look at each of these objections and evaluate them in light of all the evidence.

OBJECTION 1: THE REAL STORY WAS SUPPRESSED

There are many people who question the accuracy of the New Testament account of the resurrection. They contend that the true story was never told because the facts had been suppressed by those later in power. Any evidence to the contrary would have been burned or destroyed. The answer to this view is simple—there were unbelievers who gave alternative theories to the resurrection, their writings were not suppressed. We do have writings from unbelievers who all argue that the body was stolen—they all admit the body was gone the third day.

THEY HAD NO BETTER EXPLANATION

However, they had no better explanation than Jesus' disciples stole His body. The Christians certainly did not suppress this popular theory. To the contrary, Matthew records this theory in his gospel as the official explanation given by unbelievers.

OBJECTION 2: THE STORY BECAME EMBELLISHED

One of the most popular explanations has been to say the stories about Jesus have been embellished. The problem with this theory is that there is not enough time for this to happen. Paul's earliest letter, First Thessalonians, refutes that. The fact that Christ was killed is stated in First Thessalonians 2:15 and 4:14. The fact that He was raised is stated in First Thessalonians 4:14. This was written about A.D. 51, less than twenty years after the resurrection.

OBJECTION 3: JESUS DID NOT DIE ON THE CROSS

A favorite objection is that Jesus did not die on the cross, but rather He fainted from exhaustion. When He appeared to His disciples, it was not as the resurrected Lord but rather as one who had been resuscitated.

Therefore, what we have is resuscitation, not a resurrection. Like the other objections to the resurrection, there are many problems with this theory.

THE ROMANS DID THEIR JOB WELL

Crucifixion was common in Jesus' time and the Roman soldiers had become experts at it. They had reduced it to a science with a set of rules to be followed. There is no possible way Jesus could have survived the crucifixion, scourging, and lance thrust.

Since the governor had personally condemned Jesus to death, it is highly unlikely the soldiers would make a mistake and not finish the job. Furthermore, we have Pilate cross-examining the centurion to make certain that Jesus had died. Mark records the following.

> This all happened on Friday, the day of preparation, the day before the Sabbath. As evening approached, Joseph of Arimathea took a risk and went to Pilate and asked for Jesus' body. (Joseph was an honored member of the high council, and he was waiting for the Kingdom of God to come.) Pilate couldn't believe that Jesus was already dead, so he called for the Roman officer and asked if he had died yet. The officer confirmed that Jesus was dead, so Pilate told Joseph he could have the body (Mark 15:42-45 NLT).

Jesus was dead. There is no doubt about this.

THE BREAKING OF JESUS' LEGS WAS NOT NECESSARY

Crucifixion was a slow, painful way to die, with the person usually dying of asphyxiation. The victim had to push his body up in order to breathe.

Therefore, breaking of the legs would hasten the death of the victim. The legs of the two robbers that were crucified next to Jesus were broken because the Passover was drawing near.

Passover began at sunset, and according to Jewish law, bodies could not be left on the cross on that Holy Day. Jesus' legs were not broken because He was obviously dead. In addition, Pilate would not have given permission for Joseph to take Jesus' body for burial if He were not already dead.

BLOOD AND WATER CAME OUT FROM HIS SIDE–A SIGN OF DEATH

We are told that at Jesus' death, blood and water came out from His side when it was pierced with a spear. John writes.

> But one of the soldiers pierced His side with a spear, and immediately blood and water came out (John 19:34 NKJV).

The purpose of the spear thrust was to ensure that Jesus was dead. This is eyewitness detail—which shows that death did indeed occur. The blood and water coming out is an outward sign that someone has died.

HOW DID JESUS GET OUT OF THE TOMB?

Another question that needs to be addressed is, "How did Jesus get out of the tomb in the first place?" He had been wrapped in grave clothes and the spices would have hardened around Him in a few hours. This would make His escape difficult, if not impossible—assuming He was still alive. There was also a large stone rolled in front of the tomb that is virtually impossible to move from the inside. In addition, the guards had to have been conveniently asleep for Jesus to get by them.

JESUS WOULD HAVE BEEN PERPETRATING A DELIBERATE HOAX

If this theory is correct, then Jesus would have been guilty of perpetrating a deliberate hoax by passing Himself off as one who had risen from the dead. He did not tell His disciples that He narrowly escaped death, He told them He had risen. This would make Jesus a liar—contrary to everything we know about Him and His character.

WOULD THIS CONVINCE THE DISCIPLES?

If Jesus had survived His crucifixion, He would have been in an extremely weak condition. It is not possible to believe that a man who was half-dead, crawling around weak and needing immediate medical treatment, could have given His disciples the impression that He had just conquered death. This type of appearance of Jesus would not have changed their sorrow into enthusiasm, and caused them to worship Him as risen from the dead.

WHEN DID HE DIE?

If it were a mere resuscitation, then we are faced with the question of when did He die? Where, if anywhere, was He buried? Why wasn't His other tomb venerated?

SUMMARY TO THE CLAIM JESUS DID NOT DIE ON THE CROSS

The evidence is clear—Jesus died on Calvary's cross. Therefore, any theory that attempts to explain away the resurrection must take this fact into account.

OBJECTION 4: THE STOLEN BODY THEORY

Many argue the body of Jesus was removed from the tomb before Easter Sunday morning. Since the evidence proves the tomb was empty the question is, "What caused it to be empty?" The empty tomb means two possibilities: the body of Jesus was removed by either: (1) human hands or (2) supernatural power.

DID HUMAN HANDS STEAL JESUS' BODY?

If the body of Jesus was removed by human hands, then we have four basic possibilities as to who did it. The suspects include.

1. The Jews

2. The Romans

3. Joseph of Arimathea

4. Jesus' disciples

Two questions immediately arise about the stolen body theory. First, concerning His enemies and Joseph of Arimathea, "Would they have stolen the body?" Next we ask this question of His disciples, "Could they have stolen the body?"

THE JEWS

The Jews could have had the body of Jesus removed from the tomb, yet they had no motivation for such an act. Some have argued they may have removed the body to keep the site from becoming a place of pilgrimage for Jesus' disciples. Yet this would have caused the sort of problem they were trying to avoid—rumors that Jesus had risen.

The Jewish religious rulers are the ones who asked for the guard because they were afraid His disciples would come and steal the body. If they had taken the body, then certainly they would have produced it fifty days later when Peter, in the same city of Jerusalem, proclaimed that Jesus had risen. The fact that they did not produce the body of Jesus shows they did not remove it.

THE ROMANS

A second possible group, that could have removed Jesus' body, was the Romans. Since they were in charge of keeping law and order, it is possible that they could have taken the body from the tomb. The problem with them is also lack of a motivation. Why would they do such a thing? They wanted to keep the peace. Stealing the body of an executed religious leader would only add to the rumors about Him. It would stir up greater conflict. Consequently, there is no motivation for them to steal the body.

Furthermore, when the Christian faith began to grow, they could have easily stopped it by producing the body. But they did not do this.

JOSEPH OF ARIMATHEA

He obviously had access to Christ's body since He is the one who requested it from Pilate. It is argued that he may have had second thoughts about placing the body of Jesus in his family tomb. Thus he could have removed Jesus' body after the initial burial and placed it elsewhere—possibly in an unmarked grave.

Again, we have no motivation for him to do such a thing—especially since he and Nicodemus took the time and expense to prepare Jesus for burial. If he removed the body, then why didn't he tell anyone?

However, there is another problem. It was not the empty tomb that caused the other disciples to believe in Jesus—it was seeing the risen Christ.

DID JESUS' DISCIPLES STEAL HIS BODY?

The oldest alternative explanation to the resurrection is that His disciples stole the body of Jesus while the guard was sleeping. Matthew tells us this was the story the bribed Roman guard was to tell, even though they knew it was false. He wrote.

> As they were on their way, some of the guard came into the city and reported to the chief priests everything that had happened. After the priests had assembled with the elders and agreed on a plan, they gave the soldiers a large sum of money and told them, "Say this, 'His disciples came during the night and stole Him while we were sleeping.' If this reaches the governor's ears, we will deal with him and keep you out of trouble." So they took the money and did as they were instructed. And this story has been spread among Jewish people to this day (Matthew 28:11-15 HCSB).

The idea that the disciples stole the body is inadequate for the following reasons.

COULD THEY GET PAST THE GUARDS?

To begin with, the disciples would have had to get by the guards at the tomb. This theory has the guard members conveniently asleep. The disciples would have had to move the large stone away from the tomb without waking any of them. While this is not impossible, it certainly is inconsistent with the facts as we know them.

WHY LEAVE THE GRAVE CLOTHES BEHIND?

If the Roman guard was asleep you need to move fast. The position of the grave clothes shows the impossibility of the theft of the body. Why take the time to remove the grave clothes and leave them behind? It would have been much easier to remove the body, grave clothes and all, especially if time were a factor. The explanation that the Roman guard was asleep does not help solve this problem.

HOW COULD THE GUARD TESTIFY?

Furthermore, the guard story doesn't stand up to cross-examination. What does anyone know about what is occurring when they are asleep? If the Roman guard were sleeping, how did they know the disciples stole the body? How can you determine anything that's going on while you are asleep? Couldn't Jesus, just as easily, have risen from the dead while they were asleep without the guards knowing it?

THE DISCIPLES WOULD HAVE BEEN LIARS

The stolen body theory would make the disciples deliberate liars. These are the same disciples who gave us the New Testament—the same New Testament where they reported Jesus was sinless. They testified He never lied—rather He always told the truth. Yet this theory wants people to believe that His disciples, while spreading the message of the truth-telling Jesus, lied and continued to lie about the most important event in His life! On the one hand, they proclaimed to the world the story of the most perfect man who ever lived. On the other hand, according to the stolen body theory, they pulled off this gigantic deception. Their character testifies against this idea.

Even if they could have gotten past the Roman guard to get to the body, they would have had to live with that lie for the rest of their lives, proclaiming it, suffering for it, and dying for it. They would have been preaching the resurrection in direct contradiction to their own knowledge of the truth.

THEY HAD NO MOTIVATION FOR LYING

Assuming the disciples could have stolen the body, another question arises, "What motivated them to do it?" By proclaiming Christ had risen, they subjected themselves to beatings and jail. They eventually died for their testimony. If they had stolen the body, they would have been liars as well as thieves. They would not only have lied for the cause, they would have died for their lie. What advantage would there have been for doing this? Their Lord's body received a proper burial. They had nothing to gain and everything to lose by stealing His body.

Thus we can find no motivation for the disciples stealing the body. Their leader was buried with loving hands in a tomb of a rich man. Since they were not expecting Him to rise from the dead, this would have been the best end to Jesus' life—all things considered.

THERE WAS NO TIME TO STEAL THE BODY

There is also the problem of time. Jesus was betrayed on Thursday night and brought to trial Friday morning. His crucifixion took place from approximately 9:00 a.m. to 3:00 p.m. on Friday. At sundown on Friday the Sabbath began and the disciples, as observant Jews, would rest. The end of the Sabbath was on Saturday night. The first visit to the tomb realistically would have been on Sunday morning. By then Jesus had risen. There was simply no time to steal the body.

THE MENTAL STATE OF THE DISCIPLES NEEDS TO BE CONSIDERED

The mental state of Jesus' disciples also needs to be considered. They were now leaderless for the first time in three years. All the disciples left Jesus at the Garden of Gethsemane. Later Peter denied Jesus and John was looking after Jesus' mother. Being afraid and leaderless, did they suddenly become brave? After the surprise betrayal and crucifixion, is it really possible to think they concocted a plan late Friday afternoon to have the body removed by Sunday morning? No, it does not seem possible.

THE TRANSFORMED LIVES OF THE DISCIPLES HAS TO BE EXPLAINED

The mere removal of Jesus' body from the tomb could not have transformed their sadness into gladness. In less than thirty-six hours, they went from the depths of despair to the heights of joy. They had lost hope when Christ died, but they immediately went from hopelessness to certainty, from cowards to eventual martyrs. Something gave them the power to sustain their preaching during persecution and martyrdom. A stolen body would not have changed their lives in this manner.

LIARS ARE USUALLY CAUGHT

There is another important point—liars are usually caught in their lies. This is especially true when a number of different people are lying. Cover-ups have a way of becoming public, yet none of the disciples ever denied the resurrection. If Jesus had not risen, one would have expected the eventual confession of at least some of them. But they all went to their deaths proclaiming Christ had risen. Why?

WHY WEREN'T THE DISCIPLES PROSECUTED?

According to Roman law, the body of a condemned criminal belonged to the state. That is why Joseph of Arimathea had to ask for Jesus' body. To steal a body was a serious offense and it is odd that neither the Romans nor Jews did anything to substantiate the charges if the body had been stolen. The disciples were never prosecuted for this alleged crime. Why?

JESUS WOULD ALSO HAVE BEEN A LIAR

If Jesus did not rise, that would make Him a liar because He predicted His resurrection. As we have seen, lying is totally contrary to everything we know about His character.

WHY WAS THERE NO VENERATION OF HIS BURIAL PLACE?

The Jews venerated the graves of their religious leaders. If Christ were not buried in Joseph's tomb, then He must have been buried elsewhere, yet there is no trace of any burial place in Jerusalem for the body of Jesus. No tradition exists anywhere that Jesus remained buried.

WHY WERE THEY MARTYRED?

Finally, there is the ultimate question, "Why did they die for their testimony of Jesus?" If they had stolen the body, they would have died for a lie knowing that it was a lie. The disciples who would have "died for a lie" included Simon Peter (crucified); Andrew (crucified); James, son of Alphaeus (crucified); Philip (crucified); Simon (crucified); Thaddaeus (killed with arrows); Thomas (died by a spear thrust); Bartholomew (crucified); and James, the son of Zebedee (killed with the sword). Jesus' disciples were transformed from cowards to martyrs. Why?

It is one thing to lie—it is quite another thing to die for a lie if you know that it is a lie. The disciples sealed their testimony in their own blood. To save their own life they would only have had to confess to lying, yet they never recanted their testimony.

THEY DIED SEPARATELY

Furthermore, they died separately. It is one thing to die as a member of a group—strength could be gained from each other as you are awaiting death. However, each of the disciples died separately, apart from one another, apart from any type of moral support. Again, we ask the question, "Why?"

THE STOLEN BODY THEORY IS INADEQUATE

These different factors make the popular stolen body theory inadequate at best. The disciples were no longer capable of raiding the tomb and the other possible culprits had no motivation for stealing Jesus' body.

OBJECTION 5: THE WOMEN WENT TO THE WRONG TOMB ON EASTER SUNDAY

Kirsopp Lake, the great textual scholar, came up with this ridiculous theory. Simply stated, the women were not certain where Jesus was buried. Thus they went in the semi-darkness to an empty tomb thinking it was the tomb where Jesus was actually buried. When they found the tomb empty they assumed He had risen.

Supposedly the young man they saw that dark morning confirmed that they were at the wrong tomb. Mark 16:6 says.

> And he said to them, "Do not be alarmed. You seek Jesus of Nazareth, who was crucified. He has risen; he is not here. See the place where they laid him (Mark 16:6 ESV).

Professor Lake omits the words "he has risen" from the text. Therefore, the young man is saying to the women, "He is not here, He is over there. Come see where they have placed Him."

Let's consider the problems with this theory.

THE BODY WOULD HAVE STILL BEEN IN THE TOMB

There are so many problems with this theory—not the least of which is that the body would still have been in Joseph of Arimathea's tomb. When Peter preached the resurrection on the Day of Pentecost, it would have been a simple thing to go to the correct tomb and produce the body.

IT WOULD HAVE BEEN TOO DARK FOR THE GARDENER

In addition, if it were too dark for the women to find the right tomb, it would have been too dark for a gardener or caretaker to be working.

THERE IS NO REASON TO OMIT THE WORDS HE HAS RISEN

Furthermore, to argue for this theory, you have to omit from the text the words, "He has risen." There is no justification for this omission for every manuscript we possess has these crucial words.

THE EMPTY TOMB DID NOT CAUSE BELIEF

Finally, it was not the empty tomb that convinced the disciples that Jesus had risen from the dead. On the contrary, it was the fact they saw Him after His death. No one really takes this theory seriously.

OBJECTION 6: THE DISCIPLES EXPERIENCED HALLUCINATIONS

Another objection to the resurrection is the contention that His disciples experienced hallucinations. This does not make them liars as much as fools. The disciples only thought they saw Jesus, for He had not really risen. Hallucinations often occur when someone wishes for something so much. This theory holds the disciples saw exactly what they wanted to see.

We respond to this theory as follows.

THE BODY OF JESUS WOULD STILL HAVE BEEN IN THE TOMB

The hallucination theory does not explain how the tomb became empty, or why the authorities failed to produce a body. Since they did not produce a body, it leaves open the question what happened to Jesus. The authorities could have produced the body, ending any testimony that Jesus had risen. The hallucination theory does not explain the missing body.

HALLUCINATIONS ARE NOT COLLECTIVE

Furthermore, hallucinations are not collective—only individuals experience them. Five hundred people at one time do not have the same hallucination!

HALLUCINATIONS DO NOT JUST COME AND GO

Hallucinations tend to increase in intensity and occur on a regular basis over a long period. They become worse, not better. According to Scripture, it was after forty days that the appearances of Jesus stopped and He did not appear again. This is inconsistent with the nature of hallucinations.

WHO GAVE THEM THE POWER TO WORK MIRACLES?

If the disciples were only hallucinating about seeing the risen Christ, then how were they able to perform miracles? Who gave the disciples the power to heal the sick and raise the dead?

WHAT HAPPENED TO SAUL?

Saul of Tarsus, who became the Apostle Paul, was converted as an unbeliever. Are we to assume that he had the same hallucination?

THEY DID NOT EXPECT JESUS TO RISE

According to the New Testament, the disciples did not expect Jesus to rise because they had not expected Him to die. When Jesus appeared to them it was unexpected, they were not ready for it. The disciples did not convince themselves that Jesus was alive, it was Jesus Himself who convinced them. This was the exact opposite of what they were expecting.

HE WAS NOT WHO THEY ORIGINALLY THOUGHT

For example, Mary Magdalene did not see a gardener near the empty tomb and think it was Jesus, she saw Jesus and thought at first it was a gardener. The two disciples on the road to Emmaus did not talk with a stranger and then assume they were conversing with Jesus. Instead, they talked with Jesus and thought they were conversing with a stranger. Finally, in the upper room, the disciples of Jesus did not see a ghost and believed it was Jesus—they saw Jesus and thought they had seen a ghost.

ONLY CERTAIN TYPES OF PEOPLE SUFFER HALLUCINATIONS

Usually it is highly imaginative people who suffer hallucinations. The appearances of Jesus were to a diverse group of people of different psychological makeup. This included: fishermen, a tax collector, and a Rabbi.

HE APPEARED AT DIFFERENT TIMES AND PLACES

The appearances of Christ occurred at different times and places: early in the morning, late afternoon, in the evening, at the garden tomb, in a crowded room, at the Sea of Galilee, on top of a mountain, and on the Emmaus road. This is not consistent with hallucinations.

SUMMARY TO THE HALLUCINATION THEORY

Again, we have a theory that just does not fit all the facts. Jesus' disciples saw much more than mere hallucinations—they saw the risen Savior.

OBJECTION 7: JESUS ONLY APPEARED TO BELIEVERS

One of the objections is that Jesus appeared only to believers—people who already had a desire to believe the marvelous stories about Him. Again, the facts say otherwise.

THE DISCIPLES WERE THE FIRST UNBELIEVERS OF THE RESURRECTION

We are told that the first unbelievers of the resurrection story were none other than the disciples themselves. Luke writes.

> But the story sounded like nonsense, so they didn't believe it (Luke 24:11 NLT).

The disciples were not expecting a resurrection. Not only were the disciples not expecting Jesus to rise from the dead, they did not believe the story of His resurrection when it was first told to them!

DOUBTING THOMAS DID NOT BELIEVE AT FIRST

Thomas did not believe—even when the other disciples told him they had seen the risen Christ. John writes.

> The other disciples therefore said to him, "We have seen the Lord." So he said to them, "Unless I see in His hands the print of the nails, and put my finger into the print of the nails, and put my hand into His side, I will not believe" (John 20:25 NKJV).

Eventually, Thomas did see and believe.

OTHERS DOUBTED HIS RESURRECTION

We are even told that when Jesus met His disciples in Galilee, there were some who doubted. Matthew writes.

> When they saw Him, they worshiped, but some doubted (Matthew 28:17 HCSB).

There were still some who had doubts.

PAUL WAS AN UNBELIEVER WHEN JESUS APPEARED TO HIM

Saul of Tarsus was not a believer when the resurrected Christ appeared to Him. He had to be convinced from his position of unbelief.

Therefore, it is clear that Jesus appeared to more than merely believers.

OBJECTION 8: THE RESURRECTION REPORTS ARE CONTRADICTORY

Often it is charged that the accounts of the resurrection, as contained in the four gospels, are so contradictory that they cannot be reconciled. However, a reasonable reconciliation of the resurrection accounts is as follows.

1. After the resurrection, but before dawn on Easter Sunday, an earthquake occurred, an angel rolled away the stone from the entrance to the tomb and then sat upon it (Matthew 28:2-4).

2. As Sunday morning was beginning to dawn three women approached the tomb (Mary Magdalene, Mary the mother of James and Joses, and Salome). Their intent was to anoint the body of Jesus with perfumed oil. The oil was to be brought by a second group of women who set out later to the tomb (Matthew 28:1; Mark 16:1-4; John 20:1). The first group was amazed to find the stone rolled away when they arrived.

3. At least one of the women entered into the tomb and announced that the body of Jesus was not there. This is an inference from John 20:2.

4. Mary Magdalene immediately returned to inform Peter and John that someone had removed Jesus' body (John 20:2).

5. Mary, the mother of James and Joses, along with Salome saw an angel inside the tomb. The angel had the appearance of a young man. The angel announced that Jesus had risen and that they should go tell Jesus' disciples that He would meet them in the Galilee (Matthew 28:5-7; Mark 16:5-7).

6. These two women returned to the city without greeting anyone along the way. They were left speechless by the events which transpired (Matthew 28:8; Mark 16:8).

7. Another group of women from the Galilee, along with Joanna (see Luke 8:3), arrived at the tomb carrying perfumed oil to anoint the

body of Jesus. They met the angel, along with another angel (Luke 24:4,23). They then returned to report the angel's message of the resurrection to the eleven as well as to other disciples that had gathered together (Matthew 26:56; Luke 24:1-9; 22:23).

8. Having been informed by Mary Magdalene that the body was gone, Peter and John (and possibly others Luke 24:24) ran to the tomb without encountering Mary and Salome. They saw the grave clothes and then went back home (John 20:3-10; Luke 24:12). The grave clothes caused John to believe that something had happened.

9. Mary Magdalene followed Peter and John to the tomb. She saw two angels inside, and then met Jesus after supposing Him to be the gardener (Mark 16:9; John 20:11-17).

10. Mary Magdalene then returned to inform the disciples that Jesus had risen (Mark 16:10,11; John 20:18).

11. Mary, the mother of James and Joses, along with Salome meet Jesus on their way back from the tomb. Jesus commands them to tell His disciples that He will meet them in Galilee.

12. The disciples, who had reports of the empty tomb and resurrection from three sources—Mary Magdalene, Joanna and the women from Galilee, and Mary and Salome, still refused to believe these witnesses (Mark 16:11; Luke 24:11).

13. During that same afternoon, Jesus appeared to two disciples on the way to Emmaus. They returned to Jerusalem to report the appearance to the eleven and the other disciples (Mark 16:12-13; Luke 24:13-35).

14. Jesus appeared to Peter sometime before these two disciples returned to speak to the eleven.

15. That evening Jesus appeared to ten disciples—Judas was dead and Thomas was absent (Mark 16:14; Luke 24:33; 36-43; John 20:19-23; 1 Corinthians 15:5).

16. Eight days later, Jesus appeared to the eleven with Thomas being present (John 20:26-29).

17. Sometime later, seven disciples encountered Jesus on the Sea of Galilee (John 21:1-22).

18. Still later, the eleven met Jesus on a mountain in Galilee (Matthew 28:16-20; Mark 16:15-18).

19. Jesus appeared to more than five hundred people at one time (1 Corinthians 15:6).

20. Jesus appeared to James (1 Corinthians 15:7).

21. Before His ascension, He appeared to the eleven near Bethany (Mark 16:9-20; Luke 24:50-52; Acts 1:6-11; 1 Corinthians 15:7).

22. Finally, Jesus appeared to the Apostle Paul on the Damascus road (Acts 9, 22, 26).

This is a reasonable scenario of the events surrounding the resurrection of Jesus. The fact that we are not exactly certain of their order only goes to prove there was no collusion between the various authors. If the story would have been made up, the different writers would have made certain that the stories matched detail for detail.

However, when four different people tell any story, they will all give the same basic account, but there will always be slight differences in the details. The differences only point to the independence of each author.

OBJECTION 9: WE WILL NEVER KNOW WHAT HAPPENED AND IT DOES NOT MATTER

Finally, there is the argument that we will never know what happened to the body of Jesus. It is a mystery that does not have an explanation. Furthermore, it does not really matter what happened.

This argument ignores the facts. It does matter what happened and we can know—if we are willing to look at the evidence.

CONCLUSION TO THE OBJECTIONS OF THE RESURRECTION

In the last two thousand years many theories have been presented that attempt to give an alternative explanation to the one given in Scripture— Christ rose from the dead. As we have seen, none of them are adequate, for they do not fully explain all the different lines of evidence.

The theory that best fits all the facts is that Jesus Christ was alive three days after His death and that He is Lord of all!

THE SIGNIFICANCE OF THE RESURRECTION SO WHAT IF HE DID RISE?

If we concur that the resurrection did take place, then so what? What does it mean? There are a number of important observations to make.

THE RESURRECTION VALIDATES JESUS' CLAIMS

First, the resurrection demonstrates that Jesus is the One whom He claimed to be. Paul wrote the following to the Romans.

> This letter is from Paul, Jesus Christ's slave, chosen by God to be an apostle and sent out to preach his Good News. This Good News was promised long ago by God through his prophets in the holy Scriptures. It is the Good News about his Son, Jesus, who came as a man, born into King David's royal family line. And Jesus Christ our Lord was shown to be the Son of God when God powerfully raised him from the dead by means of the Holy Spirit (Romans 1:1-4 NLT).

The resurrection validates Jesus' claims to be a prophet (Matthew 26:8), Lord, and Messiah (Acts 2:36). Everything He claimed to be has been validated by the resurrection.

THE RESURRECTION DEMONSTRATES THE TRUTH OF THE CHRISTIAN FAITH

The resurrection also proves the truth of the Christian faith. At the beginning of this book we looked at the various options that humans have about believing if God or gods exist. The resurrection of Jesus Christ from the dead settles the matter as to which of these beliefs is true. It is the Christian faith!

Therefore, there is only one God who exists, and only one way to reach the one God, through Jesus Christ. The resurrection of Jesus demonstrates this to be true.

THE RESURRECTION OF CHRIST GIVES PURPOSE FOR LIFE

Therefore, the fact that Jesus rose from the dead, gives humanity the answers to the three basic questions about life, "Who am I? Why am I alive? What will happen to me when I die?"

IT PROVIDES US WITH AN IDENTITY

The resurrection of Jesus solves our identity problem. Humans need no longer wonder who we are. We now realize that we are created in the image of God. This means we have the ability to think, love and communicate. We have the chance to know the one true God because He has given us these abilities. We now know that human beings are special.

IT GIVES US A PURPOSE FOR LIVING

Along with identity comes a genuine purpose for living. Instead of living life without any real purpose, we can now know the reason we have been created—to love God and enjoy Him forever. Jesus Christ, and His resurrection from the dead, has provided the answer to what our purpose is here upon the earth. We not only know who we are, we also know why we are here.

IT TELLS US OF OUR DESTINY

Finally, the truth of the resurrection of Jesus provides us with an answer about our future destiny. We now know that this life is not all that there is. We are beings made for eternity, and belief in Jesus allows us to spend eternity in the presence of God. Thus, the grave has no ultimate terror for us because we know that there is a better existence beyond this life. Belief in Jesus gives us a destiny to which we can look forward.

IT PROVIDES EVERLASTING LIFE FOR THE BELIEVER

The resurrection of Jesus is the factual basis for everlasting life for those who believe in Him If a person believes in Jesus Christ, then one of the provisions is eternal life. Jesus said.

> In a little while the world will no longer see me, but you will see me; because I live, you also will live (John 14:19 NRSV).

This everlasting life is based upon His resurrection. Jesus made this astounding claim.

> I am the resurrection and the life. Those who believe in me, even though they die, will live (John 11:25 NRSV).

He Himself is the resurrection and the life.

JESUS IS THE FIRST OF MANY TO BE RAISED

Christ's resurrection is the first in a long line of resurrections of those who believe in Him. Paul wrote.

> But in fact Christ has been raised from the dead, the first fruits of those who have died (1 Corinthians 15:20 NRSV).

His resurrection also serves as a prototype of the resurrection of believers. Twice Christ is referred to as the firstborn from the dead (Colossians 1:18; Revelation 1:5). This means that He was the first to have an eternal resurrected body. Our resurrection bodies, like His, will be different from our earthly bodies. Paul says our resurrection bodies will be related to our former ones (1 Corinthians 15:35-41).

In eternity, we will be like Him. John wrote.

> Dear friends, we are God's children now, and what we will be has not yet been revealed. We know that when He appears, we will be like Him, because we will see Him as He is (1 John 3:2 HCSB).

Someday we will have a new body—a body like His.

THE RESURRECTION BRINGS COMFORT TO BELIEVERS

The realization that Christ has risen provides comfort to the believer. After writing to the church at Thessalonica on the matter of the resurrection of Christ and the eventual resurrection of the believer, the Apostle Paul exhorted the church to "comfort one another with these words" (1 Thessalonians 4:18). The knowledge that this life is not all that there is brings comfort to the believer.

Because of this, we do not fear death in the same way as unbelievers do. The Apostle Paul wrote to the Corinthian church.

> O Death, where is your sting? O Hades, where is your victory? The sting of death is sin, and the strength of sin is the law. But thanks be to God, who gives us the victory through our Lord Jesus Christ (1 Corinthians 15:54-57 NKJV).

The resurrection is comfort for believers.

THE RESURRECTION GIVES HOPE TO THOSE WHO ARE ALIVE

Because Christ has risen from the dead and granted eternal life to those who put their trust in Him, there is hope for the future.

One of the simplest prayers and earliest creeds of the church were the Aramaic words maran atha "our Lord come" (1 Corinthians 16:22). The hope of the church is the return of Jesus Christ to the earth.

WE ALL NEED HOPE

It has been said that a human being can live about five minutes without air, three days without water, and about thirty days without food, but a person cannot live one second without hope. We all need to hope for something better than what this life offers. The resurrection of Christ provides the basis for that hope.

THE RESURRECTION PROVIDES THE BASIS FOR A SATISFYING LIFE

Another benefit of the resurrection is that it provides the believer with the basis to live a satisfying life. Paul wrote that believers could now experience this life. He said.

> I pray that you will begin to understand the incredible greatness of his power for us who believe him. This is the same mighty power that raised Christ from the dead and seated him in the place of honor at God's right hand in the heavenly realms (Ephesians 1:19,20 NLT).

Abundant life is available right now because Christ has risen. The power of the resurrected Christ is experienced in the life of the believer.

THE RESURRECTION IS MORE THAN A SIMPLE HISTORICAL EVENT

Therefore, we conclude that the resurrection of Jesus Christ is more than a historical event. It does the following things.

1. It validates Jesus' claims.

2. The resurrection proves the truth of the Christian faith.

3. It gives humanity a purpose for living.

4. It provides the basis for eternal life.

5. It gives the believer comfort.

6. The resurrection offers a genuine hope for the future.

7. All these things result in a satisfying life right now.

THE EVIDENCE IS LOUD AND CLEAR

The evidence testifies that Jesus Christ has risen! The only rational explanation for these historical facts is that God raised Jesus in bodily form, forever triumphant over sin and death.

Lord Darling, the former chief law officer in England, has said it well.

> We as Christians are asked to take a very great deal on trust; the teachings, for example, and the miracles of Jesus. If we had to take all on trust, I, for one, should be skeptical. The crux of the problem of whether Jesus was, or was not, what he proclaimed himself to be, must surely depend upon the truth or otherwise of the resurrection. On that greatest point we are not merely asked to have faith. In its favour as a living truth there exists such overwhelming evidence, positive and negative, factual and circumstantial, that no intelligent jury in the world can fail to bring in a verdict that the resurrection story is true.[2]

As we examine the totality of the evidence we render the following verdict:

---

2. Lord Darling cited by Michael Green, *The Day Death Died*, Intervarsity Press, 1982, p. 15

JESUS CHRIST IS RISEN INDEED!

We have seen the overwhelming evidence for Jesus' claims—miracles, fulfilled prophecy, and Jesus' resurrection. Taken together they present an irrefutable case for Jesus as the One whom He claimed to be—God's Son.

Next, we will look at how Jesus viewed Scripture. How did He view the Old Testament? What did He think about His own teachings? Did He make any promises regarding the writings of the New Testament?

Our last part of the book will discover that the entire Bible is the Word of God because Jesus says so.

CHAPTER 11

Jesus' View Of The Old Testament: He Totally Trusted Its Contents

---

This chapter logically follows what we have learned so far. If Jesus is the Christ, God the Son, then He speaks authoritative on every matter. Therefore, we want to find how He viewed the Old Testament, His own teachings, and the New Testament. This chapter looks at Jesus' view of the Old Testament.

We will find that Jesus totally trusted its contents. The people actually existed, and the stories found in the Old Testament literally occurred. This includes some of the most controversial stories recorded in the Old Testament such as Adam and Eve, Noah, and Jonah. We also find that Jesus spoke of the necessity of Old Testament prophecy being fulfilled.

These facts will lead us to conclude that Jesus totally trusted the Old Testament. To Him, it is God's divinely inspired Word to the human race.

Now that we have seen that the evidence is sufficient for believing that Jesus is the One whom He claimed to be, we now come to the question of the divine inspiration and authority of the Bible. This chapter will deal with the Old Testament. Did the stories recorded in the Old Testament actually occur? In what sense does it speak authoritative to us? Jesus is the one who can provide us the answer.

JESUS IS THE FINAL AUTHORITY

To find the answer we examine the view of Jesus Christ, since He has already demonstrated that He speaks with ultimate authority. Paul wrote the following to the church at Rome about Christ.

> And Jesus Christ our Lord was shown to be the Son of God when God powerfully raised him from the dead by means of the Holy Spirit (Romans 1:4 NLT).

Therefore, we go to Jesus to find the answers to questions about the Old Testament's reliability. For the believer, Christ's view of the Old Testament should be our view.

HE HAD TOTAL TRUST IN THE OLD TESTAMENT

In examining the four gospels we have a great amount of information to work with concerning Jesus' view of the Old Testament. His view can be simply stated in two words, "total trust." Jesus accepted the Old Testament Scriptures as being divinely inspired—He never cast doubt on any of the accounts. Jesus assumed the people were actual people and the events literally occurred. We never find Him giving the slightest hint of anything but the complete acceptance of the Old Testament as the Word of God.

JESUS BELIEVED THE PEOPLE WERE ACTUAL PEOPLE

The first thing we find Jesus confirming about the Old Testament is that the people mentioned in its pages truly did exist. They were not mythical characters.

ABRAHAM

Jesus confirmed the existence of Abraham. He said.

> Your father Abraham rejoiced to see my day: and he saw it, and was glad (John 8:56 KJV).

Jesus accepted the fact that Abraham was an historical character.

ISAAC AND JACOB

The patriarchs, Isaac and Jacob, were real people according to Jesus. Matthew records Him saying the following.

> I tell you, many will come from east and west and will eat with Abraham and Isaac and Jacob in the kingdom of heaven (Matthew 8:11 NRSV).

According to Jesus, Isaac and Jacob truly existed

THE QUEEN OF SHEBA

The Queen of Sheba actually came to visit Solomon. Scripture records Him saying.

> The queen of the south will rise up at the judgment with this generation and condemn it, because she came from the ends of the earth to hear the wisdom of Solomon; and look—something greater than Solomon is here! (Matthew 12:42 HCSB).

Jesus accepted her existence as factual and her visit to Solomon was an historical event.

SOLOMON

Solomon himself, the great king, was an historical person. Jesus said.

> Yet I tell you that not even Solomon in all his splendor was adorned like one of these! (Matthew 6:29 HCSB).

According to Jesus, Solomon did indeed exist.

ELIJAH

Elijah was a genuine prophet. When asked about Elijah returning to this earth, Jesus clearly said that he was returning. Matthew writes.

> Jesus answered, "Elijah is coming and will put everything in order again" (Matthew 17:11 God's Word).

Elijah existed. Someday, he will come back to the earth.

ELISHA

Jesus also confirmed the story about Elisha the prophet and Naaman the leper. Luke records Jesus saying.

> There were also many lepers in Israel in the time of the prophet Elisha, and none of them was cleansed except Naaman the Syrian (Luke 4:27 NRSV).

Elisha the prophet, likewise, existed.

ZECHARIAH

Jesus also acknowledged Zechariah the prophet. He said.

> From the murder of Abel to the murder of Zechariah, who was killed between the altar and the sanctuary. Yes, it will surely be charged against you (Luke 11:51 NLT).

Jesus believed that Zechariah truly lived.

SODOM AND GOMORRAH

Jesus believed that Sodom and Gomorrah were genuine cities that were punished by God. He said.

> I can guarantee this truth: Judgment day will be better for Sodom and Gomorrah than for that city. (Matthew 10:15 God's Word).

Sodom and Gomorrah were actual cities. They were not mythical places.

TYRE AND SIDON

The account of Tyre and Sidon, the cities that were judged in the Old Testament, was confirmed by Jesus. He said.

> Woe to you, Chorazin! Woe to you, Bethsaida! For if the deeds of power done in you had been done in Tyre and Sidon, they would have repented long ago in sackcloth and ashes. But I tell you, on the day of judgment it will be more tolerable for Tyre and Sidon than for you (Matthew 11:21,22 NRSV).

According to Jesus, the cities of Tyre and Sidon were punished by the Lord just as the Old Testament said.

JESUS BELIEVED THE STORIES WERE FACTUAL

As we look at the way Jesus treated the Old Testament, we discover that He assumed the various stories to be factual.

GOD GAVE THE RITE OF CIRCUMCISION

Jesus stated that it was God who gave the people the rite of circumcision through Moses. John records Him saying.

> Moses gave you circumcision (it is, of course, not from Moses, but from the patriarchs), and you circumcise a man on the sabbath (John 7:22 NRSV).

Circumcision was a God-given rite.

GOD PROVIDED THE MANNA IN THE WILDERNESS

The provision of the manna, given to the children of Israel while they were in the wilderness, was confirmed by the Lord Jesus. He said.

> Our fathers ate the manna in the desert; as it is written, 'He gave them bread from heaven to eat' (John 6:31 NKJV).

Therefore, the account of the manna, being given by God to the people, is historical.

DAVID EATING THE BREAD OF PRESENTATION

The story of David and his men eating the bread of presentation was acknowledged by Jesus. Scripture says.

> But He [Jesus] said to them, "Have you not read what David did when he was hungry, he and those who were with him: how he entered the house of God and ate the showbread which was not lawful for him to eat, nor for those who were with him, but only for the priests?" (Matthew 12:3,4 NKJV).

Jesus accepted this account as historically accurate.

DAVID WAS THE WRITER OF CERTAIN PSALMS

Jesus taught that David was the writer of certain of the Psalms. Matthew records Jesus saying.

> How is it then that David by the Spirit calls him Lord, saying (Matthew 22:43 NRSV).

David wrote the Psalms which were attributed to him.

MOSES WROTE THE LAW

According to Jesus, the Law was indeed given by Moses. Jesus said the following to a man whom He healed of leprosy.

> See that you tell no one; but go your way, show yourself to the priest, and offer the gift that Moses commanded, as a testimony to them (Matthew 8:4 NKJV).

Moses was the writer of the books attributed to him.

THE SUFFERING OF THE PROPHETS

The fact that the prophets suffered was used by Jesus as an example of how His disciples will suffer. In the Sermon on the Mount, Jesus said.

> Rejoice and be exceedingly glad, for great is your reward in heaven, for so they persecuted the prophets who were before you (Matthew 5:12 NKJV).

The various accounts of the suffering of the Old Testament prophets are historically accurate.

THE EPISODE WITH LOT'S WIFE

The story of Lot's wife, turning into a pillar of salt, was used by Jesus as an example of not looking back. Luke records Jesus saying.

REMEMBER LOT'S WIFE (LUKE 17:32 KJV).

Lot's wife actually existed.

JESUS CONFIRMED SOME OF THE MOST CONTROVERSIAL STORIES FOUND IN THE OLD TESTAMENT

In addition, Jesus confirmed some of the most ridiculed stories in the Old Testament. It is almost as though He went out of His way to put His stamp of approval on them.

ADAM AND EVE

Jesus believed in the Genesis account of creation—which includes the direct creation of Adam and Eve. Matthew records Him saying.

> "Haven't you read the Scriptures?" Jesus replied. "They record that from the beginning 'God made them male and female.' And he said, 'This explains why a man leaves his father and mother and is joined to his wife, and the two are united into one' (Matthew 19:4-5 NLT).

He used Adam and Eve as an example of God's purpose in marriage.

CAIN AND ABEL

The account of Cain killing Abel is rejected today in many circles, but Jesus believed it occurred. We read of this in Luke's gospel.

> From the murder of Abel to the murder of Zechariah, who was killed between the altar and the sanctuary. Yes, it will surely be charged against you (Luke 11:51 NLT).

This early story, recorded in the Book of Genesis, is historically accurate.

THE FLOOD IN NOAH'S DAY

Was there really a Flood, in the days of Noah, which God sent to destroy the earth? Jesus assumed there was. He said.

> For as were the days of Noah, so will be the coming of the Son of Man. For as in those days before the flood they were eating and drinking, marrying and giving in marriage, until the day when Noah entered the ark, and they were unaware until the flood came and swept them all away, so will be the coming of the Son of Man (Matthew 24:37-39 ESV).

Jesus compared the circumstances surrounding Noah's Flood as similar to those at His Second Coming.

JONAH AND THE GREAT SEA CREATURE

Jesus also believed the story of Jonah and the great sea creature as having literally occurred. In fact, He used it as a sign of His resurrection.

> But Jesus replied, "Only an evil, faithless generation would ask for a miraculous sign; but the only sign I will give them is the sign of the prophet Jonah. For as Jonah was in the belly of the great fish for three days and three nights, so I, the Son of Man, will be in the heart of the earth for three days and three nights. The people of Nineveh will rise up against

> this generation on judgment day and condemn it, because they repented at the preaching of Jonah. And now someone greater than Jonah is here—and you refuse to repent" (Matthew 12:39-41 NLT).

Contrary to the view of many modern skeptics, Jonah actually existed. Jesus testified to this fact.

DANIEL

Though the authorship of Daniel is often rejected today, Jesus believed that he was a true prophet. He said.

> Therefore, when you see the 'abomination of desolation,' spoken of by Daniel the prophet, standing in the holy place (whoever reads, let him understand) (Matthew 24:15 NKJV).

All of these disputed and ridiculed accounts of the Old Testament were confirmed by Jesus as actually occurring. Furthermore, He used certain of them as illustrating some of the most important events in His own ministry—including His resurrection and Second Coming. Since He demonstrated Himself to be God's Son, His testimony settles the matter —these stories did occur.

JESUS SPOKE OF PROPHECY BEING FULFILLED

Jesus also said that certain predictions, recorded in the Old Testament, were fulfilled in His life and ministry. We read the following in the Gospel of Luke.

> Then he said to them, "This passage came true today when you heard me read it" (Luke 4:21 God's Word).

Jesus spoke of John the Baptist as the fulfillment of Old Testament prophecy. Matthew records Jesus saying.

> John is the man to whom the Scriptures refer when they say, 'Look, I am sending my messenger before you, and he will prepare your way before you' (Matthew 11:10 NLT).

Jesus also said that what was written about Him must be fulfilled. Mark records Jesus saying.

> Elijah is indeed coming first to restore all things. How then is it written about the Son of Man, that he is to go through many sufferings and be treated with contempt? But I tell you that Elijah has come, and they did to him whatever they pleased, as it is written about him (Mark 9:12,13 NRSV).

In another example, when predicting judgment on the city of Jerusalem, Jesus said the following.

> For those will be days of God's vengeance, and the prophetic words of the Scriptures will be fulfilled (Luke 21:22 NLT).

Jesus considered the predictions of the Old Testament as being authoritative—He assumed they needed to be fulfilled.

CONCLUSION TO JESUS' ATTITUDE TOWARD THE OLD TESTAMENT

As we examine the attitude of the Lord Jesus toward the Old Testament we find Him viewing it as totally trustworthy. Jesus believed the people actually existed and the stories literally occurred. This includes some of the most controversial accounts such as Adam and Eve, Noah, and Jonah. He never cast doubt on any of parts of the Old Testament. To the contrary, He believed all of it was equally authoritative. Consequently, Christians, to be consistent, should have the same view as Jesus.

Next we will look at Jesus' view concerning His own teachings. How did He view them?

CHAPTER 12

Jesus' View Of His Own Teachings: They Were Absolutely Authoritative

This chapter establishes what Jesus thought about His own words. We discover that He considered them to be absolutely authoritative on every subject in which He spoke about. He had no doubts that His words were to be listened to and obeyed. We give eleven different reasons why this is so. The obvious conclusion is that Jesus expects us to heed His teachings and to obey everything which He said.

We have seen that Jesus viewed the Old Testament as the authoritative Word of God. He trusted everything that was written in it. Indeed, He confirmed many of the accounts including some of the most disputed ones. Now we examine how He looked at His own teachings. How did He consider His own words? Did He view them as authoritative?

JESUS BELIEVED HIS WORDS WERE AUTHORITATIVE

From the New Testament, we find that Jesus also considered His own words as binding. When He spoke, He spoke as the voice of authority. Jesus claimed complete truth for all His teaching. The evidence is as follows.

1. HIS WORDS WOULD NEVER PASS AWAY

Jesus said that His words would remain eternally. Matthew records Jesus saying the following.

> Heaven and earth will pass away, but my words will not pass away (Matthew 24:35 ESV).

Jesus said that His words would exist eternally—they would never pass away. We should note that this prediction has been literally fulfilled.

2. HE CONTRASTED HIS WORDS WITH THOSE OF OTHERS

Jesus made certain statements where He contrasted His words with those previously written and spoken by others. He put His own words on an entirely new level. We find many such statements—like the following from the Sermon on the Mount. Jesus said.

> You have heard that the law of Moses says, 'Do not murder. If you commit murder, you are subject to judgment.' But I say, if you are angry with someone, you are subject to judgment! If you call someone an idiot, you are in danger of being brought before the high council. And if you curse someone, you are in danger of the fires of hell (Matthew 5:21, 22 NLT).

Here Jesus contrasts His words with those written earlier.

3. JESUS' STATEMENTS WERE PREFACED BY "TRULY, TRULY"

Jesus made solemn statements prefaced by the "attention getting" phrase "truly, truly." John recorded Jesus saying.

> Very truly, I tell you, no one can enter the kingdom of God without being born of water and Spirit (John 3:3 NRSV).

The words of Jesus were meant to be heeded, not ignored.

4. WISE PEOPLE LISTENED TO HIS WORDS

Jesus compared those who obeyed His words to a wise person. He said that those who did not pay attention to His teachings were to be compared to a foolish person. He concluded the Sermon on the Mount with the following words.

> Anyone who hears and obeys these teachings of mine is like a wise person who built a house on solid rock. Rain poured down, rivers flooded, and winds beat against that house. But it did not fall, because it was built on solid rock. Anyone who hears my teachings and doesn't obey them is like a foolish person who built a house on sand (Matthew 7:24-26 CEV).

Notice the contrast. The wise person listened to Jesus while the foolish one did not.

5. HE WILL BE ASHAMED OF THOSE WHO ARE ASHAMED OF HIM

Jesus words were of such high value that those who were ashamed of them, He Himself would be ashamed of these people. Mark records Jesus saying.

> If people are ashamed of me and what I say in this unfaithful and sinful generation, the Son of Man will be ashamed of those people when he comes with the holy angels in his Father's glory (Mark 8:38 God's Word).

Jesus will be ashamed of those who are ashamed of Him.

6. THOSE WHO UNDERSTAND JESUS' TEACHING BEAR SPIRITUAL FRUIT

In the parable of the sower, those who are fruit bearers are the ones who understand Jesus' teaching. He said.

> But the seed planted on good ground is the person who hears and understands the word. This type produces crops. They produce one hundred, sixty, or thirty times as much as was planted (Matthew 13:23 God's Word).

The ones who understand the teachings of Jesus will bear spiritual fruit.

The Apostle Paul later explained what the fruit of the Spirit consisted of.

> But the fruit of the Spirit is love, joy, peace, patience, kindness, goodness, faithfulness, gentleness and self-control. Against such things there is no law (Galatians 5:22-23 NIV).

The disciples of Jesus will produce these qualities.

7. THEY WERE BLESSED TO SEE AND HEAR JESUS

Jesus told His disciples that their eyes were blessed to see Him and their ears were blessed to hear His words. He said.

> But blessed are your eyes, for they see, and your ears, for they hear. Truly I tell you, many prophets and righteous people longed to see what you see, but did not see it, and to hear what you hear, but did not hear it (Matthew 13:16,17 NRSV).

According to Jesus, many prophets, kings, and righteous men had desired to hear the things His own disciples heard. Yet they had not heard them because Jesus did not appear at that time in history.

8. HIS WORDS ARE TRUE

Jesus considered His words were true. Matthew records Jesus saying the following.

> At that time Jesus said, "I praise you, Father, Lord of heaven and earth, for hiding these things from wise and intelligent people and revealing them to little children. Yes, Father, this is what pleased you. "My Father has turned everything over to me. Only the Father knows the Son. And no one knows the Father except the Son and those to whom the Son is willing to reveal him" (Matthew 11:25-27 God's Word).

His true words are revealed to the humble, not the arrogant.

9. ALL AUTHORITY HAS BEEN GIVEN UNTO HIM

The last thing that Matthew records Jesus commanding His disciples is that they should go and preach His message. Jesus claimed that all authority had been given over to Him. He said.

> Go therefore and make disciples of all the nations, baptizing them in the name of the Father and of the Son and of the Holy Spirit (Matthew 28:19 NKJV).

His authority is over everything. This is a fantastic claim!

10. ETERNAL LIFE IS DEPENDENT UPON BELIEVING HIS WORDS

Jesus also made the monumental statement that eternal life depended upon believing His words. He said.

> Very truly, I tell you, anyone who hears my word and believes him who sent me has eternal life, and does not come under judgment, but has passed from death to life. Very truly, I tell you, the hour is coming, and is now here, when the dead will hear the voice of the Son of God, and those who hear will live (John 5:24,25 NRSV).

Where we spend eternity will be determined by how we view Jesus' words.

11. HIS TEACHING HAD ITS ORIGINATION FROM ABOVE

According to Jesus, His teaching originated from heaven. We read the following in John's gospel.

> The Jewish leaders were surprised when they heard him. "How does he know so much when he hasn't studied everything we've studied?" they asked. So Jesus told them, "I'm not teaching my own ideas, but those of God who sent me. Anyone who wants to do the will of God will know whether my teaching is from God or is merely my own" (John 7:15-17 NLT).

Jesus' teaching was heavenly in origin, not earthly.

CONCLUSION TO JESUS' VIEW OF HIS OWN TEACHINGS

From the biblical evidence we discover that Jesus considered His teaching to be authoritative on whatever subject He dealt with. When He spoke, He expected people to listen and obey—because His words were the words of God.

We learn the following about Jesus' view of His own words.

1. His words would never pass away.

2. He made certain authoritative statements where He contrasted His words with those of others.

3. Jesus made solemn statements which were prefaced by the "attention getting" phrase, "Truly, truly."

4. Wise people listened to His words, foolish people did not.

5. Jesus will be ashamed of those who are ashamed of Him.

6. The ones who understand the teachings of Jesus will bear spiritual fruit.

7. The eyes of Jesus' disciples were blessed to see Him and their ears were blessed to hear His words.

8. Jesus believed His words were true.

9. He claimed that all authority had been given to Him.

10. He said eternal life depended upon how one responded to His words.

11. He said His teaching originated from heaven.

Now that we know how Jesus viewed His own teachings, the next section looks at what Christ had to say with respect to the New Testament.

CHAPTER 13

Jesus' View Of The New Testament: He Confirmed It Ahead Of Time

This is the final chapter in which we present new material—our next chapter is merely a summary of what we have learned in the entire book.

In this chapter, we look at how Jesus confirmed the New Testament before it was written. He not only gave His approval to the Old Testament as the Word of God, and His own teachings as the last word on every matter, He also pre-approved the contents of the New Testament.

We will show that Jesus hand-picked certain disciples to continue on with His ministry. These disciples were given special promises that applied to them and to them alone. Jesus told them that after He went away the Holy Spirit would come and teach them. He would lead them into "all truth."

Furthermore, He promised that the Holy Spirit would bring back to their remembrance all things which Jesus said or did. Thus, when they spoke about Jesus, or put in writing their teaching and preaching, they were guaranteed complete accuracy. This means that the final result, the New Testament, has had its contents guaranteed ahead of time by Jesus.

Therefore, we can read and study the New Testament with confidence since it gives us an accurate record of the words and deeds of Jesus.

When we put this together with what Jesus taught about the Old Testament and His own teachings, we can thus conclude that the entire Bible is the divinely inspired, inerrant Word of God.

Thus far we have seen that Jesus taught that the Old Testament was divinely inspired of God, and that His own teachings were absolutely authoritative. We now come to Christ's view with respect to the New Testament. We will discover that He confirmed it ahead of time so that we can be assured that it too, is the Word of God.

JESUS HAND-PICKED HIS DISCIPLES

Jesus selected and trained certain disciples that would be the authorized teachers of His New Covenant. He chose well the men who would be His disciples and who would pass on His teachings to us—particularly the men whom He chose to record the account of His life.

THERE IS AN OLD TESTAMENT PRECEDENT FOR WRITTEN SCRIPTURE

There was already the precedent of written Scripture (the Old Testament) that would have been available to the disciples. Since God had given a written account of His words and deeds before the time of Jesus, it makes perfect sense that He would continue with a written account of the One to whom the Old Testament looked forward.

JESUS WORDS WERE CONSIDERED AUTHORITATIVE ON EVERY ISSUE

As we have also seen, since Jesus' words were considered by Him to be absolutely authoritative on whatever issue in which He spoke, there would have been the need to eventually see them in some permanent form.

HE MADE SPECIAL PROMISES TO HIS DISCIPLES

Jesus made some special promises to His disciples which deal directly with this issue of the divine inspiration and authority of the New Testament. John records Jesus saying the following.

> But the Advocate, the Holy Spirit, whom the Father will send in my name, will teach you everything, and remind you of all that I have said to you. Peace I leave with you; my peace I give to you. I do not give to you as the world gives. Do not let your hearts be troubled, and do not let them be afraid (John 14:26, 27 NRSV).

Jesus promised that after He left this world, the Holy Spirit would come in His place and teach His disciples. We note specifically the promise of Jesus with respect to what the Holy Spirit will do. He will teach them all things and bring back to their remembrance all things that Jesus said and did. What we have is a promise from Jesus, to His disciples, of a supernatural gift of total recall. Everything that Jesus said and did would be brought back to them in a miraculous way. Therefore, we can be assured that the final outcome of their teaching and eventual writing (the New Testament) would be correct in all that it said.

THE DISCIPLES WOULD BEAR WITNESS OF JESUS

The Bible also says that the Holy Spirit, and the disciples of Jesus, will bear witness of the Lord. We read the following in the Gospel of John. Jesus said.

> But I will send you the Counselor—the Spirit of truth. He will come to you from the Father and will tell you all about me. And you must also tell others about me because you have been with me from the beginning (John 15:26,27 NLT).

Those who had been with Jesus from the beginning would bear witness of Him.

THE HOLY SPIRIT WILL GUIDE THEM INTO ALL TRUTH

There is another promise from Jesus that was given to His disciples. John records Jesus saying the following. He said.

> When the Spirit of truth comes, he will guide you into all the truth; for he will not speak on his own, but will speak

> whatever he hears, and he will declare to you the things that are to come (John 16:13 NRSV).

This has to do with the guidance of the Holy Spirit. It will be into "all truth" that He will "guide" Jesus' disciples.

THE THINGS JESUS PROMISED HIS DISCIPLES

When we consider these verses, we have the following promises from Jesus.

1. Jesus is going to leave His disciples.

2. Yet, He will not leave them without a Teacher or Helper. He will give them the Holy Spirit.

3. The Holy Spirit will be sent by God the Father to remind them of all things that Jesus both said and did.

4. This contains a promise of total recall of all the words and deeds of Jesus which they personally experienced.

5. Both the Holy Spirit, and the disciples, will testify about Jesus.

6. These specific disciples will testify about Jesus because they had been with Him from the beginning of His ministry.

7. In addition, the Holy Spirit will guide these disciples into "all truth" when they preach the message about Jesus.

8. This will continue when their preaching and teaching is recorded in a more permanent form (the New Testament).

In a sense, Jesus authenticated the New Testament ahead of time by the various promises that He gave His disciples. Therefore, we can have confidence in what the New Testament says. Our confidence is based upon the promises of Jesus.

We now move to our last chapter—a summary of the things we have studied so far in this book.

CHAPTER 14

Summary And Conclusion: The Christian Faith Is True

This chapter summarizes what we have learned in this book. It is not a long chapter, but it is essential that, by this time, you are fairly familiar with the arguments we have given. Thus, the different points listed should be mere repetition of what you have already learned. Basically, it repeats the outline in chapter three. However, at this time, you have already looked at the evidence that backs up these points.

We began our study by assuming nothing about the truthfulness of the Christian faith—rather we built our argument from only the facts that could be demonstrated. Our examination of the case for Christianity has now led us to the following conclusions.

POINT 1: THE NEW TESTAMENT IS RELIABLE IN ITS TEXT AND HISTORY

The first thing we discovered is that the New Testament has come down to us in a reliable manner in both its text and history. When we apply the same tests to the New Testament as we would to any other document, we find it to be trustworthy. The text has been transmitted in an accurate way so that we can have confidence that the message has not been changed.

We also found the events recorded in the New Testament match up to known historical events. According to the "ancient documents rule," the New Testament should be accepted as true until some evidence is brought to the contrary.

POINT 2: JESUS CLAIMED HE IS THE ONLY WAY TO GET TO THE ONE TRUE GOD

We then looked at the New Testament to discover its message. We found that it claimed that there is only one God and only one way to approach the one God—through the person of Jesus Christ. It is the unanimous testimony of the New Testament that Jesus is the way, the truth, and the life. We find this from His own teaching, and the teachings of His disciples. Their claim is that salvation comes no other way.

POINT 3: THE CLAIMS OF CHRIST CONSIDERED: THE VARIOUS POSSIBILITIES

Because the claims of the New Testament have been recorded in a document that is historically reliable, they must be dealt with. There are three possible ways in which we could understand them.

A. HE NEVER MADE THE CLAIMS—LEGEND

This view holds that the claims of the New Testament did not come from Jesus but rather from His disciples who exaggerated the things He said and did. We found many problems with this view—not the least of which is there is not enough time for this to happen.

B. HE MADE THE CLAIMS AND THEY WERE NOT TRUE: LIAR OR LUNATIC

Since it is clear that He made the claims recorded in the New Testament, they must be either true or false. If His claims were false, then He either knew them to be false or He did not know them to be false.

HE MAY HAVE BEEN A LIAR

This view holds that Jesus knew His claims were false, but He made them anyway. As we observed, this is totally contrary to everything we know about His character. There is no evidence whatsoever that Jesus lied about anything.

HE COULD HAVE BEEN A LUNATIC

If Jesus really believed Himself to be the Son of God, and He was not whom He believed Himself to be, then He would have been a lunatic. Again, we find that this is totally contrary to everything we know about His character and teachings. There is nothing in Jesus' behavior that remotely suggests that He was deluded.

HE MADE THE CLAIMS AND THEY WERE TRUE—LORD

The only possibility that makes sense is that Jesus is Lord. Yet if this is the case, then there needs to be some evidence to substantiate this claim.

POINT 4: THE EVIDENCE FOR HIS CLAIMS

The New Testament not only makes claims about Jesus, it provides evidence to substantiate these claims. The New Testament offers three different lines of proof.

THE MIRACLES OF JESUS

The miracles of Jesus provide the first line of evidence. We saw that they were an essential part of His ministry. There were a sufficient number of miracles to cause us to believe that they occurred. Furthermore, His contemporaries never denied the miracles of Jesus. The evidence is clear that Jesus did indeed perform miracles.

FULFILLED PROPHECIES BY JESUS AND FROM JESUS

The prophecies fulfilled in the life of Jesus provide further convincing evidence that the Christian faith is true. There were prophecies fulfilled by Jesus Himself when He came to the earth, as well as prophecies He gave, that have been fulfilled. These were supernaturally fulfilled without any human manipulation. The only rational way to explain these prophecies is that there is an all-knowing God who has told us what will happen in the future.

JESUS' RESURRECTION FROM THE DEAD

The final line of evidence is Christ's resurrection from the dead. Three days after His death on Calvary's cross, the New Testament says that Jesus was alive again. The evidence for the resurrection of Jesus is overwhelming for all of those who are willing to take the time and consider it.

POINT 5: THE BIBLE IS GOD'S WORD–JESUS SAID SO

We can now make some conclusions with respect to the Bible. Because Jesus demonstrated Himself to be the Son of God, the way, the truth, and the life, and the only hope of humanity for salvation, we go to Him to discover exactly what kind of book the Bible is.

JESUS' VIEW OF THE OLD TESTAMENT: IT IS THE WORD OF GOD

Jesus believed the entire Old Testament was God's Word. He confirmed some of the most controversial stories such as Adam and Eve, Noah, and Jonah. He totally trusted everything that it said. Therefore, we also should trust the Old Testament as being the Word of God since He trusted it as being authoritative and true.

JESUS' VIEW OF HIS OWN TEACHINGS: THEY ARE ABSOLUTELY AUTHORITATIVE

Jesus' own teachings show that He believed that He was the Son of God —the way, the truth, and the life. He claimed absolute authority on any subject in which He spoke about. When He spoke, He expected people to listen and obey.

JESUS' VIEW OF THE NEW TESTAMENT: IT WOULD BE TOTALLY TRUE

Finally, as we look at Jesus' view of the New Testament, we find that He confirmed it ahead of time. Jesus promised His disciples the Holy Spirit would guide them into all truth and that all things which He said would supernaturally be brought back to their remembrance. This includes everything His disciples would teach and then later write. This gives the New Testament a pre-approval before it was written.

CONCLUSION

The evidence is clear and convincing. The Christian faith is not a blind faith but rather an intelligent faith based upon the facts of history. The truth of Jesus' claims can be proven beyond a reasonable doubt or to a moral certainty to all those who are willing to honestly consider the evidence.

A FINAL ISSUE: HAVE YOU TRUSTED HIM?

As we have seen, God has given us sufficient evidence to believe. But there is more. Australian attorney/theologian Ross Clifford states the matter well.

> The fact that the Creator in his grace has preserved such an abundance of evidence shows that he wants no-one to avoid the issue of who Jesus is. The evidence would impress a court of law, but ultimately it amounts to little unless it results in a commitment to Christ and the changed life the risen Lord through the Holy Spirit produces.[1]

If you have not made a decision for Jesus Christ, there is no better time than right now. If you would like to become a Christian, pray a simple prayer like this.

Lord Jesus, I know that I'm a sinner. Thank you for dying for me. Right this moment, in the best way that I know how, I trust you as my own Savior and Lord. Thank you Lord, for saving me. In Jesus' Name, Amen.

If you just prayed this prayer, congratulations! You have decided for Jesus Christ and for eternal life. If you prayed this prayer, be sure to tell others of your decision. Also, find a church that believes and teaches the Bible.

---

1. Ross Clifford, *The Case For The Empty Tomb*, Albatross Books, Sutherland, New South Wales, Australia, 1991, p. 142

About The Author

Don Stewart is a graduate of Biola University and Talbot Theological Seminary (with the highest honors).

Don is a best-selling and award-winning author having authored, or co-authored, over seventy books. This includes the best-selling *Answers to Tough Questions*, with Josh McDowell, as well as the award-winning book *Family Handbook of Christian Knowledge: The Bible*. His various writings have been translated into over thirty different languages and have sold over a million copies.

Don has traveled around the world proclaiming and defending the historic Christian faith. He has also taught both Hebrew and Greek at the undergraduate level and Greek at the graduate level.

Made in the USA
San Bernardino, CA
05 March 2017